Cognitive-Bel
Treatment for
Generalized Anxiety
Disorder

Practical Clinical Guidebooks Series

Rosqvist	*Exposure Treatments for Anxiety Disorders: A Practitioner's Guide to Concepts, Methods, and Evidence-based Practice*
Marshall, Marshall, Serran and Fernandez	*Treating Sexual Offenders: An Integrated Approach*
Emmelkamp and Vedel	*Evidence-Based Treatments for Alcohol and Drug Abuse: A Practitioner's Guide to Theory, Methods, and Practice*
Dugas and Robichaud	*Cognitive-Behavioral Treatment for Generalized Anxiety Disorder: From Science to Practice*

Cognitive-Behavioral Treatment for Generalized Anxiety Disorder

From Science to Practice

Michel J. Dugas
Melisa Robichaud

Routledge
Taylor & Francis Group
New York London

Routledge is an imprint of the
Taylor & Francis Group, an informa business

Routledge
Taylor & Francis Group
711 Third Avenue, 8th Floor
New York, NY 10017

Routledge
Taylor & Francis Group
27 Church Road
Hove
East Sussex BN3 2FA

Printed in the United States of America on acid-free paper
10 9 8 7

International Standard Book Number-10: 0-415-95211-5 (Softcover) 0-415-95210-7 (Hardcover)
International Standard Book Number-13: 978-0-415-95211-8 (Softcover) 978-0-415-95210-1 (Hardcover)

Library of Congress Cataloging-in-Publication Data

Dugas, Michel J. (Michel Jospeh), 1961-
Cognitive-behavioral treatment for generalized anxiety disorder : from science to practice / Michel J. Dugas, Melisa Robichaud.
p. ; cm. -- (Practical clinical guidebooks series)
Includes bibliographical references.
ISBN 0-415-95210-7 (hb : alk. paper) -- ISBN 0-415-95211-5 (pb : alk. paper)
1. Cognitive therapy. 2. Anxiety disorders--Treatment. I. Robichaud, Melisa. II. Title. III. Series.
[DNLM: 1. Anxiety Disorders--therapy. 2. Cognitive Therapy--methods. WM 172 D866c 2007]

RC489.C63D84 2007
616.89'142--dc22 2006014598

Visit the Taylor & Francis Web site at
http://www.taylorandfrancis.com

and the Routledge Web site at
http://www.routledgementalhealth.com

À Céline, Jérémie et Sophie — M.J.D.
To Carolyn and Antony — M.R.

Contents

Preface

As scientist-practitioners, we strive to carry out research that has direct clinical implications and to provide clinical services that are consistent with our research findings: hence the title of this book — *Cognitive-Behavioral Treatment for Generalized Anxiety Disorder: From Research to Practice*. Over the years, however, we have heard both clinicians and scientists criticize the scientist-practitioner model. On the one hand, many clinicians are quick to point out that they do not keep up with the scientific literature because the writings are not sufficiently relevant to their day-to-day clinical work. On the other hand, many clinical scientists have been confronted with the reality of research funding where granting agencies are reticent to provide support for clinical research that emphasizes issues of external validity such as "generalizability" and clinical usefulness. Although we acknowledge the challenges inherent to the scientist-practitioner model, we also believe that it can produce the most positive outcomes in terms of both clinical research and practice. Thus, in writing this book, we hope to make a small (but significant) contribution to bridging the gap between clinical scientists and practitioners. Specifically, by presenting a theoretical model and a treatment protocol based on the model, we hope to convey the merits of moving from science to practice (and back again).

This book is intended for psychotherapists working with individuals with generalized anxiety disorder (GAD). As such, we have done our best to ensure (although one can never be sure of anything, but more on that later) that the content and style of the book reflect the needs of clinicians. In Chapter 1, we present general information on GAD that sets the stage for the remainder of the book. In Chapter 2, we introduce a cognitive model of GAD and review the research supporting the model components. We have made every effort to present the research findings in a way that "talks to clinicians" and is not overly technical (or overly statistical). We then describe an assessment strategy and present the main instruments for the evaluation of clients with GAD in Chapter 3. Again, although we typically use a comprehensive assessment strategy in our clinical trials, we have limited the presentation of instruments to those that therapists might find most useful in their day-to-day clinical practice. In Chapter 4, we present an overview of the treatment protocol and attempt to give the reader a sense of the "spirit" of therapy. Chapter 5 goes on to provide a step-by-step guide to treatment, with many examples of therapist–client dialogue that make the treatment "come to life." To increase the clinical usefulness of the guide to treatment, Chapter 5 also includes handouts for all between-session exercises. In Chapter 6, we review the data bearing on the treatment's efficacy. Specifically, the main results from four clinical trials are presented, and secondary findings with regard to treatment mechanisms are also reviewed. Finally, in Chapter 7, we present some of the main factors that can complicate treatment and discuss ways that therapists can address these factors. Throughout the book, we have attempted to strike a balance between the complexity of the research findings and the need for clinicians to have a clearly articulated model and treatment protocol for those suffering from GAD. In a sense, we have endeavored to "translate" our research findings into clinical principles and procedures that both therapists and clients can relate to, and we sincerely hope we have reached this goal.

Acknowledgments

Many people have directly and indirectly contributed to this book. After all, our model and treatment are the result of 15 years of collaborations! Although it is not possible to mention everyone, we would like to acknowledge those who have worked most closely with us. From 1992 to 1998, the GAD research program described herein was based at l'Université Laval in Quebec City. At that time, Robert Ladouceur, Mark Freeston, Eliane Léger, and Patrick Gosselin played key roles in shaping the ideas put forth in this book. Since 1998, much of the research has been carried out at Concordia University and Sacré-Cœur Hospital in Montreal. At Concordia University, all of the members of the Anxiety Disorders Laboratory have made valuable contributions to our clinical research program on GAD. In particular, we would like to thank Nicole Gervais for her invaluable help during the final stages of preparation of this book. We would also like to acknowledge the research team at Sacré-Cœur Hospital, and especially Renée Leblanc, who has made substantial contributions to the clinical applications of our model of GAD. To those listed above, and to all those not listed who have contributed to our thinking on GAD, we sincerely thank you for your work, enthusiasm, and friendship. Without you, this book could not have been written.

CHAPTER 1

Description of Generalized Anxiety Disorder

Catherine was the first of three children. During her childhood, she had often been reminded that, as the eldest child, she should look out for her two younger siblings. By the time Catherine reached the third grade, she had begun worrying about her younger brothers. For example, if it was raining, she worried about whether one of them might catch a cold, or if they played rough games, she worried whether one of them might injure himself. Although her worrying was not a problem, she was clearly less carefree than most of her friends. In high school, Catherine succeeded very well in academics and athletics. She always had good grades and was a member of the swimming and track teams. Despite worrying less about her younger brothers, she noticed that she had begun to worry more about the health of her parents, in particular her mother. For example, she had started calling her mother at work, sometimes several times a day, to ensure she was all right. Again, although Catherine did not feel that her worrying was a problem, she had definitely noticed that moderate levels of worry and anxiety were something she often had to deal with.

It was only when Catherine went away to college that her worry and anxiety began to get noticeably out of hand. Being away from home, she found herself worrying more than ever about her family. She had also begun to worry about other things such as her grades, financial situation, and friendships. She started having trouble sleeping, often lying in bed for hours before finally falling asleep. Although she continued to do well in school, she found that preparing for exams was extremely stressful, and this would typically result in Catherine speaking to her teachers or classmates several times to ensure her course notes were correct. In addition, writing papers seemed to take longer than usual because Catherine would read over what she had written several times to reassure herself that she had made no spelling or grammar mistakes.

After college, Catherine began a successful career in marketing, and eventually got married and had two children. Following the birth of her second child, her worry and anxiety began to "spiral out of control," and she decided that it might be time to receive some type of treatment. She described experiencing nearly constant feelings of fatigue, insomnia, and anxiety about "anything and everything." She also noted that these feelings were beginning to interfere with her family and work life. Although she loved her children very much, she was so worried about their health and safety that she was usually tense and on edge while spending time with them. She found this to be extremely distressing, and she said that she could no longer enjoy happy moments in her life because she was so worried about any negative events that might take place in the future. She was also beginning to feel overwhelmed at work, yet she refused to delegate any responsibilities to other employees, stating that she could only be sure that the work was "done properly" if she did it herself.

Catherine was skeptical about the benefit of any form of psychological treatment, since she thought she had "the worrying gene" and was unlikely to change this part of her character. However, she was tired of "always feeling stressed out and anxious" and was willing to try anything to stop feeling this way. When she presented for treatment, she received an in-depth assessment. Based on her report of excessive worry about a number of daily life events, and her endorsement of somatic symptoms such as fatigue, sleep difficulties, and feelings of restlessness, she was given a diagnosis of generalized anxiety disorder (GAD).

As can be seen from the preceding illustration of Catherine, GAD can easily become quite debilitating and greatly reduce one's quality of life. Unfortunately, people afflicted with GAD rarely seek professional help, and when they do, clinicians often have difficulty recognizing the symptoms as being those of GAD. For these reasons, we will attempt to accomplish two major goals in this introductory chapter. The first is to provide a relatively thorough description of the characteristics of GAD. Specifically, we will discuss the history of the diagnostic category, the prevalence and associated features of the disorder, and the impairment that GAD typically engenders. The second goal is to present a "picture" of what GAD looks like from the clinician's point of view. What do we mean when we say "excessive worry and anxiety about a number of situations?" What is daily life like for someone with GAD? The above description of Catherine is only one example of the many ways in which GAD clients can present for treatment. It is our hope that, by thoroughly presenting information gathered over the course of our clinical practice, we can begin to provide a detailed picture of this interesting and complex disorder.

DIAGNOSIS OF GAD

Generalized anxiety disorder is a relatively new diagnostic category that has undergone several changes within the last few editions of the *Diagnostic and Statistical Manual of Mental Disorders* (*DSM*; American Psychiatric Association, 1980, 1987, 1994). As such, it should come as no surprise that the diagnosis of GAD is at times confusing, even for anxiety disorder specialists. In the following section, we will review the evolution of GAD in the *DSM*, we will describe the many changes that have been made to the criteria, and we will discuss the reasons behind these changes. The reader will likely note that while the current diagnostic definition is greatly improved from earlier editions, there is still much work to be done to arrive at a set of clear and reliable criteria that will increase the ease with which GAD is diagnosed.

History of the Diagnostic Category

The term *GAD* first emerged with the publication of the *DSM-III* (American Psychiatric Association, 1980). At that time, GAD was viewed essentially as a residual disorder because the diagnosis was not made if symptoms of panic disorder, obsessive–compulsive disorder, or phobias were present. The fundamental feature of the disorder was "persistent anxiety" for at least one month, with clients also required to endorse symptoms from three out of four categories, including motor tension, autonomic hyperactivity, apprehensive expectation, and vigilance/scanning.

To improve upon the broad and vague nature of the *DSM-III* diagnostic criteria for GAD, several important changes were made with the *DSM-III-R* (American Psychiatric Association, 1987). First, the core feature of the disorder shifted from persistent anxiety to excessive or unrealistic worry. Moreover, GAD could now be diagnosed in the presence of another mental disorder, so long as the worry and anxiety were unrelated to the other condition, thereby changing GAD from a residual problem to a primary diagnostic entity. The minimum duration required for a diagnosis was changed from one to six months, which is more consistent with the chronic nature of GAD. Despite these improvements, the vague somatic criteria remained, with clients requiring six out of eighteen varied symptoms to meet diagnosis.

GAD in the *DSM-IV*

With the introduction of the *DSM-IV* in 1994, the diagnostic criteria for GAD became significantly streamlined and began to adequately reflect

TABLE 1.1 *DSM-IV* Diagnostic Criteria for Generalized Anxiety Disorder

Excessive anxiety and worry (apprehensive expectation), occurring more days than not for at least six months, about a number of events or activities (such as work or school performance).
The person finds it difficult to control the worry.
The anxiety and worry are associated with three (or more) of the following six symptoms (with at least some symptoms present for more days than not for the past six months). Note: Only one item is required in children.
Restlessness or feeling keyed up or on edge.
Being easily fatigued.
Difficulty concentrating or mind going blank.
Irritability.
Muscle tension.
Sleep disturbance (difficulty falling or staying asleep, or restless unsatisfying sleep).
The focus of the anxiety and worry is not confined to features of an Axis I disorder, e.g., the anxiety or worry is not about having a panic attack (as in panic disorder), being embarrassed in public (as in social phobia), being contaminated (as in obsessive–compulsive disorder), being away from home or close relatives (as in separation anxiety disorder), gaining weight (as in anorexia nervosa), or having a serious illness (as in hypochondriasis), and the anxiety and worry do not occur exclusively during posttraumatic stress disorder.
The anxiety, worry, or physical symptoms cause significant distress or impairment in social, occupational, or other important areas of functioning.
The disturbance is not due to the direct physiological effects of a substance (e.g., a drug of abuse, a medication) or a general medical condition (e.g., hyperthyroidism) and does not occur exclusively during a mood disorder, a psychotic disorder, or a pervasive developmental disorder.

Source: American Psychiatric Association. (1994). *Diagnostic and statistical manual of mental disorders* (4th ed.). Washington, D.C., pp. 435–436.

the independence of the disorder (see Table 1.1 for the complete *DSM-IV* diagnostic criteria for GAD). Although excessive worry and anxiety was retained as the main feature of GAD, the term *unrealistic* was dropped and replaced with the notion that the worry is "difficult to control." In addition, the minimum duration requirement of six months was retained. Taken together, these two criteria clearly reflect the fundamental nature of GAD as a chronic condition that distinguishes itself from nonclinical worry by a *quantitative* difference in worry frequency and intensity, rather than by a qualitative difference (as was suggested by the term *unrealistic*). The criterion of "excessive and uncontrollable" worry reflects the clinical reality that individuals with GAD generally worry about the same types of things as everyone else does. The difference is that they worry more about them and it is harder to stop worrying once they have started. Indeed, the criterion of "uncontrollable" worry and anxiety was incorporated to distinguish GAD from nonpathological worry (Barlow & Wincze, 1998), highlighting the fact that the difference between GAD and "non-GAD" worry is primarily a matter of degree, not content.

Another notable revision to the criteria in the *DSM-IV* was the exclusion of many somatic symptoms from the diagnosis. Specifically, all the autonomic hyperactivity symptoms were removed, as well as a number of items from the motor tension and vigilance/scanning categories. The exclusion of the hyperactivity symptoms was particularly beneficial because they are more likely to be seen among individuals with panic disorder than those with GAD. As such, prior to this revision, distinguishing between panic disorder and GAD was a significant challenge for clinicians. At present, there are only six somatic symptoms linked to a GAD diagnosis, and although all but one (that is, muscle tension) can also be endorsed by clients suffering from other mood or anxiety disorders, the six symptoms are reliably found among GAD clients.

A final noteworthy change to the *DSM-IV* was the inclusion of "significant distress and impairment" to the GAD criteria. Earlier editions of the DSM described GAD as a disorder that engenders only mild social and occupational impairment. The prevailing perception of individuals with GAD was as the "worried well;" that is, people who worry excessively, yet are still able to accomplish most of their daily activities while maintaining acceptable levels of well-being and quality of life. Given that worry is a universal experience, it is not surprising that excessive worry would not be viewed as particularly disabling in one's day-to-day life. Yet, both research and clinical experience stand in contradiction to this belief. In fact, a more apt description of people with GAD is as "the walking wounded." Not only do they typically endure symptoms for many years without receiving treatment, but they may also experience significant social and economic disadvantages. For example, individuals with GAD are often unmarried or divorced, are more likely to have received disability payments at some time in their lives, and typically have very low annual incomes (e.g., Blazer, Hughes, George, Schwartz, & Boyer, 1991; Hunt, Issakidis, & Andrews, 2002). In addition, they frequently experience significant dissatisfaction with their professional and personal lives, as well as a diminished sense of well-being (Stein &

Heimberg, 2004). As such, the *DSM-IV* revision to the impairment and distress criterion for GAD is more reflective of the actual presentation of the disorder.

It is striking that GAD was, and to some extent still is, viewed as a relatively mild disorder despite its association with poor quality of life, as well as social and occupational impairment. This inaccuracy is most likely due to the fact that the impairment associated with GAD is often compared to that seen in other anxiety disorders. For example, when discussing the interference in the daily lives of individuals with panic disorder, social anxiety disorder (that is, social phobia), or obsessive–compulsive disorder, the associated impairment is quite obvious. Specifically, individuals with these disorders will often engage in time-consuming and fear-driven behaviors as well as physical avoidance of specific places or events, rendering the disability apparent to both themselves and those around them. For example, individuals with obsessive–compulsive disorder characterized by contamination concerns might wash his or her hands so excessively that they bleed, or an individual with panic disorder might become so fearful of having a panic attack that he or she rarely leaves the house. In contrast, the majority of individuals with GAD do not engage in behaviors that visibly demonstrate marked interference, nor do they necessarily appear particularly distressed or impaired by their symptoms. Rather, the lives of GAD clients are more typically fraught with subtle interference. For example, they might have difficulty concentrating on specific tasks at work because they are worrying about their retirement, or fail to enjoy a weekend get-together with friends because they are concerned about the upcoming work week. Because these types of worries are commonplace among GAD clients, they have a considerable negative impact on productivity on a professional level (more on that later) and pleasure on a personal level (for example, clients are too preoccupied with potential problems to enjoy the pleasures of life). Further, due to the longstanding nature of the disorder, there is an additive effect to these interferences, and feelings of demoralization and exhaustion are often the end result of years of worrying. Consequently, although the impairments caused by GAD are sometimes less obvious, they are no less detrimental to one's quality of life and are therefore of significant clinical concern.

In summary, it is clear that the way in which GAD is conceptualized (and ultimately diagnosed), has undergone sweeping changes since 1980 when it first appeared in the *DSM*. Successive editions of the *DSM* have attempted to define GAD in terms that are more specific, as well as more reflective of basic and applied research on worry, anxiety, and GAD. However, although our current ability to diagnose the disorder has definitely improved with each revision, GAD remains the anxiety disorder with the lowest diagnostic reliability (Brown, Di Nardo, Lehman, & Campbell, 2001). In other words, clinicians have considerable difficulty agreeing on the presence or absence of GAD, more so than for any other anxiety disorder. Thus, although the field has come a long way, much remains to be done before the reliability of the diagnosis of GAD reaches an ideal level. On a final note, a text revision to the *DSM-IV* was published (American Psychiatric Association, 2000); however, no changes were introduced to the GAD diagnostic criteria. As such, the *DSM-IV* criteria will be referred to throughout the remainder of this book.

CLINICAL PICTURE: WHAT DOES GAD LOOK LIKE?

As is evident from the prior section, the *DSM-IV* sets out diagnostic criteria that are quite helpful for the purposes of diagnosis; however, it does not fully capture the clinical presentation of GAD. In the following sections, we will therefore describe some of the subtleties of the clinical picture of clients with GAD, with a special emphasis on their subjective experience.

Worry Themes

As noted previously, the cardinal feature of GAD in the *DSM-IV* is excessive and uncontrollable worry and anxiety about a number of situations. What exactly does that mean, and how does someone with GAD present for treatment? The criterion of excessive worry about "a number of situations" can be confusing to clinicians unfamiliar with GAD. Would an individual who worries excessively and uncontrollably about two situations (for example, health and social interactions) meet this diagnostic criterion? In our experience, the answer to this question is most often "no." We have observed that clients who report worry about a very limited number of subjects usually do not have GAD. As a result, it is best to be vigilant for other disorders that may better capture the presenting symptoms. For example, for someone who worries only about health and social interactions, separate diagnoses of hypochondriasis and social anxiety disorder may be warranted.

Clients with GAD really do tend to worry about many different things. Often, when asked what they worry about, GAD clients will reply: "What *don't* I worry about?" In this sense, "generalized" anxiety is an apt moniker, as the content of their worries is generalized to almost everything in their lives. There are of course exceptions to this, where a client's worries focus on only two or three particular topics, but this is not the case for most GAD clients. Typically, a diagnosis of GAD implies that the client worries about "almost everything." In addition, the worries of GAD clients can spiral from one topic to another. For example, a client might begin worrying about his health ("What if I get cancer?") and subsequently worry about his family and finances (for example, "Who will take care of my kids if I die? Will they be well provided for? What if my family can't afford the funeral?").

Clinicians will often ask what exactly do GAD clients worry about. The short answer to this question is that they worry about the same things that everyone else does (hence, they worry about daily life situations). That is, they frequently cite worry themes that include family, relationships, work/school, health, and finances. Both research findings and clinical experience indicate that the worries of GAD clients generally are not different in content from the worries of nonanxious individuals. There are, however, two subtle differences that have been observed in terms of GAD worry. First, it appears that people with GAD consistently worry more about *minor matters* than both nonclinical individuals and people with other anxiety disorders (Brown, Moras, Zinbarg, & Barlow, 1993; Hoyer, Becker, & Roth, 2001). In fact, minor matters seem to be the worry topic that is most specific to GAD. Indirect support for this was provided by Di Nardo (1991, cited in Brown, O'Leary, & Barlow, 1993), who found that a negative response to the question "Do you worry excessively about minor matters?" could effectively rule out a diagnosis of GAD. In practical terms, this means that when a person worries excessively about minor matters (for example, what kind of toaster to buy, which book to read), that person is likely to have GAD.

GAD clients also tend to worry more about unlikely or remote future events than do other anxious individuals (Dugas, Freeston et al., 1998). For example, they might worry about their plane crashing even though the likelihood of this occurring is very slight, or worry about how to pay for their unborn children's university education. Despite these differences (i.e., worry about minor matters and unlikely/remote future events), it can be said that individuals with GAD do not generally worry about topics that are particularly different or unique. Rather, for the most part, they simply worry more about the same things as everyone else.

Living in the Future

Individuals with GAD almost always report a poor quality of life, and much of this has to do with their tendency to live "in the future." Stated differently, they have great difficulty living in the moment. Even when they are involved in something pleasant, they often do not enjoy themselves because they are too busy worrying about various future events. For example, a client with GAD might spend an evening at a party worrying about the clean-up afterward, or have difficulty falling asleep the night before a dental appointment because she is worried about being late for the appointment. The future orientation of individuals with GAD is often apparent right from the first therapy session. For example, the client might ask "Will this therapy work for me?" or "How long will it take before I feel better?" It may even be difficult for the clinician to obtain information about the client's current state because of this tendency to discuss the future.

Although some would argue that living in the future has advantages such as being better prepared for situations that might occur, it is clear that an excessive future orientation prevents one from enjoying moments in the here and now. In fact, many clients with GAD report that they are unable to enjoy themselves because they are constantly thinking about what might happen next. Research has shown that individuals with GAD tend to have thoughts beginning with "What if...?" Clearly, it is difficult to enjoy the present moment when one is thinking thoughts such as, "What if I can't meet my deadline at work?"; "What if my child gets terribly sick?"; and "What if my husband decides to leave me?"

GAD Client Presentation

Although this topic will be discussed in greater detail in chapter 3, it is of interest to know how GAD clients appear upon presentation. In terms of initial contact during assessment, many GAD clients do not appear particularly anxious or nervous. Unlike patients with panic disorder or obsessive–compulsive disorder, where the anxiety associated with presenting for treatment is often immediately visible (for example, the client is nervous/fidgety and expresses feelings of anxiety at the outset), GAD clients might initially appear calm and composed. However, one is struck by the second impression that begins to form once GAD clients are encouraged to discuss their worries. Some clients might disclose having gotten little or no sleep the night before as a result of worrying all evening about being late for the appointment. They may also describe elaborate worry chains and a nearly constant background of anxiety due to the frequency of their worries. Moreover, diagnostic interviews conducted with GAD clients can be quite lengthy because they often wish to provide exhaustive detail to all questions out of fear of providing insufficient or inaccurate information (e.g., "What if I forgot to mention something important? What if treatment does not go well because of something I didn't explain?").

An additional noteworthy point relates to the presentation of excessive worry in GAD clients. Specifically, clients will sometimes *not* use the term *worry* when describing their symptoms; therefore, clinicians will occasionally need to inquire about symptoms using different terminology. For example, in general it can be said that much of the excessive and uncontrollable worry that GAD clients engage in is done in an attempt to control and prepare for any eventuality in the future. As such, GAD worry can be seen as extensive "scenario building," which usually takes the following form: "What if X happens? Well, then I could do.... But what if Y happens? Well, then I might do...." As such, if the clinician suspects the presence of GAD, even though the client denies worrying, then the clinician can inquire about scenario building.

So if clients do not always describe their symptoms as worries, what do they refer to instead, and why? Some GAD clients will describe their worries as fears, thereby making their problem appear to be a phobia rather than GAD. For example, an individual with GAD might describe a "fear" of driving, but upon further questioning the client voices this fear as a series of "what if" statements: "What if I get into an accident and end up in the hospital? What if we can't pay the hospital bills and have to sell the house? What if I lose my job from being out of work due to an accident?" Although the use of words such as *fear* or *anxiety* rather than *worry* is simply the particular way in which some clients express their symptoms, the avoidance of the term *worry* can also be due to the belief that worry is not a legitimate mental health complaint. That is, some clients might choose to describe their distress as *fear* or *anxiety* since these words may appear to be more indicative of a mental health disorder than the term *worry*.

The Case of Catherine

In keeping with our description of the clinical presentation of GAD, we will briefly review the course of Catherine's symptoms as depicted in the case illustration at the beginning of this chapter. Generally speaking, we can see an escalation of Catherine's worries and anxiety throughout her life. As a child, she worried about the health of her siblings, and although these worries diminished over the years, she developed new concerns consistent with the changes in her life. For example, her worries focused on academic performance when she was attending college; however, her concerns shifted to work and the health of her children after she was employed and married with two kids. Her somatic symptoms also appear to have progressively increased over the years. While in college, Catherine began to experience significant sleep disturbance, "often lying in bed for hours before she finally fell asleep." After the birth of her second child, Catherine's somatic symptoms increased to an unmanageable level, as she reported near constant feelings of fatigue, tension, and restlessness. In our experience, it is the presence of increasingly severe and unmanageable somatic symptoms that often serves as the impetus for clients to ultimately seek treatment. This appears to be the case with Catherine, who stated that she was "sick and tired of always feeling stressed out and anxious." In fact, it is unlikely that she expected treatment to address her excessive worries in any way, as she stated that she believed herself to have "the worrying gene."

It is of interest to note the many worry-related behaviors that Catherine engaged in over the years in an attempt to deal with, or reduce, her worries. For example, when her worries about her mother's well-being escalated, she began calling her repeatedly during the day to ensure that she was all right. In addition, while in college, she began seeking excessive reassurance from her classmates and professors to ensure that her notes were correct, and she would often reread her papers to make sure that there were no mistakes. These worry-related behaviors later continued when she started working, where despite feeling overwhelmed by her responsibilities at work, Catherine would not delegate any tasks to other employees in order to ensure that the work was "done properly." These types of behaviors not only served to maintain her symptoms, but were likely to have exacerbated her feelings of fatigue and general anxiety.

One of the most noteworthy points in Catherine's case is the interference and distress caused by her symptoms. Specifically, we see a gradual decrease in her quality of life throughout the years, despite the high standard of performance she maintained in her professional and personal life (i.e., academic excellence, successful career, and rewarding family life). Early on, she described herself as feeling "less carefree" than other children who were her age, and as she advanced through high school and college, she appeared to be constantly struggling with chronic stress and anxiety. The decrease in her quality of life reached an apex following the birth of her second child, when she began feeling "tense and on edge" whenever she spent time with her children. Although some GAD clients will exhibit interference in their lives through social or occupational impairment (for example, interpersonal difficulties or job loss), Catherine's decreased joy and quality of life, despite her noticeable successes, is a good example of an alternate presentation of GAD. That is, some clients will outwardly present as high functioning through their ability to maintain a good career and family life, but are nevertheless quite impaired by their symptoms (albeit in a different manner). Specifically, individuals like Catherine might report extreme fatigue from overwork and a need "to do everything" themselves. Ultimately, they can experience feelings of "burnout" as a result of their chronic worry and anxiety.

EPIDEMIOLOGY

Given that GAD is a chronic disorder that often leads to significant distress and impairment, research on the prevalence and associated features of the disorder can provide answers to vitally important questions. That is, how many people suffer from GAD? Are women or men more likely to be diagnosed with the disorder? When do symptoms typically begin to occur, how long do they last, and do they occur in isolation? The following sections will address these questions by presenting epidemiological data on GAD obtained in both community and clinical settings.

Prevalence in the General Population

Given the numerous changes to the diagnostic criteria of GAD over the years, and the fact that the current *DSM-IV* definition appeared relatively recently, one might expect that it would be difficult to report GAD prevalence ratings with any accuracy. Specifically, many of the large-scale epidemiological studies on prevalence were conducted using the *DSM-III* and *DSM-III-R* criteria, which are quite different from the criteria seen in the *DSM-IV*. As such, it would not be surprising if the prevalence rates changed markedly from study to study. However, this does not appear to be the case. In terms of community studies, where individuals from the general population are queried about symptoms for various mental health disorders, the prevalence ratings are *relatively* uniform. In terms of one-year prevalence rates, the likelihood of GAD is approximately between 2 and 4%, whereas lifetime prevalence rates hover between 4 and 7% (see Table 1.2 for actual ratings across studies). In other words, 2 to 4% of the population will meet criteria for GAD in any given year, whereas 4 to 7% of the population will develop GAD at some point in their lives. While this does not make GAD the most common mental health problem, it is clear that a considerable proportion of the general population is at risk for either having GAD or developing it at some point in the future. In fact, the aforementioned ratings might be an underestimation of the actual prevalence of GAD in the community. As noted by Kessler and colleagues (Kessler, Walters, & Wittchen, 2004) in their excellent review on the epidemiology of the disorder, some uncertainty still remains about the basic epidemiological characteristics of

GAD. This appears to be the result of difficulties in cross-study comparisons due to changing DSM criteria, as well as continued debate over the appropriate criteria and thresholds for a diagnosis of GAD. The authors conjecture that the true current prevalence of the disorder in the community might actually be as high as 5 to 8%. Further studies are needed to determine the precise rate of GAD among the general population.

Prevalence in the Clinical Population

When we move from the community to primary care settings, it appears that there is a dramatic increase in the prevalence of GAD. Based on several investigations, including a multicenter study conducted by the World Health Organization, it appears that 8% of all people who seek primary care treatment meet diagnostic criteria for GAD (Maier et al., 2000; Üstün & Sartorius, 1995). Moreover, among individuals seeing their physicians for a psychological problem, 25% have a diagnosis of pure GAD (that is, no comorbid conditions). Indeed, GAD is the *most frequent* anxiety disorder, and the *second most frequent* of all mental disorders, in primary care facilities (Barrett, Oxman, & Gerber, 1988;

TABLE 1.2 Prevalence Ratings for GAD in Three Large-Scale Community Studies Using *DSM-III*, *DSM-III-R*, and *DSM-IV* Criteria

Study	One-Year GAD (%)	Lifetime GAD (%)
Epidemiologic Catchment Area (ECA) study[a] (*DSM-III* criteria)	2–3.6	4.1–6.6
National Comorbidity Survey (NCS)[b] (*DSM-III-R* criteria)	3.1	5.1
Australian National Survey of Mental Health and Well-Being[c] (*DSM-IV* criteria)	3.6	n/a

[a]*Blazer, Hughes, George, Schwartz, & Boyer (1991).*
[b]*Wittchen, Zhao, Kessler, & Eaton (1994).*
[c]*Hunt, Issakidis, & Andrews (2002).*

Wittchen et al., 2002). GAD is therefore not only a debilitating disorder that is associated with poor quality of life, it is also a highly common problem, particularly in clinical settings.

Age of Onset, Course, and Remission

When is GAD most likely to develop? It appears that the age of onset for GAD has a bimodal distribution. In other words, there are two periods when individuals are at greatest risk for developing the disorder. Approximately two-thirds of individuals with GAD experience an early onset of the disorder that occurs between the ages of 11 and the early 20s. However, a significant minority experience a late onset of the disorder that develops in middle adulthood (Blazer, Hughes, & George, 1987; Brown, Barlow, & Liebowitz, 1994). In early onset GAD, there is usually no dramatic life stressor or shift from an earlier condition that precipitates the development of the disorder, although a gradual increase in responsibilities and transitional challenges characteristic of adolescence might play a significant role (Cole, Peeke, Martin, Truglio, & Seroczynski, 1998; Sprujit-Metz & Sprujit-Metz, 1997). In contrast to the insidious development of early-onset GAD, it appears that a significant life stressor (for example, the death of a loved one or a major life transition) is more likely to be the precipitating factor for late-onset GAD (Hoehn-Saric, Hazlett, & McLeod, 1993).

Irrespective of the age at which the disorder developed, the symptoms of GAD are generally chronic and unremitting in nature. Moreover, although there are fluctuations in the severity of GAD over time, with increases in GAD severity usually occurring in response to life stressors, episodes of the disorder commonly persist for over 10 years (Kessler, Keller, & Wittchen, 2001; Stein, 2004). Yet, despite the unremitting course of the disorder, many individuals with GAD will wait over 25 years before presenting for treatment (Rapee, 1991).

In terms of remission, GAD symptoms rarely abate naturally over time. In a large-scale study conducted by the Harvard/Brown Anxiety Research Program (HARP; Yonkers, Warshaw, Massion, & Keller, 1996) to investigate the natural history of GAD, only 15% of the participants showed full remission of their symptoms after one year, 25% showed remittance at two years, and 38% at five years. However, remission was determined if the participants were symptom-free for eight consecutive weeks. As GAD symptoms can wax and wane over time, these percentages are underestimations of actual remission rates. In fact, a substantial number of participants were later found to have "relapsed," highlighting the persistence of GAD symptoms and the chronicity of the disorder. In essence, unless individuals with GAD receive some form of treatment for their symptoms, they will likely continue to experience excessive worry and anxiety throughout most of their lives.

Age and Gender Differences

In terms of the gender makeup of GAD, it seems that the disorder is more commonly seen among women than it is among men, and this finding has been reliably and consistently shown in a great deal of research. For example, in both the National Comorbidity Survey (NCS) and the Epidemiologic Catchment Area (ECA) study, both of which are large-scale U.S. investigations of mental health prevalence rates in the community, women reported virtually double the rates of GAD than men. Specifically, in terms of one-year prevalence ratings, approximately 4% of women were identified with GAD compared to 2% of men (Blazer et al., 1991; Wittchen, Zhao, Kessler, & Eaton, 1994).

The finding that women are more likely to have a diagnosis of GAD than men is consistent with the findings obtained for many other anxiety disorders. In the NCS, prevalence rates were found to be higher among women for panic disorder, agoraphobia without panic disorder, social anxiety disorder, and simple phobia. In fact, prevalence rates for having any anxiety disorder ranged from 22 to 30% for women, compared to 12 to 20% for men (Kessler et al., 1994). A host of psychosocial and biological theories have been advanced to account for this gender difference, all of which may have an additive effect on the report of anxiety among women, but no definitive answer as to why women report more anxiety concerns than men has yet been found.

Although the relationship between gender and GAD seems to be relatively clear, age has a more complicated association with the disorder. For example, although several epidemiological studies found the highest prevalence ratings for GAD in middle age (ages 35 to 55) and the lowest ratings among older adults over the age of 55 (e.g., Blazer et al., 1991; Wittchen et al., 2002), studies on GAD and aging have revealed a different pattern. Specifically, GAD appears to be the most common disorder among older adults, and there might in fact be a steady increase of GAD rates with age, even for those over 65 (Beekman et al., 1998; Carter, Wittchen, Pfister, & Kessler, 2001). To further complicate the issue of age and GAD, a study on worry among older adults found that those in the 75 or older age category were significantly less worried than those in the 65 to 74 age category (Doucet, Ladouceur, Freeston, & Dugas, 1998), thereby contradicting the notion that GAD rates steadily increase into old age.

These discrepancies in the reported presence of GAD according to age group might be due to several factors. First, since GAD is a chronic disorder with a low rate of remission, it would be expected that middle aged adults would have a higher lifetime risk for developing the disorder than others in younger age groups. Second, in terms of the discrepancy in the prevalence ratings for older adults, it appears that anxiety disorders go undiagnosed in many older adults because they may also have health problems with symptoms that are similar enough to those seen in anxiety disorders to mask the presence of GAD (Stanley & Novey, 2000). As a result, the identification of GAD, and ultimately the reported rates, might differ from study to study, depending on the accuracy with which GAD is differentiated from physical health complaints. In practical terms, it is difficult to state with any confidence which age group is most likely to have a diagnosis of GAD. However, since we know that the disorder frequently begins in adolescence or early adulthood, and is both chronic and unlikely to remit on its own, we can assume that from middle adulthood onward, the rates of GAD are likely to be relatively high.

Comorbidity

Does GAD occur in isolation? In epidemiological studies of GAD, a consistent finding has been that the vast majority of people with the disorder have other diagnosed problems as well. Specifically, over 90% of individuals who meet criteria for GAD in a given year will also have at least one other *DSM-IV* diagnosis (see Table 1.3 for a list of comorbid conditions). Mood disorders such as major depression and dysthymia are the most common comorbid conditions; however, more than half of GAD clients will have an additional anxiety disorder as well (for example, social anxiety disorder, panic disorder).

The fact that GAD has such a high rate of comorbidity with other disorders has led several anxiety disorder experts to debate whether GAD can actually be considered a distinct disorder in its own right. That is, because individuals with GAD rarely present without other problems, there is some controversy as to whether GAD is an independent disorder or simply a "prodromal" condition that serves to promote the development of other anxiety or mood disorders (e.g., Akiskal, 1998; Maser, 1998; Roy-Byrne & Katon, 1997). Through several independent lines of inquiry, including studies on the specificity of symptoms to GAD (e.g., Brown, Chorpita, & Barlow, 1998; Maier et al., 2000), the contention that the disorder is not a unique diagnostic entity has been largely disproved. First, when lifetime prevalence is considered, the rate of comorbidity among individuals with GAD is not any greater than what is seen

TABLE 1.3 Prevalence of Comorbid *DSM-IV* Disorders for Individuals with GAD

***DSM-IV* Disorder**	**One-Month GAD(%)[a]**	**One-Year GAD(%)[b]**
Alcohol abuse/dependence	08.2	06.4
Nicotine dependence	n/a	14.0
Drug abuse/dependence	5.8	1.4
Major depression	39.3	59.0
Dysthymia	17.7	36.2
Panic disorder	13.9	21.5
Agoraphobia without panic	5.2	11.3
Social anxiety disorder	21.2	28.9
Specific phobia	n/a	29.3
Phobia NOS	n/a	10.6
Obsessive–compulsive disorder	5.8	10.0
Posttraumatic stress disorder	12.4	n/a
Any somatoform disorder *	n/a	48.1
Any eating disorder	n/a	2.5
Any depressive disorder	44.9	70.6
Any anxiety disorder	37.4	55.9
Any of the above disorders	67.8	93.1

[a]*Data taken from the Australian National Survey of Mental Health and Well-Being:* Hunt, Issakidis, & Andrews (2002).

[b]*Data taken from the Mental Health Supplement of the German National Health Interview:* Carter, Wittchen, Pfister, & Kessler (2001). One-year prevalence of subthreshold and threshold *DSM-IV* generalized anxiety disorder in a nationally representative sample.

* *The category "any somatoform disorder" includes pain disorder, hypochondriasis, and somatization.*

in individuals with other anxiety disorders. In the NCS, although the great majority of individuals with lifetime GAD had at least one lifetime comorbid disorder, this was equally the case for those with other anxiety and mood disorders. Second, research has shown that the temporal priority of GAD is similar to that seen for most other anxiety and mood disorders. In other words, the onset of GAD does not *systematically* precede or follow the onset of comorbid conditions. The one exception to this rule appears to be that GAD often emerges as the first disorder for individuals who experience comorbid depression (Kessler et al., 2004). Because of the chronic and unremitting nature of GAD, it should certainly come as no surprise that a longstanding struggle with GAD symptoms might have negative repercussions on one's mood. Put simply, feeling constantly worried and anxious for an extended amount of time is most likely quite depressing. To some extent, the fact that GAD often occurs prior to depression is consistent with this hypothesis.

THE COST OF GAD

Although the cost of GAD to the individual in the form of functional impairment has been debated due to its subtle (yet insidious) presentation, there is little disagreement as to the high cost that the disorder exerts on society. When examining the economic burden of mental health problems, two broad categories have typically been considered: direct and indirect costs (Dupont et al., 1996; Greenberg et al., 1999). Direct costs refer to health care utilization, including consultations with various medical and mental health practitioners, emergency room visits, and use of medication. Indirect costs typically relate to poor work productivity, absenteeism in the workplace, financial dependence (for example, social assistance, employment insurance), and caregiver burden. For GAD, the cost to society, both direct and indirect, is surprisingly substantial (see Koerner et al., 2004, for a review).

Direct Costs

Taking all anxiety disorders into consideration, it appears that a diagnosis of GAD is associated with one of the highest rates of health care use. In the NCS, 66% of individuals with GAD reported seeking professional help for their symptoms (Wittchen et al., 1994). A similar finding emerged in the Australian National Survey of Mental Health and Well-Being, where over half of individuals with a GAD diagnosis reported consulting with health care professionals. Interestingly, of those seeking help, only

14% consulted a mental health specialist (Hunt et al., 2002). Rather, when individuals with GAD seek help, they typically seek out the services of family physicians, nurses, and medical specialists, which often results in numerous unnecessary medical tests that are highly costly. In fact, GAD clients overuse these primary care resources at a surprisingly high rate, as they have been found to report double the average number of visits to primary care facilities when compared to depressed clients (Wittchen et al., 2002). In terms of visits to nonmental health specialists, the data show that individuals with GAD have very high consultation rates, in particular with cardiologists and gastroenterologists (Kennedy & Schwab, 1997; Logue et al., 1993). Most disturbing though is that despite their numerous medical visits, less than 10% of GAD clients receive adequate psychological or pharmacological treatment (Wittchen, 2002). This is likely to be due to the fact that the diagnosis of GAD is often "missed" in frontline care. In practical terms, these findings highlight the fact that a misdiagnosis of GAD is costly not only to the individual, who ends up suffering for years from a treatable condition, but also to society, as untreated GAD costs the health care system dearly in terms of time, money, and medical resources.

Indirect Costs

In addition to the burden of GAD on the health care system, undiagnosed and untreated GAD also has a deleterious impact on work productivity. In the Australian epidemiological study, more than half of the sample had taken at least one disability day in the past month that they attributed to their anxiety (Hunt et al., 2002). Another study showed that approximately one-third of individuals with GAD showed a reduction in work productivity of 10% or more, and 11% decreased their work productivity by half as a result of their anxiety (Wittchen, Carter, Pfister, Montgomery, & Kessler, 2000). The impact of these indirect costs was underscored in a U.S. study on the annual cost of anxiety disorders in 1990. It was determined that $42 to $47 billion was spent that year alone as a result of anxiety disorders. Although most of that cost was attributed to psychiatric and nonpsychiatric medical treatment, reductions in work productivity accounted for 10% of that amount (that is, more than $4 billion; Greenberg et al., 1999). Despite the fact that these figures represent the cost of all anxiety disorders, the contribution of GAD is substantial. Given that a diagnosis of GAD is associated with the overuse of health care services and reduced productivity over years of employment (given the chronicity of the disorder), it represents a significant burden on the economy and an important public health concern.

SUMMARY AND CONCLUDING REMARKS

GAD is unique among the anxiety disorders in that it is a relatively new diagnostic category. Its first official introduction into the mental health vernacular was in 1980 with the third edition of the *DSM*. Since then, GAD has gone through several revisions in its criteria, and it has been the subject of much debate, particularly in terms of its place in the *DSM* as a distinct diagnostic entity. Most interestingly, basic research and epidemiological studies have gradually changed the perception of GAD from a residual disorder with mild associated impairment to a highly prevalent, chronic, and disabling disorder that exerts a high economic burden on society.

GAD is also a disorder that exhibits the lowest diagnostic reliability of all the anxiety disorders, and is frequently misdiagnosed and either treated inappropriately or not at all. Because so many GAD clients seem to be "slipping through the cracks" of the health care system (despite their overuse of that system), it is vital that clinicians become adept at identifying, understanding, and ultimately treating GAD. As such, the following chapters will be devoted to the following:

- We will endeavor to give clinicians an understanding of the cognitive processes that underlie the disorder through the exposition of an empirically supported model of GAD.
- We will provide helpful strategies and guidelines that will aid clinicians in recognizing the symptoms of GAD and enable them to conduct a thorough assessment.
- We will describe a treatment for GAD based on our cognitive model, with primary importance being placed on the role of intolerance of uncertainty in the maintenance of the disorder.
- We will review the data on the treatment's efficacy and provide potential solutions to the factors that can complicate treatment.

It is our hope that this book will be a helpful resource for clinicians working with GAD clients. Although their unique presentation is at times subtle, and a learning curve can be expected in terms of gaining proficiency in the assessment and treatment of the disorder, we believe that increased familiarity with the presentation and inner workings of

GAD will properly demystify the disorder. We have attempted to incorporate as many practical tips and strategies as possible for the diagnosis and treatment of GAD, in order to maximize the benefit of this book for clinicians working with individuals suffering from GAD.

CHAPTER 2

A Cognitive Model of Generalized Anxiety Disorder

In this chapter, we will present the theoretical and empirical basis of our cognitive model of generalized anxiety disorder (GAD). Given that our main goal is to prepare the reader for subsequent chapters describing our cognitive-behavioral treatment, we have chosen not to present other models of GAD here. The reader should keep in mind, however, that other biological, environmental, and psychological models of GAD have received considerable empirical support. By not formally presenting these models, we do not mean to imply that they have less scientific and clinical value than ours; only that they are not germane to the treatment described in this book. We will refer to the work of others, of course, in instances where we have integrated their ideas into our model. This is particularly the case for the final component of our model, cognitive avoidance, which draws heavily upon the research of others.

Our cognitive model of GAD has four main features: intolerance of uncertainty, positive beliefs about worry, negative problem orientation, and cognitive avoidance. Although we have used the term *cognitive-behavioral model* in past writings (e.g., Dugas, Gagnon, Ladouceur, & Freeston, 1998; Robichaud, Dugas, & Conway, 2003), our recent work suggests that the term *cognitive model* is a more appropriate label for our conceptualization of the main processes involved in GAD. Even if behavioral and emotional (subjective affect and physiological responses) factors certainly play a role in GAD, it is our contention that cognitive factors play a more central role in its etiology. Specifically, our model states that beliefs about uncertainty are pivotal to the development and maintenance of GAD. As highlighted by cognitive models of psychopathology (e.g., Beck & Clark, 1997), fundamental beliefs direct the way individuals process information from their environment. This basic premise is central to our conceptualization of the etiology of GAD, thus making the term *cognitive model* more suitable for our model.

INTOLERANCE OF UNCERTAINTY

Intolerance of uncertainty, the central feature of our model, refers to *a dispositional characteristic that results from of a set of negative beliefs about uncertainty and its implications.* For example, individuals who are intolerant of uncertainty believe that uncertainty is stressful and upsetting, that being uncertain about the future is unfair, that unexpected events are negative and should be avoided, and that uncertainty interferes with one's ability to function. Although we have previously defined intolerance of uncertainty in other ways (e.g., Dugas, Gosselin, & Ladouceur, 2001; Freeston, Rhéaume, Letarte, Dugas, & Ladouceur, 1994), data from converging lines of research suggest that the term *dispositional characteristic* best describes its fundamental nature (much as anxiety sensitivity can be viewed as a dispositional characteristic of individuals at risk for panic disorder).

Before reviewing the research on intolerance of uncertainty, we will briefly describe the clinical and empirical considerations that led us to this construct. As recently as the 1980s, behavioral and cognitive treatments for GAD fell primarily into two categories: (1) general anxiety reduction techniques such as progressive muscle relaxation and anxiety management training, and (2) cognitive interventions such as general cognitive restructuring or reevaluation. Although these interventions are efficacious for many clients with GAD, both the empirical literature and our clinical experience have led us to the conclusion that they are not sufficient for the long-term management of GAD. In terms of general anxiety reduction interventions such as progressive muscle relaxation, data from treatment studies (e.g., Barlow, Rapee, & Brown, 1992; Öst & Breitholtz, 2000) suggest that relaxation techniques lead to notable changes in GAD symptoms but that many clients are left with considerable residual symptoms. Our clinical experience (as well as some of our recent data) has led us to a similar conclusion; namely, that although many clients make significant gains early on in therapy, they often reach a plateau and find themselves continuing to experience important residual GAD symptoms following treatment.

As for general cognitive interventions, data from the same multitreatment studies cited above (i.e., Barlow et al., 1992; Öst & Breitholtz, 2000) suggest that their efficacy is similar to that of relaxation techniques. In other words, general cognitive interventions appear to lead to notable but insufficient change for many clients with GAD. One way to account for this may be that although there are many forms and variations of cognitive therapy for anxiety, most emphasize the reevaluation of probability and cost estimates related to feared outcomes. One of the aims of cognitive therapy is therefore to help anxious clients reevaluate both the probability that a feared outcome will take place and the consequences should it occur. For example, imagine a client who fears job loss. The client might overestimate the probability of this loss taking place ("If I don't handle every assignment perfectly, I will lose my job"), as well as the probability of never finding another job should his or her current employment be terminated ("Other employers will know that I was fired from this job and will not want to hire me"). When using cognitive therapy, the therapist helps the client to reevaluate these thoughts and arrive at more realistic estimates of both the probability of job loss and the chances of never finding another job should he or she get fired. According to the cognitive theory of anxiety, the reevaluation of the probability and costs of the feared outcome should lead to a corresponding decrease in worry and anxiety about the potential outcome. Specifically, the client might conclude that an occasional good but imperfect performance would probably not lead to being fired and that the person would most likely be able to find another job if his or her current employment were lost.

When using "standard" cognitive therapy with GAD clients, we observed something that we had not expected. Specifically, we found that following the reevaluation of probability and cost estimates, our clients often reported that their worry and anxiety had *not* decreased. For example, one client had this to say about his fear of taking the airplane once he had reevaluated the chances of his plane crashing during his upcoming trip: "I know that there is only about one chance in three million that my plane will crash, but as long as there is a chance, no matter how small, I can't help but worry." Another client reported the following regarding her performance at work: "I know that I could probably deal with my boss being disappointed in my work performance, but I can't stop worrying about it because I just might be devastated." These examples illustrate what we have experienced time and time again in our work with GAD clients: in order to not worry, they seem to require absolute *certainty* that either a given event will not occur or that they will be able to deal with it should it take place. Thus, we have come to the conclusion that standard cognitive therapy is insufficient for most individuals with GAD because the usual conclusion of cognitive reevaluation (that is, that a negative event is unlikely to happen and that the person would probably be able to cope with the occurrence of the event) is insufficient to help most clients with GAD significantly decrease their worry and anxiety about the event. Stated differently, the reevaluation of probability and cost estimates typically does not lead them to the conclusion they are looking for; namely, that a potential negative event would *definitely* not occur or that they would *unquestionably* be able to deal with the event should it occur. This line of reasoning led us to the idea that individuals with GAD might be *intolerant of uncertainty*.

Since coming to the conclusion that intolerance of uncertainty might play an important role in GAD, we have tested this idea using a variety of approaches. In the following sections, we present the main research findings that bear on the relationship between intolerance of uncertainty, worry, and GAD. As a general rule, the research on intolerance of uncertainty (and all other model components) has progressed from nonclinical studies to investigations in clinically anxious populations. The rationale behind this research strategy is the following: because nonclinical studies offer the advantage of testing new ideas in a relatively quick and cost-efficient fashion, they should be carried out first; clinical studies, which are much more time consuming and expensive, can then focus on replicating and extending key nonclinical findings. Generally speaking, the literature on GAD supports this research strategy, as nonclinical findings have proven extremely useful in designing studies in clinical populations. Moreover, the vast majority of the results pertaining to the processes involved in nonclinical worry have been replicated in samples of clients with GAD, suggesting that nonclinical research can be quite valuable in terms of understanding the etiology of GAD.

We begin our review with studies examining the *specificity* of the relationship between intolerance of uncertainty and GAD. We then turn our attention to the research that has looked into the *nature* of their relationship; that is, the studies that address the question of whether intolerance of uncertainty is a risk factor for GAD. Finally, we summarize the research on potential mechanisms that link intolerance of uncertainty and GAD. These latter investigations have attempted to identify cognitive, behavioral, and emotional pathways leading from intolerance of uncertainty to GAD.

Specificity of Intolerance of Uncertainty

In our initial studies, we tested the relationship between intolerance of uncertainty and excessive worry in nonclinical individuals. Because worry is a universal phenomenon, we reasoned that if intolerance of uncertainty is involved in the etiology of GAD, we should be able to see a relationship between intolerance of uncertainty and worry in people from the general population. Our early studies confirmed that intolerance of uncertainty and worry were in fact highly related among nonclinical individuals (e.g., Freeston et al., 1994). We also wanted to ensure that the relationship between intolerance of uncertainty and worry was not simply the result of their respective relationships with anxiety and depression. The findings from our early studies also confirmed that this was clearly not the case: the relationship between intolerance of uncertainty and excessive worry was largely independent of their respective relationships with both anxiety and depression (e.g., Dugas, Freeston, & Ladouceur, 1997).

To further examine the issue of specificity, we were interested in knowing if the relationship between intolerance of uncertainty and nonclinical worry could be accounted for by personal dispositions that are known to be related to worry and anxiety. To address this question, we examined the associations between worry, intolerance of uncertainty, perfectionism, and need for control (Buhr & Dugas, 2006). As expected, we found that worry was more highly related to intolerance of uncertainty than to perfectionism and need for control. In addition, the relationship between intolerance of uncertainty and worry was largely independent, whereas the relationships between worry and both perfectionism and need for control were for the most part accounted for by intolerance of uncertainty. Put simply, the contribution of perfectionism and need for control to the tendency to worry is largely explained by intolerance of uncertainty. From a theoretical perspective, these findings imply that perfectionism and need for control are not essential components within a cognitive model of GAD. From a clinical perspective, this suggests that helping clients with GAD become more tolerant of uncertainty should also help them to decrease their perfectionism and need for control.

We were also interested in knowing if intolerance of uncertainty was more highly related to worry than to other types of anxious symptoms. By and large, this line of research has supported the idea that the relationship between intolerance of uncertainty and worry is unique. Although intolerance of uncertainty is related to other anxious symptoms, which is not surprising given that different types of anxiety share common vulnerabilities, it appears to be more highly related to excessive worry. For example, intolerance of uncertainty is more highly related to worry than to obsessions and panic symptoms in nonclinical individuals (Dugas, Gosselin et al., 2001). Because worry and depression are related, we also compared the relationships between intolerance of uncertainty, worry, and depressive symptoms. Again, we found that although intolerance of uncertainty was related to level of depressive symptoms in nonclinical individuals, it was more highly related to worry (Dugas, Schwartz, & Francis, 2004). Although we are aware of one nonclinical study in which the association between intolerance of uncertainty and worry was not significantly higher than the relationship between intolerance of uncertainty and a subset of obsessive–compulsive symptoms (e.g., Holaway, Heimberg, & Coles, 2006), the weight of the evidence indicates that intolerance of uncertainty is specifically related to excessive worry in the nonclinical population. In the following paragraphs, we present the findings of our research examining intolerance of uncertainty in samples of clinically anxious clients.

In an initial clinical study, we compared levels of intolerance of uncertainty in clients with GAD, clients with various other anxiety disorders, and nonclinical control participants (Ladouceur et al., 1999). The other anxiety disorders group was primarily comprised of clients with obsessive–compulsive disorder, although social anxiety disorder, panic disorder, specific phobia, and posttraumatic stress disorder were also represented. As expected, we found that both clinically anxious groups had higher levels of intolerance of uncertainty than the nonclinical control group. More importantly, however, clients with GAD were more intolerant of uncertainty than were clients with other anxiety disorders. Although these findings are instructive, they are limited by the fact that they do not provide information about levels of intolerance of uncertainty in specific non-GAD anxiety disorders.

Since this initial clinical study, we have compared levels of intolerance of uncertainty in GAD clients to those of panic disorder clients (Dugas, Marchand, & Ladouceur, 2005). As expected, we found that relative to the clients with panic disorder, those with GAD were more intolerant of uncertainty (i.e., they reported more negative beliefs about uncertainty and its implications). Interestingly, when both groups were combined, intolerance of uncertainty was related to level of worry but unrelated to panic-like symptoms. This implies that having difficulty tolerating and dealing with uncertainty predicts GAD-like symptoms in anxious clients who do not necessarily meet diagnostic criteria for GAD (at least, those with panic disorder). Consequently, intolerance of uncertainty shows some evidence of both diagnostic and symptom specificity. Further research is required, however, before any conclusions can be drawn with regard to other anxiety disorders.

In a further clinical test of specificity, we examined whether level of intolerance of uncertainty could predict the severity of symptoms in a group of individuals with GAD (Dugas et al., in press). Given that the variability of symptoms and processes within a group of GAD clients is limited (all have high levels of worry, anxiety, and intolerance of uncertainty), we did not necessarily expect to find any significant relationships. Nonetheless, we found that clients with severe GAD had more difficulty tolerating uncertainty than those with less severe forms of the disorder, lending further support to the sensitivity of the relation between intolerance of uncertainty and GAD.

In summary, the bulk of the research conducted in both nonclinical and clinically anxious populations suggests that intolerance of uncertainty has a sensitive and specific relationship to the symptoms of GAD (in particular chronic, excessive, and uncontrollable worry). Given these findings, we now turn our attention to the literature bearing on the *nature* of the relation between intolerance of uncertainty and GAD.

Evidence for Causality of Intolerance of Uncertainty

Before addressing the question of a potential causal link between intolerance of uncertainty and GAD, the criteria for establishing such a link will be reviewed. In 1997, Helena Chmura Kraemer and her colleagues proposed a set of conditions to establish causality. The authors convincingly argued that the term *causal risk factor* should be used when describing a factor that has a causal influence on another because the term *cause* inaccurately suggests that only one factor is involved in the etiology of a second factor (which is almost never the case). Thus the term *causal risk factor* will be used throughout this book when addressing the notion of causality. According to Kraemer and her associates, four conditions must be met for one factor (Factor A) to be considered a causal risk factor for a second factor (Factor B): (1) Factor A must be correlated with Factor B; (2) Factor A must precede Factor B; (3) Factor A must be modifiable (or else it would be considered a fixed marker; e.g., year of birth, gender); and (4) the manipulation of Factor A must lead to changes in, or the occurrence of, Factor B. Given our hypothesis that intolerance of uncertainty is a causal risk factor for GAD, we have begun to test these conditions. Although the previously reviewed studies show that intolerance of uncertainty and worry are closely related (Condition 1), they do not address the other three conditions required to establish that intolerance of uncertainty is a causal risk factor for GAD. We have begun to address these issues by experimentally manipulating level of intolerance of uncertainty and by examining change mechanisms during the treatment of GAD.

In a nonclinical laboratory study, we attempted to experimentally manipulate level of intolerance of uncertainty and assess the impact of changes in intolerance of uncertainty on level of worry (Ladouceur, Gosselin, & Dugas, 2000). Specifically, we used a gambling procedure to place participants in a situation that included uncertainty and asked them to place a series of bets where the chances of winning were one out of three. For half of the participants, we sought to *increase* their intolerance of uncertainty by having the experimenter repeatedly mention that the chances of winning were poorer in the present study compared to previous studies. The goal of this procedure was to have participants interpret their chances of winning as *unacceptable*. For the other half of the participants, we aimed to decrease their intolerance of uncertainty by having the experimenter frequently mention that the chances of winning in the current study were better than in previous studies. The goal of this procedure was to have participants interpret their chances of winning as *acceptable*. Unbeknownst to the participants, however, the gambling outcomes were programmed to be identical for everyone. All participants were told that if they managed to "break even," a donation would be made to a foundation for disadvantaged children. Following the gambling procedure, where none of the participants managed to break even, all were asked to complete a measure of intolerance of uncertainty (manipulation check) as well as a measure of worry about the financial needs of the foundation. The results showed that the experimental manipulation was successful as participants in the increased intolerance of uncertainty condition reported higher levels of intolerance of uncertainty than those in the decreased intolerance of uncertainty condition. Further, participants in the increased intolerance of uncertainty condition reported more worry about the needs of the foundation than did participants in the decreased intolerance of uncertainty condition. Thus, this study provided support for the notion that level of intolerance of uncertainty can be modified and that change in intolerance of uncertainty leads to change in worry, thereby satisfying Conditions 3 and 4 for a causal risk factor as set out by Kraemer and her colleagues (1997).

In another test of the causality hypothesis, we investigated precedence of change over the course of treatment for clients with GAD. We reasoned that if intolerance of uncertainty is a causal risk factor for GAD, changes in intolerance of uncertainty should precede changes in worry during treatment. Stated differently, if intolerance of uncertainty is among the factors that lead to worry, it follows that individuals with GAD would have to succeed in better tolerating uncertainty before they could succeed in decreasing their worry. We addressed this issue by examining treatment data for 16 clients who received cognitive-behavioral therapy (CBT) for GAD (Dugas, Langlois, Rhéaume, & Ladouceur, 1998). Participants were asked to rate their levels of intolerance of uncertainty and worry on a daily basis over the course of therapy (14 to 18 weeks). Following treatment completion, we used the statistical technique of time-series analysis to examine the temporal relationship between intolerance of uncertainty and time spent worrying. We found that changes in intolerance of uncertainty preceded changes in level of worry for 11 clients, whereas changes in time spent worrying preceded changes in intolerance of uncertainty for only one client (no significant relationships were observed for four clients). Therefore, it appears that changes in intolerance of uncertainty typically precede changes in worry during the treatment of GAD. Returning to the conditions set out by Kraemer and her colleagues (1997), the findings reviewed in this section show that three of the four conditions for identifying a causal risk factor have been satisfied. Specifically, intolerance of uncertainty is closely related to worry (Condition 1), intolerance of uncertainty can be modified (Condition 3), and changes in intolerance of uncertainty typically precede changes in worry over the course of treatment (Condition 4). However, research has yet to address Condition 2, which states that Factor A (intolerance of uncertainty) must precede Factor B (excessive worry and GAD). We are currently conducting a five-year longitudinal study in adolescent samples to address this issue.

Pathways from Intolerance of Uncertainty to GAD

Given that the data accumulated thus far is consistent with the idea that intolerance of uncertainty is a causal risk factor for GAD, we now turn our attention to the issue of *how* intolerance of uncertainty might lead to GAD. Stated another way, what are the different pathways leading from intolerance of uncertainty to GAD? In the following paragraphs, we review two lines of research that address this question. The first involves studies of information processing and the second is made up of research on decision making. Together, these lines of research begin to paint a portrait of the many interacting and dynamic pathways leading from intolerance of uncertainty to GAD.

Research on the way in which anxious individuals process information from their environment has the potential to elucidate the role of intolerance of uncertainty in GAD. In particular, studies of interpretational biases in anxious individuals suggest a potential pathway leading from intolerance of uncertainty to high levels of worry and GAD. Specifically, these studies show that individuals with GAD have an exaggerated tendency to make threatening interpretations of ambiguous information (e.g., Eysenck, Mogg, May, Richards, & Mathews, 1991; Mogg, Bradley, Miller, & Potts, 1994). Thus, when faced with a situation that contains the possibility of two or more outcomes, individuals with GAD tend to conclude that a negative outcome will ensue. For example, he or she might conclude that their plane will crash if they experience turbulence during a flight or that they will be late for a meeting if their taxi is temporarily stuck in traffic.

On the surface, the finding that individuals with GAD tend to make threatening interpretations of ambiguous information certainly seems consistent with the notion that they have difficulty tolerating uncertainty. In fact, it may be that strongly held negative beliefs about uncertainty are "responsible" for the tendency to make threatening interpretations of information that is unclear. In other words, intolerance of uncertainty may be the factor that best explains this interpretational bias in individuals with GAD.

To test this hypothesis, we have begun to examine the relationship between intolerance of uncertainty and the tendency to make threatening interpretations of ambiguous information. In an initial study, we looked at the relationship between intolerance of uncertainty and interpretations of ambiguous information in nonclinical volunteers (Dugas, Hedayati et al., 2005). Participants were instructed to read a series of fictional diary entries, imagine them as though they were their own, and rate each entry in terms of its threat value. Half of the diary entries were ambiguous ("While on my way out tonight I was stopped in the street") and the other half of the entries were divided between positive ones ("I was really pleased when I passed my driving test today; this calls for a big celebration") and negative ones ("We had invited some friends to join us for a barbecue, but no one turned up"). As expected, the participants with high levels of intolerance of uncertainty rated the ambiguous diary entries as more threatening. More importantly, threat ratings of ambiguous entries were more highly related to intolerance of uncertainty than to levels of anxiety, depression, and worry. Furthermore, the relation between intolerance of uncertainty and threat ratings was independent of mood ratings. Thus, it appears that in nonclinical individuals, intolerance of uncertainty may be at the root of the biased interpretations of ambiguous information. This conclusion is in line with the cognitive theory of psychopathology that states that fundamental beliefs (and not symptoms such as anxiety or depression) have a direct impact on the way we process information from our environment (Beck & Clark, 1997). *Therefore, one potential pathway leading from intolerance of uncertainty to GAD is that individuals who are intolerant of uncertainty have a strong tendency to make threatening interpretations of ambiguous information, which may lead to elevated levels of worry and anxiety about the implications of their interpretations.*

Related to the study of information processing, a number of researchers have examined the impact of level of worry and anxiety on laboratory decision making. Although intolerance of uncertainty was not assessed in many of these studies, they are nonetheless quite informative in terms of understanding the potential role of intolerance of uncertainty in GAD.

Richard Metzger and his colleagues (Metzger, Miller, Cohen, Sofka, & Borkovec, 1990), set out to examine differences between high and low worriers in terms of decision making, by comparing both groups of participants on a categorization task that varied in level of ambiguity. Participants were asked to decide whether or not variations in figures were members of a novel category. The level of ambiguity was manipulated by modifying one or more features of the figures. The results showed that high worriers did not differ from low worriers when the level of ambiguity was low (manipulation of only one feature). However, for elevated levels of ambiguity (manipulation of more than one feature), the high worriers took longer that the low worriers to reach a decision. Thus, it appears that high worriers have greater difficulty dealing with the uncertainty of highly ambiguous situations.

In a related study, Frank Tallis and his colleagues (Tallis, Eysenck, & Mathews, 1991) used a computerized search task to compare high and low worriers. Participants viewed randomly distributed letters on the computer screen and were asked to determine if a target (the letter "E") was among the displayed letters. When the target was present, there were no differences between the groups. However, when the target was absent, the high worriers took longer to respond than did the low worriers. Tallis and colleagues concluded that high worriers required more evidence than did low worriers when making a decision involving greater levels of ambiguity or uncertainty. Although both studies reviewed above did not specifically address the role of intolerance of uncertainty, their findings can be interpreted as showing that high worriers have difficulty dealing with the uncertainty inherent in ambiguous situations. Because high worriers typically have elevated levels of intolerance of uncertainty, one can speculate that intolerance of uncertainty is closely related to the disparity in performance on the unambiguous and ambiguous tasks.

Having considered the findings of the decision-making studies described above, we chose to directly examine the impact of intolerance of uncertainty on decision making. In an initial study, we used a series of three laboratory tasks to investigate the relationship between intolerance of uncertainty and decision making in nonclinical participants (Ladouceur, Talbot, & Dugas, 1997). In the first task, we varied the level of difficulty, whereas in the second and third tasks, we manipulated the level of ambiguity. As expected, we found that intolerance of uncertainty was unrelated to performance at all levels of difficulty on the first task. However, intolerance of uncertainty was related to performance at moderate levels of ambiguity on the second and third tasks, with the high intolerance of uncertainty participants doing more poorly. Thus, it appears that intolerance of uncertainty has its greatest effects in moderately ambiguous situations. This seems logical when one considers that unambiguous situations generally present little threat to all individuals (including those high in intolerance of uncertainty) and that highly ambiguous situations are typically threatening for most people (including those low in intolerance of uncertainty). Unfortunately, for individuals who have high levels of intolerance of uncertainty, many situations in everyday life are characterized by moderate levels of ambiguity or uncertainty. *Therefore, a second potential pathway leading from intolerance of uncertainty to GAD is that individuals who are intolerant of uncertainty may require more information when making decisions in moderately ambiguous situations, which may lead to prolonged worry and anxiety about these situations.*

In line with other cognitive models of psychopathology, our model is based on the idea that beliefs (in this case, about uncertainty) are fully activated when the individual is in a negative mood state. Others (e.g., Beck & Emery, 1985) have referred to this as the activation of latent schemas. Although we prefer the term *belief* to *schema*, we agree with the notion that negative cognition and emotion can interact to contribute to the development and maintenance of psychopathology. Given the potential interaction between beliefs and emotional state, we examined the interaction between intolerance of uncertainty and state anxiety in nonclinical participants (Talbot, Dugas, & Ladouceur, 1999). In this study, half of the participants were subjected to the Public Speaking Task, a state anxiety manipulation where they were told that they would be speaking in front of a small group of graduate students (although they did not actually have to make the speech). Participants then completed a laboratory task that included various levels of ambiguity. Although level of intolerance of uncertainty and state anxiety were unrelated to task performance at all levels of ambiguity, they were related to certainty about having made correct decisions on the task. In particular, participants with high levels of intolerance of uncertainty who had received the anxiety manipulation were less confident about their performance than were the other participants, including those who had received the anxiety manipulation but were low in intolerance of uncertainty. These results imply that the combination of high intolerance of uncertainty and high anxiety leads to lower levels of certainty (confidence) in at least some decision-making situations. *Consequently, a third potential pathway leading from intolerance of uncertainty to GAD is that individuals who are intolerant of uncertainty, when anxious, have less confidence in their decisions in ambiguous situations, which may lead to worry about the implications of their decisions.*

In summary, the data accumulated thus far suggest that individuals who are intolerant of uncertainty may be at risk for developing GAD because they tend to: (1) make threatening interpretations of ambiguous information; (2) perform poorly in moderately ambiguous situations;

and (3) have particularly low confidence in their decisions when anxious. Although future research will undoubtedly uncover many other pathways leading from intolerance of uncertainty to GAD, there is good reason to believe that investigations into the way individuals with varying levels of intolerance of uncertainty process information will continue to be highly useful in furthering our understanding of the etiology of GAD.

POSITIVE BELIEFS ABOUT WORRY

The beliefs that individuals with GAD hold about worry have also received considerable study. In this section, we focus on the research on positive beliefs about worry because this line of study has direct implications for the treatment that is presented in the following chapters. However, the reader should keep in mind that negative beliefs about worry have received formidable empirical support (e.g., Wells & Carter, 1999), and that other cognitive-behavioral treatments focus on changing these beliefs to help individuals with GAD.

Our research on positive beliefs about worry was initially the result of our interest in conditioning theory. In line with operant conditioning principles, we reasoned that positive beliefs about worry could develop and be maintained by the processes of positive and negative reinforcement. Specifically, if a person notices that the act of worrying is followed by the attainment of desired outcomes (positive reinforcement) or the avoidance of undesirable outcomes (negative reinforcement), that person would be likely to develop positive beliefs about worry (and continue to worry). With this in mind, we set out to examine positive beliefs about worry in nonclinical and clinical populations.

First Generation Studies of Positive Beliefs

In our initial studies, we assessed positive beliefs about worry that fell into two broad categories: (1) worrying can prevent or minimize negative outcomes (negative reinforcement), and (2) worrying is a positive action for finding a solution (positive reinforcement). We first found that nonclinical individuals meeting some GAD criteria reported greater positive beliefs about worry than did nonclinical individuals meeting none of the criteria (Freeston et al., 1994). We also found that the relationship between positive beliefs and level of worry was independent of anxiety and depression, which suggests that these beliefs make a unique contribution to the explanation of how much people worry. In a second study, we assessed the same positive beliefs about worry and found that GAD clients reported stronger beliefs than did nonclinical moderate worriers (Ladouceur, Blais, Freeston, & Dugas, 1998). Subsequently, we examined these positive beliefs in GAD clients, other anxiety disorder clients, and nonclinical individuals (Ladouceur et al., 1999). Although the GAD clients reported more positive beliefs about worry than did the nonclinical individuals, both clinical groups reported similar levels of these beliefs. These results suggest that although GAD clients have higher levels of worry than do clients with other anxiety disorders, they do not hold stronger beliefs about the usefulness of worrying. These findings have since been replicated in a study comparing GAD clients to panic disorder clients (Dugas, Marchand et al., 2005), lending further support to the idea that positive beliefs about worry are a characteristic of clinically anxious individuals as opposed to being a GAD-specific characteristic.

If positive beliefs about worry are not specific to a diagnosis of GAD, why are they one of the components of our cognitive model? Simply put, because specificity and causality are different constructs (although many people confuse the two). In other words, the fact that positive beliefs about worry are not exclusively related to GAD does not mean that they are not involved in the development and maintenance of the disorder. In fact, although at least one of the model components should be specific to GAD (otherwise it would not be a GAD model), there is no need for all components to show evidence of diagnostic specificity. As discussed previously, given that intolerance of uncertainty is for the most part specific to a diagnosis of GAD, the model can already be said to be GAD-specific.

Having acknowledged the distinction between specificity and causality, we turn to the issue of the evidence suggesting that positive beliefs are involved in the etiology of GAD. Because experimental manipulations and longitudinal studies of positive beliefs about worry have yet to be carried out, the only evidence that these beliefs play a role in the etiology of GAD is indirect at best. For example, the data show that a treatment that targets positive beliefs about worry not only leads to a decrease in these beliefs, but also to a reduction in GAD symptoms (Laberge, Dugas, & Ladouceur, 2000). Furthermore, the *degree* to which the beliefs change predicts the *extent* of improvement in GAD symptoms. Although these findings are certainly enticing, their implications are rather unclear given that the treatment targets all model components and not only positive beliefs. Nonetheless, further study into the nature of the relation between positive beliefs about worry and GAD is clearly warranted.

Second Generation Studies of Positive Beliefs

In an effort to attain a more comprehensive and clinically useful understanding of positive beliefs about worry, our group has revised our conceptualization to include five types of positive beliefs: (1) worrying helps to find solutions to problems; (2) worrying increases motivation to get things done; (3) worrying about something in advance can decrease one's negative reaction should the event actually occur; (4) worrying, in and of itself, can prevent bad things from happening (this has been referred to as magical thinking or thought–action fusion); and (5) worrying shows that one is a responsible and caring person. Since conceptualizing positive beliefs along these lines, we have developed and validated a questionnaire measuring these five positive beliefs about worry (the Why Worry-II, which is presented in Chapter 3). In studies using this questionnaire, we have found that the degree to which nonclinical individuals endorse the combination of these beliefs predicts the presence of excessive and uncontrollable worry (Laugesen, Dugas, & Bukowski, 2003; Robichaud et al., 2003). In terms of the specific beliefs, it appears that the fifth belief (worrying shows that one is a responsible and caring person) is the best predictor of excessive worry, at least in the general population (Bakerman, Buhr, Koerner, & Dugas, 2004).

In clinical samples, unpublished analyses of a recently completed treatment study show that four of these five positive beliefs significantly decreased over the course of therapy for clients receiving CBT. Only the second belief (worrying increases motivation to get things done) did not change during CBT. Interestingly, for clients receiving the other treatment, applied relaxation, none of the five beliefs decreased over the course of therapy. Thus, it appears that targeting positive beliefs about worry in treatment makes a difference; these beliefs do not change unless they are directly addressed by the therapist and client.

In summary, the data from a number of nonclinical and clinical studies show that positive beliefs about worry are related to level of worry and GAD. Although we believe that these beliefs play a role in the development and maintenance of GAD, the nature of their relation to GAD awaits clarification via experimental manipulations and longitudinal studies.

NEGATIVE PROBLEM ORIENTATION

According to current models of problem solving (D'Zurilla & Nezu, 1999), the problem-solving process can be broken down into two major constituents: problem orientation and problem-solving skills. Problem orientation refers to an individual's general cognitive set when faced with a problem. As such, it includes perceptions of problems, appraisals of oneself as a problem-solving agent, and expectations regarding problem-solving outcomes. Problem-solving skills, on the other hand, refer to the actual skills required to successfully solve everyday problems. These skills include: (1) defining the problem and formulating problem-solving goals; (2) generating alternative solutions; (3) choosing a solution; and (4) implementing the chosen solution and assessing its effectiveness. Overall, research has shown that worry and GAD are closely related to having a negative problem orientation, but that they are largely unrelated to knowledge of problem-solving skills. Thus, it appears that although individuals with GAD generally know how to solve their problems, they have difficulty successfully doing so because they have a negative cognitive set when faced with a problem. That is, they tend to view problems as threatening, to doubt their problem-solving ability, and to be pessimistic about problem-solving outcomes. Thus, the third component of our cognitive model of GAD is *negative problem orientation.* In the following paragraphs, we review the findings from studies using problem-solving questionnaires as well as those from a recent study using an innovative structured interview.

Questionnaire Studies of Problem Solving

In our initial studies, we assessed the relationship between problem solving and worry in nonclinical volunteers using self-report questionnaires (Dugas et al., 1997; Dugas, Letarte, Rhéaume, Freeston, & Ladouceur, 1995). In both studies, we found that although level of worry was strongly related to having a negative problem orientation, it was unrelated to knowledge of problem-solving skills. In the first study (Dugas et al., 1995), the findings showed that negative problem orientation continued to predict worry scores when anxiety and depression were statistically controlled. That is, the relationship between problem orientation and worry was not explained by their respective relationships with anxiety and depression. In the second study (Dugas et al., 1997), we added a measure of intolerance of uncertainty and found further evidence for the specificity of the relationship between negative problem orientation and excessive worry. Specifically, negative problem orientation maintained its relationship with worry when anxiety, depression, and intolerance of uncertainty were statistically controlled.

Given that negative problem orientation overlaps to some extent with the personality characteristics of pessimism, low self-mastery, and neuroticism, we recently examined their respective relationships with excessive worry (Robichaud & Dugas, 2005b). In terms of our model, the main finding was that the relation between negative problem orientation and worry was largely independent of all personality characteristics assessed in our study. In other words, negative problem orientation makes a specific contribution to the prediction of worry, which cannot simply be explained by the more general personality features of pessimism, low self-mastery, and neuroticism. Another important finding of this study was that negative problem orientation was a stronger predictor of worry than of depression when the above-mentioned personality characteristics were taken into account. Thus, although negative problem orientation has also been shown to predict depressive symptoms, it appears to be a stronger predictor of the tendency to worry. Taken together, the findings from the nonclinical questionnaire studies of problem solving suggest that negative problem orientation is a sensitive and specific marker of chronic and excessive worry.

For the most part, the findings of our nonclinical studies have been supported by those of our clinical studies. For example, we found that although clients with GAD and nonclinical control participants had relatively equivalent knowledge of problem-solving skills, the GAD clients had a more negative problem orientation (Dugas, Gagnon et al., 1998). In terms of comparisons between different clinical groups, we found that clients with GAD had a more negative problem orientation than clients with various other anxiety disorders, most of whom had primary obsessive–compulsive disorder (Ladouceur et al., 1999). Recently, however, we found that clients with GAD and those with panic disorder both had a similar problem orientation (Dugas, Marchand et al., 2005). Thus, it may be that GAD clients have a more negative problem orientation than some but not all other anxiety-disordered clients. Although the preliminary data point to this conclusion, further research including groups of clients with each anxiety disorder is required to properly address the question of diagnostic specificity.

In a previous section of this chapter, we reported a study showing that level of intolerance of uncertainty was related to the severity of GAD *within* a sample of GAD clients (Dugas et al., in press). In the same study, we found that level of negative problem orientation was also related to the severity of GAD symptoms. In fact, intolerance of uncertainty and negative problem orientation were the only model components that predicted the severity of GAD. These findings suggest that, although negative problem orientation may not be specific to a diagnosis of GAD relative to all other anxiety disorder diagnoses, it does seem to be quite sensitive to the presence and severity of GAD. Clinically, therefore, negative problem orientation appears to be an important target in the treatment of clients with GAD.

Interview Study of Problem Solving

According to D'Zurilla and Nezu's (1999) model of problem solving, individuals with adequate problem-solving skills will not be efficient problem solvers if they have a negative problem orientation, because having a negative problem orientation can interfere with the proper application of one's problem-solving skills. For individuals with GAD, this certainly appears to be the case. Although research shows that they possess problem-solving skills that are roughly equivalent to those of nonclinical individuals, clinical experience suggests that they often have difficulty dealing with relatively minor day-to-day problems. But how does having a negative problem orientation *actually* interfere with solving one's problems effectively? Does negative problem orientation always interfere with successful problem solving or does it only interfere under certain conditions? Does negative problem orientation prohibit the proper application of all problem-solving skills or only a subset of the skills? To begin addressing these questions, we recently developed a comprehensive interview procedure that allows us to examine the impact of problem orientation on each step of the problem-solving process for different types of problems.

Generally speaking, the Problem-Solving Interview asks participants to describe exactly what they would do at each stage of the problem-solving process (problem definition and goal formulation, generation of alternative solutions, decision making, and solution implementation and verification). Furthermore, participants are asked to go through the problem-solving process for two different problems: a hypothetical problem and a real-life problem they are currently experiencing. In a recently completed study, we asked nonclinical participants to complete the Problem-Solving Interview and a series of questionnaires, including the Negative Problem Orientation Questionnaire and the Intolerance of Uncertainty Scale (Robichaud, Dugas, & Radomsky, 2006). Overall, the findings showed that having a negative problem orientation was related to poor problem-solving performance under certain circumstances. In terms of specific results, three findings are particularly important for our model and treatment. First, regardless of the participants' level of intolerance of uncertainty, negative problem orientation was unrelated to performance at all problem-solving steps for the hypothetical problem. Second, for participants with low levels of intolerance of uncertainty, negative problem orientation was related to poor performance on *one* problem-solving step (that is, decision making) for the real-life problem. Finally, for participants with high levels of intolerance of uncertainty, negative problem orientation was related to poor performance on *all* problem-solving steps for the real-life problem. Consequently, it appears that having a negative problem orientation interferes most with the proper use of problem-solving skills when individuals who are intolerant of uncertainty have to deal with current problems that have personal relevance. Given that individuals with GAD typically have high levels of intolerance of uncertainty, it may be that their negative problem orientation has a particularly negative impact on their ability to deal with their personally relevant, day-to-day problems.

The findings of the interview study described above fit nicely with the clinical procedures described in chapters 4 and 5, which include training in both problem orientation and problem-solving skills. Namely, it appears that offering training in the specific steps required to successfully deal with personally relevant problems is essential when treating GAD clients (who typically have a negative problem orientation *and* are intolerant of uncertainty). Therefore, the decision to include comprehensive problem-solving training in the treatment of GAD is supported by research that takes into account the complex interrelations between negative problem orientation, problem-solving skills, intolerance of uncertainty, and problem relevance.

COGNITIVE AVOIDANCE

The final component of our model, *cognitive avoidance*, refers to a variety of strategies that lead to the avoidance of threatening cognitive and emotional content. In our view, cognitive avoidance strategies can be divided into two broad categories: (1) implicit or automatic strategies, and (2) explicit or voluntary strategies. Each one is discussed in turn in the following paragraphs.

Implicit Cognitive Avoidance Strategies

Since the late 1980s, Thomas Borkovec, a researcher at Penn State University, has studied the avoidant nature of worry. His work has shown that individuals use implicit avoidance strategies that allow them to avoid threatening cognitive content and dampen unpleasant physiological arousal. In the late 1980s and early 1990s, Borkovec observed that worry is primarily a lexical or verbal-linguistic mental activity (Borkovec & Inz, 1990). Stated differently, when individuals worry, they do so with a relative absence of mental imagery. Furthermore, it seems that the worry of individuals with GAD contains a smaller proportion of mental images than the worry of nonanxious individuals. Research also shows that the proportion of mental images contained in the worry of

GAD clients tends to increase and normalize following successful treatment (Borkovec & Hu, 1990). But what is the clinical relevance of this finding? To fully grasp the clinical implications of the lexical nature of worry, one must consider the basic nature of fear and the mechanisms of fear reduction.

Research examining the cognitive correlates of fear suggests that mental images may play a key role in the generation of the fear response. Specifically, mental images about a threatening situation are associated with a stronger emotional reaction than are verbal-linguistic thoughts about the same situation (Vrana, Cuthbert, & Lang, 1986). One way to think about this finding is that verbal-linguistic thoughts, such as worry, reduce one's emotional reaction when thinking about a feared outcome. Thus, it may be that the worry of individuals with GAD allows for a dampening of physiological reactions when contemplating threatening outcomes. In fact, this appears to be the case, as a number of studies show that GAD worry is associated with reductions in autonomic hyperactivity such as tachycardia and hyperventilation. From the perspective of operant conditioning, one could say that verbal-linguistic worry is negatively reinforced by the avoidance of threatening images and their attendant physiological activation.

According to the emotional processing theory of fear reduction, fear is reduced when two conditions are met: (1) the full fear structure in memory is accessed, and (2) information that is incompatible with the fear is integrated into the structure (Foa & Kozak, 1986). In terms of the first condition, the full fear structure is accessed when the individual experiences "full network activation." This term nicely encapsulates the idea that the individual must experience fear with all its referents: behavioral, cognitive, and emotional (both subjective affect and physiological arousal). When the full fear structure is activated, the individual can then incorporate new nonthreatening information into the structure. Although, in our view, the theory of emotional processing does not account for all instances of fear reduction, it is nonetheless a very useful framework for understanding how worry interferes with the reduction of fear.

In summary, according to Borkovec's avoidance theory of GAD, the primarily verbal-linguistic nature of GAD worry is negatively reinforcing because it leads to the avoidance of both threatening mental images and unpleasant autonomic activation. Moreover, because GAD worry impedes full network activation, individuals with GAD have difficulty completely accessing the fear structures stored in their memories. Ultimately, if the fear structures are not properly accessed, they will prove more difficult to modify via the integration of new information. The end result of the relative lack of emotional processing of fear is that individuals with GAD continue to worry about the possibility that threatening outcomes may occur.

Explicit Cognitive Avoidance Strategies

In addition to the research showing that individuals with GAD use implicit cognitive avoidance strategies such as the automatic avoidance of threatening mental images, there is also a considerable body of evidence suggesting that these individuals use a series of explicit or voluntary cognitive avoidance strategies. These include the following deliberate strategies: (1) suppressing worrisome thoughts; (2) substituting neutral or positive thoughts for worries; (3) using distraction as a way to interrupt worrying; and (4) avoiding situations that can lead to worrisome thinking. Recent findings have substantiated that all four of these cognitive avoidance strategies are independently related to excessive and catastrophic worry (e.g., Gosselin et al., 2002; Sexton, Dugas, & Hedayati, 2004).

How does the use of effortful cognitive avoidance lead to GAD? Of the cognitive avoidance strategies listed above, the first (thought suppression) has received the most research attention in terms of how it might lead to high levels of worry and anxiety. According to recent theories of thought suppression, attempts to suppress unwanted thoughts can lead to enhancement and rebound effects. Enhancement effects are observed when an individual experiences an increase in the target thought *during* attempted suppression, whereas rebound effects are witnessed when a person experiences an increase in the target thought *following* attempted suppression. For example, if you were instructed not to think about a white bear for one minute (the classic thought suppression paradigm), you might find that you had many thoughts about a white bear during the one-minute suppression period (enhancement effect). Similarly, you might find yourself thinking about a white bear from time to time over the next few days (rebound effect). Although some theorists have claimed that enhancement and rebound effects play an important role in most if not all anxiety disorders (e.g., Becker, Rinck, Roth, & Margraf, 1998; Wegner & Zanakos, 1994), most studies of suppression in GAD suggest that these effects may not be germane to the worry of individuals with GAD (e.g., Behar, Vescio, & Borkovec, 2005; Mathews & Milroy, 1994).

It is our position that thought suppression, like the other cognitive avoidance strategies mentioned above, contributes to the development and maintenance of GAD via a series of pathways, many of which involve the avoidance of unpleasant emotional reactions. In the interest of conciseness, we will discuss only two such pathways. The first involves the use of effortful cognitive avoidance strategies, which may serve the same purpose as the avoidance of mental images in GAD worry; that is, the dampening of unpleasant emotional arousal. In fact, by temporarily removing the worrisome thought, effortful cognitive avoidance may even eradicate the emotional reaction altogether, in a sense "going one step further" than the avoidance of mental images. Thus, like the automatic avoidance of images, the effortful avoidance of worrisome thoughts may interfere with the emotional processing of fear.

The second pathway involves the utilization of active avoidance strategies, which may lead to the consolidation of *negative beliefs about anxiety*. Our work, as well as the work of others, shows that individuals with GAD have a strong tendency to fear their own anxious responding (e.g., Mennin, Heimberg, Turk, & Fresco, 2002; Sexton & Dugas, 2004). As mentioned above, by actively using cognitive avoidance strategies, individuals with GAD succeed in temporarily dampening or eliminating anxious responding. This may, in turn, strengthen negative beliefs about anxiety (and fear of anxiety) because these individuals do not learn to deal with their anxious responding. Specifically, they do not learn that they can "handle" feeling anxious and they do not develop strategies to deal with the anxious responding. Thus, the use of effortful cognitive avoidance strategies may contribute to the development and maintenance of GAD by interfering with emotional arousal (much like the automatic avoidance of threatening mental images) and by strengthening negative beliefs about anxiety and the resulting fear of anxiety.

CONNECTIONS BETWEEN MODEL COMPONENTS

In this chapter, we have presented the research on the model components in separate sections. We chose this approach because it seemed like the most useful way of presenting the model to clinicians who were unfamiliar with our work. The reader should keep in mind, however, that the model components are not mutually exclusive and that they interact in complex ways that we are just beginning to understand. In particular, it appears that intolerance of uncertainty is a *higher order process* that contributes to all three other model components. From an empirical point of view, the data show that the relationship between GAD and the three other model components can be explained, at least partially, by level of intolerance of uncertainty. From a clinical perspective, these data imply that intolerance of uncertainty should be addressed at all phases of therapy and not only when it is directly targeted at the beginning of therapy.

CLINICAL IMPLICATIONS OF THE MODEL

As mentioned at the beginning of this chapter, our main objective in developing and validating a cognitive model of GAD was to come up with a framework that would assist clinicians in working with GAD clients. We have tried to achieve a balance between "following the data" and formulating a model that has heuristic value in terms of clinical work. Although our model and treatment are clearly a work in progress, we believe that the model, as it now stands, is neither too complex nor overly simplistic for most clients seeking help for their worry and anxiety.

CHAPTER 3

Diagnosis and Assessment

As discussed in Chapter 1, the identification of generalized anxiety disorder (GAD) can present quite a challenge, even for the seasoned clinician. In fact, anxiety disorder specialists can also find it difficult to recognize GAD, so it comes as no surprise that GAD has the lowest diagnostic reliability of all the anxiety disorders. Therefore, in this section, we will provide a detailed outline of strategies that are helpful for the assessment of GAD in a clinical interview format, particularly in terms of the differential diagnosis of GAD from other anxiety-related disorders. In addition, because the use of standardized instruments is very important in establishing a diagnosis of GAD, useful diagnostic interviews and self-report questionnaires will be reviewed. Finally, in presenting each instrument we will add a personal discussion of the strengths and weaknesses of each one, as well as integrate thoughts about our experience with these different measures.

THE CLINICAL INTERVIEW

When perusing the *DSM-IV*, one is quickly struck by the overlap between virtually all of the GAD somatic symptoms (that is, restlessness or feeling keyed up or on edge, being easily fatigued, difficulty concentrating or mind going blank, irritability, and sleep disturbance) and the symptoms of other anxiety and mood disorders. In fact, of all the somatic symptoms included as criteria for GAD, only muscle tension is not included in the criteria for at least one other anxiety or mood disorder. Obviously, attempting to establish a diagnosis on the basis of muscle tension alone is rather difficult. Clinicians should therefore focus their assessment on the client's worry in an attempt to establish a diagnosis, rather than focusing on the somatic symptoms. This is also a useful tip for clinicians assessing a client who has not been specifically referred for GAD. That is, simply asking whether the client has been worrying a great deal about a number of daily events can increase the chances of recognizing GAD if the disorder is in fact present.

One of the more tricky aspects involved in the diagnosis of GAD is attempting to determine whether a client's worry is *excessive and uncontrollable*, as this may not be as straightforward as it appears. Because it is fundamentally a subjective call whether a client is worrying excessively and uncontrollably, clinicians will have to rely on their own judgment to assess the pathological nature of a client's worry. Although this may seem like a daunting task, we have elaborated some useful diagnostic questions that can help clinicians to assess worry on these two dimensions.

GAD Worry

Given that the notion of excessiveness is subjective and highly dependent upon an individual's life circumstances, it is important to begin with an assessment of the stressors, changes, or difficulties in a client's life. This is necessary because a client may be worrying excessively about his mother's health, for example, but if his mother was recently diagnosed with a life-threatening illness or is slated to undergo surgery in the near future, the level of worry the client is experiencing may be appropriate to his current situation. For this reason, clients should be queried about possible stressors involving their family, interpersonal relationships, physical health, finances, and work or school. In addition, it is important to ask about changes in clients' lives, including positive ones (for example, a move, graduation from school, or a wedding), as these transitions can be stressful and it is normal that individuals might worry more in relation to these events.

So, if worry levels often increase during times of stress or change, how does one determine whether a client's worry is excessive? There are several useful and specific questions that can address this issue. Because the hallmark of GAD is worry about a number of events or activities, clinicians should take the time to go through each major life area of the client's life to get an idea of the frequency and excessiveness of each worry. This includes family, interpersonal relationships, work/school, health, finances, and day-to-day minor matters. In practical terms, clinicians should try to get an idea of how frequently clients worried about each topic *over the last six months*.

Once the frequency of worry has been established, excessiveness can be determined through several questions. First, clients can be asked whether they feel that their worry is excessive: "Does your worry about X strike you as excessive? That is, do you think that you worry too much about X?" If clients experience difficulty with this, it might be helpful to remind them that this is a subjective question and that the goal is to try to get an idea of their own perceptions. There is no right or wrong answer to this question. Second, to address any potential stressors in a client's life that may be exacerbating worry about a particular topic, clinicians might ask: "If everything is going all right with X, do you still worry a great deal about this topic?" Alternatively, a specific stressor can be incorporated into the question. For example, "I know that you mentioned your mother is ill right now, which is obviously causing you to worry a great deal about her, but do you find that you worry a lot about your family's health even when everyone is doing well?" A third way in which to tap excessiveness is to ask clients to compare their worry to that of others. That is, "If someone else were in your shoes, would they worry as much about X as you do?" The most important information to draw from these questions is whether the individual is worrying frequently about a number of events, whether the worry is longstanding and not simply the result of a particular stressor, and whether the level of worry is greater than what would be expected given the client's life circumstances.

In addition to frequency and excessiveness, the assessment of GAD worry should include an evaluation of thc client's sense of control over his or her worrisome thoughts. Individuals with GAD will often describe their worries as spinning out of control, with one worry ("What if I get into an car accident one day?") engendering others ("What if it's a serious accident and I don't recover? What will happen to my children?"). This *chaining effect* of worry, and the resultant feeling of uncontrollability that is characteristic of GAD, can be addressed through the analogy of a freight train. That is, "Is it difficult to control your worry about X? Does it feel like a freight train, in that it is difficult to put on the brakes once it has really started up?" Once again, the clinician should ask these questions about each worry topic. This is important not only to satisfy the criterion of excessive and uncontrollable worry about a number of events, but also to allow for differential diagnosis. Since individuals with various other anxiety disorders will typically report worrying about their primary fear, it is necessary to make certain that a client with suspected GAD is truly worrying about a number of topics.

GAD Somatic Symptoms

In order to be diagnosed with GAD, clients need to endorse at least three of the following six somatic symptoms: restlessness or feeling keyed up or on edge, being easily fatigued, difficulty concentrating or mind going blank, irritability, muscle tension, and sleep disturbance. As noted previously, all of these symptoms, with the exception of muscle tension, can be found among the criteria for other mental health disorders. This is particularly the case for mood disorders, where a depressed or dysthymic client might endorse concentration difficulties, fatigue, and sleep disturbance. Because of this, it is a good idea for clinicians to question clients further about these symptoms to determine whether they are in fact GAD-related. However, clinicians must first assess whether clients have experienced a given symptom chronically for it to satisfy the somatic criteria for GAD. That is, the symptom must be experienced for at least the past six months and for more days than not. Subsequent to this, specific questions for certain symptoms can also be asked to increase clinician confidence in a GAD diagnosis. Specifically, when querying about muscle tension, clients can be asked: "Do you find that most of the muscle tension is in your neck and shoulders?" Since chronic anxiety often leads to tension in that part of the body, individuals with GAD will usually endorse this symptom. In addition, specifying a particular location of tension gives clients the feeling that they are "in the right place." That is, that they are speaking with someone who really understands their specific difficulties.

When asking about concentration difficulties, clients can be asked to expand on their answer if they endorse this symptom: "Why do you think you have concentration problems? Does it feel like your mind is running at 100 miles an hour with various worries and that, as a result, it is hard to focus or concentrate?" Finally, in terms of sleeping difficulties, it is a good idea to get a sense of the type of sleeping problem (that is, problems falling asleep, staying asleep, or restless sleep), because for GAD sufferers this is most likely due to excessive worry. For example, if a client endorses difficulties falling asleep, they can be queried: "Do you find that your mind starts spinning with worries the moment you put your head to the pillow?" Alternatively, clients who endorse difficulties staying asleep or restless sleep can be asked: "Do you find that you are so preoccupied with worries that you wake up throughout the night?" By asking clients to provide additional information about how they experience their somatic symptoms, the clinician will be in a much better position to determine if the symptoms are part of the GAD syndrome or if they reflect the presence of another disorder.

Impairment and Distress

The final criterion required to ascribe a diagnosis of GAD is the presence of significant distress or interference in the individual's life as a result of his or her symptoms. This can certainly be determined by simply asking clients whether they experience mild, moderate, or severe distress and interference due to their worry and anxiety; however, this is also an opportunity to gather additional information about the impact of the disorder on the client's life. As will be discussed at length in later chapters, there is a certain amount of ambivalence that clients often experience with regard to reducing their worries. Since many view themselves as "born worriers," it can be difficult for them to imagine a life without excessive worry. As such, it will be important for clinicians to have an understanding of the negative impact that worry has had on the client's life, as this is information that can be used later in treatment.

In order to get a good picture of the GAD-related impairment, it might be helpful to probe specific aspects of the client's life. For example, how is this impacting upon the person's relationships with family and friends? Is the person constantly seeking reassurance from others to the degree that it is causing tension? Problems may also arise at work or in school. Are assignments getting done on time, or is the individual spending so much time worrying about small details that work productivity is suffering? Another highly revelatory aspect is that of quality of life. Is the client enjoying life? More specifically, when engaging in a pleasant activity, is the client so preoccupied by worries about future events that he can't enjoy the moment? Allowing clients to discuss the repercussions of their worry on their lives can strengthen their motivation for treatment and give them the feeling of being understood.

In summary, there are numerous aspects to consider when making a GAD diagnosis, the most time-consuming of which is the assessment of worry. Since worry is a universal human phenomenon, it is important to verify that the client's worries are frequent, excessive, and difficult to control, as well as related to several different events or activities of daily life. Moreover, the worry must be chronic and longstanding, and not simply the result of external stressors. The detail described herein can often result in a rather lengthy clinical interview, particularly when time is taken to gather specific information about each major worry topic. However, there are several benefits to spending a full session or two on information gathering. First, it will increase the clinician's confidence in a GAD diagnosis if one is given, and considering its low diagnostic reliability, it is important to take the time to really understand a client's presenting complaints. Second, it allows for a complete "picture" of the client, which will be quite helpful during the treatment phase. Finally, clients are more likely to feel that they are understood by the clinician, which can help to establish a good rapport right from the initial assessment stage.

OBSTACLES TO THE DIAGNOSIS OF GAD

GAD clients are like most people who present for treatment with mental health issues, in that they are rarely "textbook cases." Few, if any, will walk into the clinician's office and state that they are experiencing excessive and uncontrollable worry. Unless specifically referred for GAD, the majority of clients will not even think to mention worry as their primary complaint. The following are some obstacles to diagnosis, as well as some practical suggestions to address them.

"I'm Not a Worrier"

For various reasons, clients with GAD might deny that their problem is excessive worry. This can be due to the belief that worry is not a legitimate complaint, is socially undesirable, or does not reflect the intensity of the individual's suffering. As a result, the clinician's task will involve ascertaining what words the client is using to describe worry and providing a more expansive definition of worry that the client can accept and endorse. As mentioned in Chapter 1, frequent alternate terminologies that clients use in place of worry are: "anxiety," "fear," and "phobia." For example, "I am fearful of everything! I have a phobia about travel, storms, and even driving a car. I also get really anxious in social situations." From this description, the client could indeed have several specific phobias, as well as some social anxiety. However, by probing into the reasons underlying these fears, it can quickly become apparent that these are worries rather than phobias. For example, when asked why he is fearful about travel, the client might respond: "I'm afraid that there might be a problem with the plane. What if it crashed? What would happen to my children? How would my wife cope with being a single parent?" Given that this response looks like a worry chain, it is recommended that the clinician probe about other "fears" to determine whether they are also mislabeled worries.

When clients are reluctant to describe their problems in terms of worry, we have found it helpful to explain what we mean when we talk about worry. A useful explanation is as follows:

> When I talk about worry, I'm not referring to the kind of worrying that almost all of us do in our daily lives to some extent. I'm talking about excessive worry, which is essentially a form of *scenario building*. That is, taking anything uncertain in your life and trying to think of every possible eventuality so that nothing comes as a surprise. For example, "What if X happens? Well, then I might do this.... But what if Y happens? Well in that case, I might try to do this...." Some people

> describe this type of scenario building as "fear" or "anxiety," but it is still worry. Does this sound like what you do?

By providing an alternate way of describing worry, clinicians can not only better establish a diagnosis of GAD when that is in fact the problem, but they can also lay some of the groundwork for the forthcoming treatment. That is, clients need to be able to recognize that they are in fact worrying, or they might not see a treatment that targets excessive worry as appropriate for their particular distress.

"Yes, I Have That Too..."

Given that individuals with GAD often describe worrying about "everything," it should come as no surprise that some will be very worried about whether they are describing their symptoms properly (that is, "What if I don't explain myself well and I'm misdiagnosed?"). As a result, some GAD clients can feel the need to provide exhaustive detail in response to each question, and can also endorse symptoms from many other anxiety disorders that they are not currently experiencing. That is, if they have ever experienced symptoms from any particular diagnostic category (as we all do sometimes), they will respond in the affirmative to questions about those symptoms. For example, a GAD client queried about social anxiety might endorse fears of being negatively evaluated by others in social situations even if this is not causing any particular distress or interference. Obviously, if a client is endorsing symptoms from every diagnostic category, the interview can become extremely lengthy, and the challenge of distinguishing clinically significant problems from those that are not increases exponentially.

How can a clinician deal with a client who is endorsing virtually every symptom he or she is asked about, while still maintaining rapport and identifying multiple concurrent disorders if comorbidity is present? First, the clinician can discuss this issue at the outset. Clients can be told that they will be asked about a variety of symptoms, many of which probably will not apply to them, and only those symptoms that they are actually experiencing (or have experienced in the past) will be discussed in more detail. It is also a good idea to discuss the difference between experiencing a symptom (which is common to most people) and having the symptom be a serious problem for the individual. One way to address this is by saying the following:

> We are going to be discussing a lot of different types of symptoms today so that we can determine which ones are problematic for you and which ones aren't. I will always start off by asking some general

> questions that require a yes or no answer. If the symptom applies to you, I will ask you about it in more detail, but if it doesn't apply to you, we will simply move on to the next. I want to remind you that most of the symptoms that I will be talking to you about today are things that many people experience to some degree from time to time in their lives. For example, many people are afraid of snakes, but we wouldn't classify this fear as a "disorder" unless it significantly interfered with their lives and caused them great distress. That means that when I ask you about particular symptoms, it is best to say yes to a question only if I am describing something that you experience quite often and that is really bothering you or interfering with your life. Do you have any questions about that?

By taking the time to "set the stage" for the interview, clients are less likely to endorse almost every symptom. As a result, identifying the disorders that are actually a problem for the individual can become clearer and the length of the interview can be reduced as well. However, if clients are still endorsing virtually every symptom throughout the clinical interview, clinicians might want to ask: "Is this something that you experience excessively or severely and is it causing you great distress?" Eventually, clients can be expected to focus more specifically on their clinically significant problems. As stated beforehand, GAD clients will occasionally engage in this overreporting behavior out of a concern that if they fail to disclose anything, they might be improperly diagnosed. It is important for clinicians not to lose patience with clients, but to bring them back on course gently in order to maintain a good working relationship at this initial therapeutic stage.

Misdiagnosing Symptoms as GAD

Another common problem in diagnosis is the labeling of GAD when the disorder is not in fact present. Although this will be discussed in greater detail in the differential diagnosis section, a frequent reason for this problem is due to the introduction of mental health terms into the common vernacular. That is, more and more, clients will describe increases in anxiety as "panicking," bouts of low mood as "depression," and ruminations as "obsessing." In the case of GAD, just as it is likely for clients to describe their worries as fears, it is also common for clients with other anxiety or mood disorders to state, "I worry about many different things." Because of this, clinicians always need to subquestion clients about their worries. For example, a client might state that they worry about school, work, and social situations. On the surface, this is suggestive of worry about several different daily life events (which is characteristic of GAD), but the underlying fear for these disparate situations might be a fear of negative evaluation that is better accounted for by a diagnosis of social anxiety disorder. Such a potential misdiagnosis underscores the importance of not only being thorough in the assessment of GAD, but also in the evaluation of other anxiety and mood disorders as well.

DIFFERENTIAL DIAGNOSIS

As noted previously, of all the anxiety disorders, GAD can be one of the trickiest diagnoses to make. Even in anxiety clinics where clinicians are expecting to encounter GAD, it is not an obvious or straightforward diagnosis. Certainly, for clinicians in nonspecialized settings, it can be even more of a challenge to identify. The problem is aggravated by the fact that when medical practitioners refer anxious clients for psychological treatment, they will occasionally note only "generalized anxiety" in the referral. However, in these cases, "generalized anxiety" can refer to any of the anxiety disorders, not necessarily GAD, as the locus of the anxiety was probably not thoroughly assessed. In essence, clients who are described as having "generalized anxiety" may be suffering from an anxiety disorder other than GAD, and clients with GAD may be misdiagnosed as having another anxiety/mood disorder. For this reason, it is helpful to have some guidelines to aid in the differential diagnosis of GAD in relation to specific anxiety disorders.

Hypochondriasis (Health Anxiety)

Classified as one of the somatoform disorders, hypochondriasis has also been called health anxiety, and it is defined as an excessive preoccupation with having a serious disease or illness. The disorder is the result of the misinterpretation of physical symptoms and bodily sensations. For example, a persistent cough or a small bump on a part of the body may be erroneously interpreted as signs of cancer. Individuals with hypochondriasis will frequently consult with medical specialists for their feared illnesses, although the reassurance they receive from these visits is typically short-lived, as they tend to persist in their belief that the disease or illness is in fact present although undiagnosed.

Because of the excessive preoccupation and worry about health, hypochondriasis can resemble GAD. As such, if a client reports excessive and uncontrollable worry about her health, the clinician is faced with a dilemma: does the client have GAD, hypochondriasis, or both disorders? If a client only reports excessive worry about her health, that is, she does not list worries about any topics other than her fears about having contracted a specific disease, then a diagnosis of GAD would not be appropriate. In this case, a diagnosis of hypochondriasis would likely be warranted. However, if a client reports excessive worries about other topics in addition to concerns about health, then the primary issue becomes the discrimination between a diagnosis of GAD or a diagnosis of GAD and hypochondriasis (with the primary disorder being established based on which problem is causing the individual greater distress and interference).

To aid in this discrimination, there are several useful questions that clinicians can ask. First, a primary distinction between both disorders relates to the belief that the feared disease or illness is already present. With GAD, individuals tend to report excessive worries about one day developing a serious disease such as cancer; thus, the focus is on the *possibility* of developing the disease. With hypochondriasis, individuals tend to focus on their conviction that they may have *already developed* the disease, and as a result, numerous medical consultations are sought out to identify and begin treating the feared illness. Clients can therefore be asked the following question: "Do you think that you may already have a serious disease or illness that has simply not been diagnosed yet, or are you mostly worried about potentially getting this disease in the future?" If clients report that the main focus of their health concerns is about the possibility of developing a health condition in the future (and the consequences thereof), then a diagnosis of hypochondriasis can be ruled out, as the concerns are most consistent with a diagnosis of GAD. If clients instead report the conviction that they have already contracted a disease not yet identified, then a diagnosis of hypochondriasis might be more appropriate.

Other useful questions relate to the erroneous interpretations of physical symptoms or bodily changes. Individuals with hypochondriasis have a tendency to catastrophically misinterpret any physical change as evidence of a serious illness. As such, a slight discoloration of the skin, a rash, or a cough is taken as proof of having contracted a disease. Clients can therefore be asked the following: "Do you often perceive changes in your body or physical symptoms as evidence that you have in fact contracted a serious illness?" As stated previously, GAD clients might worry excessively about their health and the possibility of becoming ill, but they are less likely to focus on the interpretation of minor physical symptoms. In a related vein, individuals with hypochondriasis often devote excessive time to scanning their bodies for physical changes, seeking reassurance from others, obtaining information about medical conditions, and consulting with medical specialists. Body scanning can involve palpating minor lumps to the point where they become inflamed, or repeatedly checking one's body to ensure that there are no physical changes. Excessive information seeking includes reading various textbooks about the symptoms of different medical conditions and seeking out diagnostic information on the Internet.

In terms of medical consultations, individuals with hypochondriasis can present for the same tests on several occasions, out of a conviction that a specific disease is present but unidentified. Often, the medical visits are for very frivolous or minor concerns, and although individuals with GAD will also frequently consult with medical specialists, they are less likely to return for the same tests multiple times. With respect to hypochondriasis, all of these behaviors provide only brief reassurance. For example, clients might feel relieved following a medical visit where no illness was found; however, that relief is short-lived; before long, the individual with hypochondriasis will once again become convinced that the feared disease is present. GAD clients, however, might see several medical specialists for their concerns, but the worries are assuaged once the results of medical tests are provided. As a final note, if the clinician determines that a client merits a diagnosis of hypochondriasis in addition to GAD, a simple way to determine which disorder is primary is to ask the client which problem is most distressing. This can be accomplished with a pie chart, where clients are asked: "If this pie represents all the problems that you are struggling with now, how much of the pie would the health anxiety take? How much would GAD take?" In this manner, clinicians can determine whether GAD should be the focus of treatment or whether it is secondary to another condition.

Social Anxiety Disorder

Social anxiety disorder is characterized by an intense fear of social or performance situations, where one might be judged or thought of negatively. Individuals with social anxiety tend to engage in significant avoidance of feared social situations, and they typically experience extreme anxiety when anticipating an upcoming social event or activity. It is an anxiety disorder that can manifest itself in multiple situations, including parties, business meetings, one-on-one conversations, or crowded areas where one might be prone to be judged or observed by others. Because of both the heterogeneity of situations where an individual with social anxiety might feel anxious, and the tendency to worry about these situations prior to entering them, the disorder can appear quite similar to GAD.

As with hypochondriasis, if worries are relegated exclusively to concerns about being judged or negatively evaluated in social situations, then a diagnosis of GAD is likely not warranted. However, it can be a challenge to determine whether disparate worries about various situations are in fact subsumed under a diagnosis of social anxiety disorder. A primary distinction between GAD and social anxiety is the underlying fear. If, for example, a client reports worrying about several situations (e.g., work, school, interpersonal/relationships), clinicians should ask about the fear that is motivating the worry. Clients with social anxiety will consistently endorse a fear that they might be observed or evaluated by others, or that they will do something embarrassing or humiliating in front of others. Although GAD clients can also endorse this fear, they will likewise endorse other concerns as well, thereby satisfying the criterion of worries about a number of daily events.

The picture becomes more complex if clients appear to report GAD worries in addition to social concerns. The question then becomes: Does the client have a diagnosis of GAD where one of the worry topics is social/interpersonal situations, or is a secondary diagnosis of social anxiety disorder merited? A good way to determine this is to ask about avoidance behavior. One of the hallmarks of social anxiety disorder is significant avoidance of social situations, the extent of which is distressing to the individual and interferes with his or her life. For example, a client with social anxiety might avoid initiating conversations with others, attending social gatherings with friends, or eating and writing in public. Although GAD clients might engage in a certain amount of avoidance of triggers for their worries, it is their excessive worry and anxiety that is causing most of their distress and impairment, not the avoidance behavior. As such, clients can be asked the following: "When you think about your fear of social situations, what would you say is most distressing and interfering for you: the fact that you worry excessively about these situations or the fact that you avoid them?" GAD clients will frequently endorse greater distress and impairment from their worries, whereas individuals with a diagnosis (either primary or secondary) of social anxiety disorder will often endorse avoidance.

Obsessive–Compulsive Disorder

Obsessive–compulsive disorder (OCD) is an anxiety disorder characterized by the presence of obsessions or compulsions that cause significant interference and distress. Because obsessions are intrusive and recurrent thoughts, they can, at times, appear quite similar to GAD worries, once again rendering the discrimination between GAD and other anxiety disorders a challenge. In terms of overt behavioral compulsions such as excessive handwashing, touching or tapping of objects in a ritualistic manner, or excessive checking of locks and appliances, the presence of these behaviors is clearly specific to OCD. As such, if clients endorse these types of overt compulsions, a diagnosis of OCD is warranted. However, individuals with OCD can also experience solely the presence of obsessions without associated compulsions. Since both obsessions and worries are essentially cognitive intrusions, the distinction between both is not immediately evident. Although there are certain obsessions that are more obviously distinct from GAD worries, such as an obsessional impulse to stab a loved one compared to an excessive worry about completing work tasks on time, there are cognitive intrusions that are less easily distinguishable. For example, thoughts about harm occurring to one's child can be viewed as either an obsession or a worry. Discriminating between the two can be effectively done by querying clients along several dimensions about their thoughts.

First, the content of worries tends to be about real-life daily events (e.g., work or school performance, punctuality, interpersonal relationships). In contrast, obsessive thoughts are typically considered odd or inappropriate, such as sexual or blasphemous thoughts. Moreover, although obsessions can take the form of thoughts (for example, "What if I hit someone with my car while driving?"), they can also be experienced as vivid visual images (for example, an image of punching someone) or impulses (for example, an urge to scream obscenities in church). Worries, on the other hand, are experienced mostly as thoughts and rarely take the form of images or impulses. Second, obsessive thoughts are seen by the client as unwanted and intrusive. That is, they are experienced as highly unpleasant and distressing, and the client will typically make a concerted effort to resist or avoid the thoughts. This is not the case with GAD worries. The content of the worries is not typically viewed as inappropriate and is largely ego-syntonic. In fact, as will be discussed in later chapters, many worries experienced by GAD clients are viewed as serving a positive function (for example, "The fact that I worry about the health of my children shows that I am a caring mother"). Finally, the content of obsessions tends to be static in nature. That is, individuals with OCD typically experience repeated intrusions of the same distressing thought, image, or impulse. Worries, however, are largely dynamic in nature, as the content will shift from day to day, and they are experienced as a continually evolving scenario. For example, worries about the health of one's child ("What if my child gets injured at school?") will typically lead to other worries ("What if the injury is serious, and my child never recovers? What if my child's performance at school and ability to make friends is affected? How will this impact my family?"). As such, through a careful assessment of the content and the nature of a client's thoughts, clinicians can differentiate between GAD and OCD with confidence.

Major Depressive Disorder and Dysthymic Disorder

Major depressive disorder (or depression) is characterized by persistent feelings of sadness and loss of interest in previously enjoyed activities for a period of at least two weeks. Dysthymic disorder (or dysthymia) is a less severe, although more chronic form of depression, as symptoms must be present for at least two years. There are two main reasons why discriminating between these disorders and GAD can prove to be a challenge. First, there is an overlap in terms of somatic symptoms. Specifically, lack of concentration, sleeping difficulties, and fatigue are associated with both GAD and depression/dysthymia. Second, depressed or dysthymic individuals are prone to ruminations, that is, the passive and repetitive focus on one's distress and the meaning of that distress (Nolen-Hoeksema, 1998). This kind of dwelling thought process could easily resemble GAD worry. Moreover, GAD and depression/dysthymia have been found to co-occur quite frequently. As such, it is important to determine whether clients are suffering from either one or both disorders in order to begin developing a proper treatment strategy. The following are a few helpful suggestions that can be used to aid in the differentiation of these disorders.

In terms of somatic symptoms, the experience of muscle tension, particularly in the neck and shoulders, has been found to be specific to GAD. As a consequence, participants who endorse this symptom, in addition to other GAD somatic symptoms, are likely to merit a diagnosis of GAD. However, not all GAD clients endorse significant muscle tension, and because of the considerable overlap between the disorders, clinicians should ultimately place the diagnostic focus on the client's thought content rather than their somatic symptoms. That is, the emphasis should be placed on distinguishing between GAD worries and depressive ruminations. A primary distinction between worries and ruminations is the temporal focus. Individuals who worry tend to focus on potential negative events in the future (that is, negative things that *might* happen), whereas those who ruminate tend to focus on negative events that have taken place in the past (that is, negative things that have *already* happened). One potential complication with this distinction is the fact that worries can occasionally relate to past events. For example, a client might be preoccupied about an exam that they failed the week before. On its surface, this thought appears to be a depressive rumination as it involves a negative event in the past. However, whether it is a worry or a rumination will depend on why the client is focusing on that particular concern. That is, this may in fact be a GAD worry if the individual is thinking about a past event in terms of its *future* repercussions, whereas it is more likely to reflect depression if the individual is dwelling on the event as yet another example of failure. As with other disorders, the best way to confidently diagnose GAD is to obtain detailed information about the content of the client's thoughts and the reasons underlying their troublesome thoughts (see Table 3.1 for an overview of the differential diagnosis of GAD and the previously discussed disorders).

In summary, differential diagnosis with respect to GAD can be quite a challenge. This is due not only to the inclusion of relatively subjective criteria for the disorder in the *DSM-IV* (that is, excessive and uncontrollable worry), but also to the high comorbidity rates between GAD and other disorders. As such, it is extremely important to take the time to properly assess the thought content of clients. Although this process of assessment might seem lengthy, the information derived is invaluable both to clinicians and to the client. Clinicians can feel confident that when a diagnosis is made, it accurately reflects the symptom presentation of their clients, and clients can leave the assessment with a better understanding of themselves and their distress. Although the previous information was primarily described in a clinical interview format, it is our belief that the use of structured diagnostic tools is vital to a complete and thorough assessment. As such, the following section will address the various structured assessment tools that are most relevant to GAD and to our particular treatment protocol.

STRUCTURED DIAGNOSTIC INTERVIEWS

Although many clinicians prefer to use nonstructured clinical interviews when assessing their clients, our experience has been that the use of structured diagnostic interviewing is essential when attempting to identify GAD. Furthermore, we have found that clients respond very well to the structured nature of the interview, and often interpret the highly structured and in-depth nature of the interview as a sign that they are "in the right place." In fact, many clients have never had a thorough investigation of their anxiety and welcome the opportunity to discuss the many facets of their anxiety and anxiety-related problems.

The main advantage of structured diagnostic interviewing is that the clinician is less likely to make the mistake of not going beyond clients' presenting complaints. By inquiring about a broad range of emotional problems, the clinician may discover that what appeared to be a simple case of GAD is in fact a case of many comorbid conditions.

TABLE 3.1 Differential Diagnosis: Tips for Discriminating between GAD and Other Anxiety and Mood Disorders

GAD	Hypochondriasis
1. Excessive worry about several topics, which might include disease or illness 2. Worry about potentially contracting a disease in the future, but no conviction that it is already present but undiagnosed 3. May present for medical consultations, but visits are not excessive regarding feared disease 4. No presence of persistent misinterpretation of bodily symptoms or changes	1. Excessive preoccupation with disease or illness 2. Belief that one has already contracted the feared disease 3. Excessive medical consultations and reassurance-seeking; reassurance provided is short-lived 4. Physical symptoms are erroneously interpreted as signs of a serious illness (despite evidence to the contrary)

GAD	Social Anxiety Disorder
1. Worry about several different events in daily life that can include social/interactional situations 2. Worries are not confined to negative social evaluation concerns 3. Worries about social situations are more distressing and impairing than avoidance	1. Worries exclusively relate to situations where the individual might be judged negatively by others 2. Underlying fear of all worries is of being judged or evaluated negatively by others 3. Avoidance of social situations causes significant distress and impairment

GAD	Obsessive–Compulsive Disorder
1. Worries about real-life daily events 2. Worries are not seen as inappropriate; the content is often ego-syntonic (e.g., worries about family can be viewed as evidence of the individual's caring and empathy toward others) 3. Content of worries is dynamic (i.e., takes the form of a continually evolving scenario)	1. Obsessive thoughts are considered odd or inappropriate 2. Thoughts are seen as intrusive and unwanted; the content of which causes significant distress 3. Content of thoughts is typically static (i.e., repetition of the same thought, image, or impulse)

GAD	Depression
1. Muscle tension as a unique somatic symptom 2. Cognitive content is worry 3. Focus is on negative events that may occur in the future	1. Muscle tension is not associated with depression 2. Cognitive content is rumination 3. Focus is on negative events that have occurred in the past

This is particularly the case with clients who are experiencing a great deal of distress as a result of their primary presenting complaint. Their focus on the most disruptive symptoms can lead them to ignore or fail to disclose other concurrent problems unless specifically queried. As noted previously, not only is GAD a disorder with a high comorbidity rate, but disentangling GAD from other secondary diagnoses can be quite a challenge. It is therefore highly advantageous to use a structured assessment tool in order to ensure that all other relevant disorders are properly queried.

Another advantage of structured diagnostic interviewing is that it provides information that can be used to establish a "baseline," which can then be used as a comparison point for changes over treatment and thereafter. This is useful not only for the clinician to monitor progress in treatment, but also for clients themselves, as over the course of treatment they might be unaware or dismissive of the extent of positive changes they have made. A final advantage worthy of mention is that structured diagnostic interviews prevent the clinician from "drifting" away from standard diagnostic criteria to a more idiosyncratic or personal interpretation of the criteria for the specific disorders contained in the different classification systems. Thus, there are a number of important advantages to structured diagnostic interviewing that more than compensate for the disadvantages of using this methodology. There are, however, at least two disadvantages to using these interviews that are discussed below.

The first and most obvious disadvantage of structured diagnostic interviewing is that the interviews can take a considerable amount of time to administer, anywhere from 20 minutes to 2 hours depending on the interview used and the client's problems. Although this does not necessarily present a difficulty in the context of research, it is definitely an important consideration for clinicians working in nonresearch settings, whether they work in the public or in the private sector. The second disadvantage worthy of mention is that there is an important learning curve to the proper use of diagnostic interviews. Until the clinician becomes accustomed to using an interview, there is a chance that the interview will feel "artificial" and may even interfere with the establishment of a sound working relationship with the client (although, in our experience, this is quite rare). Thus, clinicians should expect that they might feel awkward the first few times that they use an interview. Overall, however, the advantages of structured diagnostic interviewing outweigh the disadvantages. It is important, though, that clinicians follow certain guidelines when using structured diagnostic interviews. In the following paragraphs, we will describe the main guidelines for using most assessment interviews. Although the list is not meant to be exhaustive (interviews typically come with clinician manuals that describe the guidelines in detail), it is meant to give the reader a sense of the "spirit" that goes into structured diagnostic interviewing.

Guidelines for Using Structured Diagnostic Interviews

When using structured diagnostic interviews, clinicians should take 5 or 10 minutes before beginning the interview to explain why a structured approach is helpful for the diagnosis and conceptualization of the client's problem. The client should be prepared for the structure and organization of the interview by the provision of a general description of how it will proceed. For example, the clinician may want to present the following notions:

> Today, I will be using a structured interview to help us to gain a better understanding of your difficulties. As you will see, I will ask a wide variety of questions, some of which will be relevant to your situation and some of which will not. It is important that I ask you all of these questions because it is easy to focus on just one problem without verifying if you have other problems that might be related to your presenting complaint. In other words, we need to ascertain if there are problems that may not be so obvious to you that are contributing to your difficulties. That is why I will be asking you about so many different things today. Does that seem reasonable to you? Do you have any questions before we proceed with the interview?

Another important point that clinicians should keep in mind is that they should not be apologetic for using a structured diagnostic interview (which is what most clinicians tend to do the first few times they conduct a structured interview). In our experience, it is important that the clinician model confidence when using a validated assessment strategy. Although lengthy, the interview should be presented as a valuable tool that will not only allow the clinician to thoroughly understand the client's problems, but also allow the client to leave the session with a better understanding of him- or herself. In terms of the actual interview process, the clinician should pose each question as it is formulated in the interview. Only if the client does not fully understand the question should a different formulation of the question be used. If the clinician is not clear on the meaning of the client's answer, additional explanations should be sought. For example, the clinician may ask what clients mean when they say that they are "panicked at work." As mentioned previously, clinicians should also not be overly reliant on clients' answers to their questions. For example, when the client's answers appear to contradict earlier information, the clinician should point this out and ask for clarification. In addition, if difficulties arise in discriminating between disorders, some of the suggestions provided in the differential diagnosis section can be used.

Description of Structured Diagnostic Interviews

What follows is a description of the main diagnostic interviews that can be used for the identification of GAD. Although the list is not exhaustive, the three interviews that are described represent the most commonly used instruments to diagnose GAD as well as various other Axis I disorders.

Anxiety Disorders Interview Schedule

The Anxiety Disorders Interview Schedule for *DSM-IV*, Current Version (ADIS-IV; Di Nardo, Brown, & Barlow, 1994), is a semistructured interview commonly used by researchers and practitioners to assess all anxiety disorders and screen for mood disorders, somatoform disorders, psychoactive substance use disorders, psychotic disorders, and medical problems. Although the ADIS-IV also exists in a Lifetime Version, the Current Version of the ADIS-IV provides sufficient information for a comprehensive assessment of most clients. The interview yields information on the presence of Axis I disorders with severity ratings on a 9-point Likert scale (0–8). Research has shown that the diagnostic reliability of the anxiety disorders obtained with the ADIS-IV is satisfactory, with improvements over the ADIS-III-R (Brown, Di Nardo, Lehman, & Campbell, 2001). The main advantage of the ADIS-IV is that it includes a Clinical Severity Rating Scale that allows for an evaluation of the severity of each condition that is identified. This information allows the clinician to establish the severity of each disorder, to determine which is the primary disorder when multiple disorders are diagnosed (with primary disorder meaning the most severe disorder), and to ascertain a baseline level of severity that can be used as a comparison point for treatment progress. In addition, the questions to be posed for the different anxiety disorders are in-depth enough to get a relatively rich picture of each of the client's problems if comorbidity is present. The main disadvantages of the ADIS-IV are that it does not cover certain disorders that are often comorbid with anxiety (such as eating disorders) and that it can take anywhere from 30 minutes to 2 hours to administer.

Structured Clinical Interview for DSM

The Structured Clinical Interview for *DSM-IV-TR* for Axis I disorders, Patient Edition (SCID-I/P; First, Spitzer, Gibbon, & Williams, 2002) contains modules for anxiety disorders, mood disorders, psychotic disorders, substance use disorders, somatoform disorders, eating disorders, and adjustment disorders. In terms of its psychometric properties, given that the SCID-I/P has only recently been updated to conform to the DSM-IV-TR, the research examining its psychometric properties is ongoing and has yet to be published. However, research with earlier versions of the SCID for Axis I disorders shows that these versions have acceptable psychometric properties (Williams et al., 1992; Zanarini et al., 2000). In addition to the Patient Edition of the SCID-I, there also exists a Clinician Version (SCID-CV: First, Spitzer, Gibbon, & Williams, 1996), which was designed for use in clinical settings. However, because the Clinician Version does not include many specifiers, subtypes, and even disorders, we recommend using the Patient Edition. The main advantage of the SCID-I/P is that it covers a broad range of Axis I disorders, not only in comparison to the SCID-CV, but also in comparison to the ADIS-IV, which focuses more extensively on the anxiety and mood disorders. The main disadvantage of both the SCID-I/P and SCID-CV is that unlike the ADIS-IV, they do not provide ratings of severity. Rather, they exclusively provide information about the presence/absence of disorders. Moreover, questions related to the assessment of the anxiety disorders, particularly GAD, are not as detailed and specific as those found in the ADIS-IV. Because of this, discriminating among the anxiety disorders may be more difficult when using the SCID.

Mini International Neuropsychiatric Interview

The Mini International Neuropsychiatric Interview for *DSM-IV*, English Version 5.0.0 (MINI; Sheehan & Lecrubier, 1998) is a brief structured Axis I diagnostic interview designed for use in clinical settings by psychiatrists and general practitioners. It includes modules for the anxiety disorders, mood disorders, substance use disorders, eating disorders, and psychotic disorders. Like the SCID, the MINI requires clients to provide yes or no answers to the clinician's questions. Unlike the SCID-I/P, however, the MINI asks few questions about each diagnosis in an effort to minimize the duration of the interview. The MINI, which is clearly the briefest of the structured diagnostic interviews reviewed here, has a mean duration of approximately 20 minutes (see Lecrubier et al., 1997; Sheehan et al., 1997). As such, the main advantage of the MINI is the brief time required for its administration. Its main disadvantage is that research has yet to clearly establish its reliability for the diagnosis of GAD (Lecrubier et al., 1997). In our own research, however, we have found that the MINI provides valid and reliable information with regards to the diagnosis of GAD.

SELF-REPORT QUESTIONNAIRES

Self-report questionnaires are an extremely useful assessment modality because they are both highly informative and very practical. As these measures are easily administered, many of them are standardized with clear guidelines for their interpretation. What follows is a selection of the main self-report questionnaires for the assessment of GAD symptoms and the model components (measures of associated anxiety, depression, and quality of life are also briefly discussed). Again, it is worth noting that we will focus solely on the measures used by our research group. Although there are many other excellent self-report questionnaires for the assessment of the symptoms and processes involved in GAD, we will restrict the following presentation to the instruments that directly map onto our treatment rather than attempting to present a comprehensive list of measures for GAD.

Guidelines for Using Self-Report Measures

In our experience, the flexible use of self-report measures greatly facilitates the assessment of treatment progress. A general strategy for using self-report questionnaires might be to administer a comprehensive battery of questionnaires before beginning treatment, to select a limited number of questionnaires that the client will complete every week or so during treatment, and to readminister all questionnaires following treatment. A typical example of this strategy would be to give the client all questionnaires described below as a between-session exercise before the first and last treatment sessions, and to have the client complete the measures of worry and intolerance of uncertainty in the waiting room before each treatment session. In our experience, filling out the measures of worry and intolerance of uncertainty on a weekly basis provides extremely useful information about the client's progress and the required treatment length. In terms of the interpretation of the client's responses to the self-report questionnaires, some general guidelines are provided below. However, clinicians should keep in mind that responses to individual items may be just as informative as the total score in terms of helping to establish treatment priorities. Moreover, the clinician should review the responses to the self-report questionnaires with the client in order to validate the client's responses and show the client that his answers are being taken into account for treatment planning. For example, simply discussing the items scored highest on each questionnaire can go a long way in helping the client see the usefulness of the comprehensive assessment.

One final point about the self-report questionnaires merits discussion. Specifically, these measures, like the structured diagnostic interviews previously discussed, should be used as complements to the information obtained during interviews. In other words, the client's responses to the questionnaires should be interpreted while keeping in mind matters such as the client's comorbid conditions, current life circumstances, and "personality style." As a general rule, one would expect that a client with many comorbid disorders, who is currently experiencing many stressors, and who has a dramatic or flamboyant personality style, would have inflated scores on the self-report questionnaires. Keeping these caveats in mind, the following is a description of the main measures used for clients with GAD at our clinic.

Self-Report Measures of GAD Symptoms

Worry and Anxiety Questionnaire

The Worry and Anxiety Questionnaire (WAQ) (Dugas, Freeston et al., 2001) is made up of 11 items covering *DSM-IV* diagnostic criteria for GAD. Items such as "Do your worries seem excessive or exaggerated?" and "To what extent does worry or anxiety interfere with your life, for example, your work, social activities, family life, etc.?" are rated on a 9-point Likert scale (0–8). The WAQ has satisfactory test-retest reliability and good known-groups validity (Dugas, Freeston et al., 2001). Our research indicates that the WAQ, when used as a diagnostic instrument, leads to many false positives but few false negatives. Stated differently, many individuals meeting GAD diagnostic criteria on the WAQ will not meet the same criteria on a structured diagnostic interview (false positive). However, rarely will an individual who does not meet GAD diagnostic criteria on the WAQ meet the same criteria on a diagnostic interview (false negative). Given that our group developed the WAQ as a screening instrument for GAD, the fact that the WAQ is more inclusive than actual diagnostic measures is consistent with our intent; there is little cost to a false positive (having to further assess the individual before rejecting the diagnosis of GAD) whereas there are great costs associated with a false negative (for example, not providing the appropriate treatment to someone suffering from GAD) (see Appendix 3.1).

Penn State Worry Questionnaire

The Penn State Worry Questionnaire (PSWQ) (Meyer, Miller, Metzger, & Borkovec, 1990) is comprised of 16 items designed to evaluate the tendency to engage in excessive and uncontrollable worry. Items are rated on a 5-point Likert scale ranging from 1 ("not at all typical of me") to 5 ("very typical of me"). Examples of items are "My worries overwhelm me" and "I know I shouldn't worry about things but I just can't help it." The PSWQ has high internal consistency ($\alpha = .86$ to $.95$), which indicates that items are responded to in a consistent manner. The PSWQ also has very good four-week test-retest reliability, $r = .74$ to $.93$, which suggests that responses remain stable over time (Molina & Borkovec, 1994). The questionnaire also shows evidence of convergent and divergent validity as it is more highly correlated with other measures of worry than with measures of anxiety and depression (Molina & Borkovec, 1994).

Since its development, the PSWQ has established itself as the gold standard for the assessment of worry. Over the past decade, the majority of studies on worry and GAD have used the PSWQ. One advantage of the PSWQ is that it offers a quick, valid, and reliable assessment of the tendency to engage in excessive and uncontrollable worry. A second advantage of the PSWQ is that a great deal of normative data on the measure is available, which makes the interpretation of the client's score easier and more meaningful. In our opinion, however, one disadvantage of the PSWQ is that it contains five inverted items (items that measure the absence of worry such as "I find it easy to dismiss worrisome thoughts" and "I never worry about anything"). Thus, clients need to be particularly attentive to the formulation of items when responding to the PSWQ, and clinicians need to ensure that they are correctly scoring the measure. A copy of the PSWQ is provided in Appendix 3.2.

Self-Report Measures of Model Components

Intolerance of Uncertainty Scale

The Intolerance of Uncertainty Scale (IUS) (Original French version: Freeston et al., 1994; English translation: Buhr & Dugas, 2002) consists of 27 items relating to the idea that uncertainty is unacceptable, reflects badly on a person, and leads to frustration, stress, and the inability to take action. Items are rated on a 5-point Likert scale ranging from "not at all characteristic of me" to "entirely characteristic of me." Items from the IUS include "It's unfair having no guarantees in life" and "When it's time to act, uncertainty paralyses me." Like the original French version, the English translation of the IUS shows excellent internal consistency, $\alpha = .94$, good test-retest reliability over a five-week period, $r = .74$, and good convergent and divergent validity when assessed with measures of worry, depression, and anxiety (Buhr & Dugas, 2002).

Since the inception of our research program on GAD, the IUS has consistently outperformed measures of other anxiety-related constructs such as perfectionism and need for control in terms of predicting levels of worry and identifying individuals with GAD. Furthermore, the IUS is sensitive to changes over treatment (Dugas, Gagnon, Ladouceur, & Freeston, 1998). Thus the main advantage of the IUS resides in its sensitivity and specificity to excessive worry as well as to the presence and severity of GAD. It is a good measure to administer weekly to clients, because reductions in IUS scores can indicate good treatment progress. The main disadvantage of the IUS relates to its fluctuating factor structure, which interferes with the possibility of identifying subscales that might reflect underlying dimensions of intolerance of uncertainty. For this reason, the IUS should be used as a global measure of intolerance of uncertainty and normative data exist only for the total score. See Appendix 3.3 for a copy of the IUS.

Why Worry-II

The Why Worry-II (WW-II) (Original French version: Gosselin, Ladouceur, Langlois et al., 2003; English translation: Holowka, Dugas, Francis, & Laugesen, 2000) is a 25-item revised English version of the Why Worry (WW) questionnaire (Freeston et al., 1994), designed to assess positive beliefs about the function of worry. Items are rated on a 5-point Likert scale from "not at all true of me" to "absolutely true of me." Its design incorporates five subscales that reflect different dimensions of beliefs about worry. These five subscales include beliefs that: (1) worry aids in problem solving (e.g., "The fact that I worry helps me plan my actions to solve a problem"); (2) worry helps motivate (e.g., "The fact that I worry motivates me to do the things I must do"); (3) worrying protects the individual from difficult emotions in the event of a negative outcome (e.g., "If I worry, I will be less unhappy when a negative event occurs"); (4) the act of worrying itself prevents negative outcomes (e.g., "My worries can, by themselves, reduce the risks of danger"); and (5) worry is a positive personality trait (e.g., "The fact that I worry shows that I am a good person"). The English version of the WW-II shows a high internal consistency ($\alpha = .93$), high test-retest reliability at six weeks ($r = .80$), and good convergent and divergent validity with other measures of positive and negative beliefs about worry (Holowka et al., 2000).

Although there exist other measures of positive beliefs about worry such as the Positive Beliefs subscale of the Consequences of Worrying Scale (Davey, Tallis, & Capuzzo, 1996), the WW-II is the only questionnaire entirely devoted to the assessment of beliefs about the usefulness of worrying (or positive beliefs about worry). Furthermore, the WW-II taps the five types of beliefs that have been identified in our previous research and that are specifically targeted by our treatment. Thus, there are some important advantages to using the WW-II for the assessment of positive beliefs about worry. The main disadvantage of using the WW-II for the assessment of positive beliefs is that self-report may not be the optimal format for identifying these beliefs. Not surprisingly, we have found that many clients are not fully aware of their beliefs about worry and that some clients who are aware may not wish to disclose these beliefs because they represent a form of secondary gain of having GAD. Thus, for a client reporting few positive beliefs about worry, the clinician may want to investigate these beliefs further during the session to ensure that the responses on the questionnaire are in fact indicative of the client's true beliefs. The WW-II is reproduced in Appendix 3.4.

Negative Problem Orientation Questionnaire

The Negative Problem Orientation Questionnaire (NPOQ) (Original French version: Gosselin, Pelletier, & Ladouceur, 2001; English translation: Robichaud & Dugas, 2005a) is a 12-item measure that assesses the dysfunctional cognitive set of negative problem orientation. Participants rate each item on a 5-point Likert scale ranging from "not at all true of me" to "extremely true of me," according to how they react or think when confronted with a problem. Sample items include "I see problems as a threat to my well-being" and "I often see problems as bigger than they really are." An initial psychometric evaluation of the measure suggests that the NPOQ is unifactorial, with excellent internal consistency ($\alpha = .92$), high test-retest reliability over five weeks ($r = .80$), and good convergent and discriminant validity (Robichaud & Dugas, 2005a).

The main reason that the NPOQ was developed was that: First, until now, there existed no stand-alone measure of problem orientation. All measures of problem orientation were embedded in questionnaires that assessed many facets of problem solving, including knowledge of problem-solving skills. Given that the self-report of problem-solving skills has been found to be unrelated to worry and GAD (Davey, 1994; Dugas, Freeston, & Ladouceur, 1997; Dugas, Gagnon, et al., 1998), it appeared that a measure exclusively assessing problem orientation was called for. The main advantage of the NPOQ is that it is brief and easy to administer. Furthermore, unlike previous self-report measures of negative problem orientation (e.g., Social Problem-Solving Inventory—Revised; D'Zurilla, Nezu, & Maydeu-Olivares, 1998), the NPOQ is comprised solely of items that reflect the cognitive process or predisposition of negative problem orientation. Specifically, it is devoid of items that reflect the potential emotional, behavioral, and cognitive *consequences* of having a negative problem orientation (e.g., feelings of frustration regarding problem solving, avoidance of solving one's problems). The main disadvantage of the NPOQ is that it has only recently been developed and that validation data using clinical samples has yet to be collected. A copy of the NPOQ is provided in Appendix 3.5.

Cognitive Avoidance Questionnaire

The Cognitive Avoidance Questionnaire (CAQ) (Original French version: Gosselin et al., 2002; English translation: Sexton & Dugas, 2004) contains 25 items assessing the tendency to use five types of cognitive avoidance strategies. The CAQ subscales measure the following strategies: (1) suppressing worrisome thoughts (e.g., "There are things I try not to think about"); (2) substituting neutral or positive thoughts for worries (e.g., "I think about trivial details so as not to think about important subjects that worry me"); (3) using distraction as a way to interrupt worrying (e.g., "I often do things to distract myself from my thoughts"); (4) avoiding actions/situations that can lead to worrisome thinking (e.g., "I avoid actions that remind me of things I do not want to think about"); and (5) transforming mental images into verbal-linguistic thoughts (e.g., "When I have mental images that are upsetting, I say things to myself in my head to replace the images"). Items are rated on a 5-point Likert scale ranging from "not at all characteristic of me" to "entirely characteristic of me." The CAQ has good internal consistency, $\alpha = .95$ for the total scale, and very good test-retest reliability over four to six weeks ($r = .85$). The CAQ also shows evidence of convergent and divergent validity when used with measures of worry, thought suppression, and dispositional coping styles (Sexton & Dugas, 2004).

The main advantage of the CAQ is that it covers a broad range of cognitive avoidance strategies. But like the NPOQ, its psychometric properties have yet to be adequately explored in clinical samples of individuals with GAD or other anxiety and mood disorders. Although the Original French version of the CAQ has shown promise in clinical samples, the English translation awaits further testing. The CAQ is reproduced in Appendix 3.6.

Self-Report Measures of Associated Symptoms

There are many ancillary self-report measures that one might want to use to complement the assessment of GAD. Generally speaking, we have found it useful to assess associated anxiety, depression, and quality of life. In our experience, it is important to assess for somatic anxiety with a self-report measure such as the Beck Anxiety Inventory (Beck, Epstein, Brown, & Steer, 1988). Even if, theoretically, GAD is not associated with exceptionally high levels of somatic anxiety, a significant minority of individuals with GAD have more of a somatic profile than would normally be expected. Furthermore, our data suggest that many individuals with GAD also present with subclinical levels of panic disorder symptoms. Thus the assessment of somatic anxiety provides valuable information in terms of treatment issues.

The second set of symptoms that should be assessed when conducting a comprehensive assessment of GAD is general depression. To this end, a self-report questionnaire such as the Beck Depression Inventory-II (Beck, Steer, & Brown, 1996) can be very useful. Data from a number of studies show that individuals with GAD often have high levels of depressive symptoms. In fact, it may be that many individuals with GAD only decide to seek professional help when they become demoralized or depressed about their constant worry and anxiety. Thus, the assessment of depression is an important part of a comprehensive assessment of GAD.

The final factor that the clinician should assess is quality of life. In the field of psychotherapy (and pharmacotherapy), there is increasing emphasis on the assessment of nondisorder specific variables such as quality of life. There is good reason for this trend because simply being free of DSM-defined symptoms does not necessarily mean that the client has attained a quality of life that is comparable to that of individuals from the general population. The assessment of quality of life with measures such as the Quality of Life Inventory (Frisch, 1994) also fits well with current models of wellness that emphasize that the absence of disorders does not necessarily imply that a person is healthy and well.

SUMMARY AND CONCLUDING REMARKS

A comprehensive assessment of GAD is important for many reasons. First, given that the diagnostic reliability of GAD is lower than that of most other anxiety disorders, a careful and complete assessment is warranted. In theory, the identification of GAD may seem relatively straightforward; however, in practice this is not usually the case. Second, because individuals with GAD often meet diagnostic criteria for other disorders as well, it is important to determine not only what, if any, other problems a given client is suffering from, but also which problem is most severe and requires immediate attention. Third, a comprehensive assessment provides a broad range of baseline scores that can be used to measure the client's progress in areas such as symptoms, processes, general psychopathology, and quality of life.

One of the criticisms of the scientist-practitioner model is that treatment research is not always informative for clinicians because the methods used in treatment research are not thought to be amenable to everyday clinical practice. Perhaps nowhere is this more apparent than for assessment. However, it may be that this situation is in part attributable to clinician perceptions of what clients are willing to engage in for the proper assessment of their difficulties. Our own experience has been that most clients appreciate receiving a thorough assessment battery and understand its importance. Moreover, by having clients complete most of the self-report measures as between-session exercises, the burden of assessment can be significantly reduced.

APPENDIX 3.1

Worry and Anxiety Questionnaire (WAQ)

1. What subjects do you worry about most often?
   a) ________________ d) ________________
   b) ________________ e) ________________
   c) ________________ f) ________________

For the following numbers, please circle the corresponding number (0–8).

2. Do your worries seem excessive or exaggerated?

0	1	2	3	4	5	6	7	8
Not at all excessive				Moderately excessive				Totally excessive

3. Over the past six months, how many days have you been bothered by excessive worry?

0	1	2	3	4	5	6	7	8
Never				1 day out of 2				Every day

4. Do you have difficulty controlling your worries? For example, when you start worrying about something, do you have difficulty stopping?

0	1	2	3	4	5	6	7	8
No difficulty				Moderate difficulty				Extreme difficulty

5. Over the past six months, to what extent have you been disturbed by the following sensations when you were worried or anxious? (Rate each sensation with the following scale.)

0	1	2	3	4	5	6	7	8
Not at all				Moderately				Very severely

____ Restlessness or feeling keyed up or on edge
____ Being easily fatigued
____ Difficulty concentrating or mind going blank
____ Irritability
____ Muscle tension
____ Sleep disturbance (difficulty falling or staying asleep, or restless unsatisfying sleep)

APPENDIX 3.1 (continued)

6. To what extent does worry or anxiety interfere with your life? For example, your work, social activities, family life, etc.?*

0	1	2	3	4	5	6	7	8
Not at all				Moderately				Very severely

* English translation of original French version, from: Dugas, M. J., Freeston, M. H., Provencher, M. D., Lachance, S., Ladouceur, R., & Gosselin, P. (2001). Validation dans des échantillons non cliniques et cliniques. [The Worry and Anxiety Questionnaire: Validation in clinical and nonclinical samples]. *Journal de Thérapie Comportementale et Cognitive, 11*, 31–36.

APPENDIX 3.2

Penn State Worry Questionnaire (PSWQ)*

Please enter a number (1 to 5) that best describes how typical or characteristic each item is of you.

1	2	3	4	5
Not at all typical		Somewhat typical		Very typical

1. ______ If I don't have enough time to do everything, I don't worry about it
2. ______ My worries overwhelm me
3. ______ I don't tend to worry about things
4. ______ Many situations make me worry
5. ______ I know I shouldn't worry about things but I just can't help it
6. ______ When I'm under pressure, I worry a lot
7. ______ I am always worrying about something
8. ______ I find it easy to dismiss worrisome thoughts
9. ______ As soon as I finish one task, I start to worry about everything else I have to do
10. ______ I never worry about anything
11. ______ When there is nothing more that I can do about a concern, I don't worry about it anymore
12. ______ I've been a worrier all my life
13. ______ I notice that I have been worrying about things
14. ______ Once I start worrying, I can't stop
15. ______ I worry all the time
16. ______ I worry about projects until they are all done

Reversed items: 1, 3, 8, 10, 11

* Reprinted from Meyer, T. J., Miller, M. L., Metzger, R. L., & Borkovec, T. D. (1990). Development and validation of the Penn State Worry Questionnaire, Behaviour Research and Therapy, 28, 487–495. (With permission from Elsevier.)

APPENDIX 3.3

Intolerance of Uncertainty Scale (IUS)

You will find below a series of statements which describe how people may react to the uncertainties of life. Please use the scale below to describe to what extent each item is characteristic of you. Please enter a number (1 to 5) that describes you best.

1	2	3	4	5
Not at all characteristic of me		Somewhat characteristic of me		Entirely characteristic of me

1. _______ Uncertainty stops me from having a firm opinion
2. _______ Being uncertain means that a person is disorganized
3. _______ Uncertainty makes life intolerable
4. _______ It's unfair not having any guarantees in life
5. _______ My mind can't be relaxed if I don't know what will happen tomorrow
6. _______ Uncertainty makes me uneasy, anxious, or stressed
7. _______ Unforeseen events upset me greatly
8. _______ It frustrates me not having all the information I need
9. _______ Uncertainty keeps me from living a full life
10. _______ One should always look ahead so as to avoid surprises
11. _______ A small unforeseen event can spoil everything, even with the best of planning
12. _______ When it's time to act, uncertainty paralyses me
13. _______ Being uncertain means that I am not first rate
14. _______ When I am uncertain, I can't go forward
15. _______ When I am uncertain I can't function very well
16. _______ Unlike me, others always seem to know where they are going with their lives
17. _______ Uncertainty makes me vulnerable, unhappy, or sad
18. _______ I always want to know what the future has in store for me
19. _______ I can't stand being taken by surprise
20. _______ The smallest doubt can stop me from acting
21. _______ I should be able to organize everything in advance
22. _______ Being uncertain means that I lack confidence
23. _______ I think it's unfair that other people seem sure about their future
24. _______ Uncertainty keeps me from sleeping soundly

APPENDIX 3.3 (continued)

25. _______ I must get away from all uncertain situations
26. _______ The ambiguities in life stress me
27. _______ I can't stand being undecided about my future*

---

* Reprinted from Buhr, K., & Dugas, M. J. (2002).The Intolerance of Uncertainty Scale: Psychometric properties of the English version, Behaviour Research and Therapy, 40, 931–945. (With permission from Elsevier.)

APPENDIX 3.4

Why Worry-II (WW-II)

Below are a series of statements that can be related to worry. Please think back to times when you are worried, and indicate by entering a number (1 to 5) to what extent these statements are true for you.

1	2	3	4	5
Not at all true	Slightly true	Somewhat true	Very true	Absolutely true

1. _______ If I did not worry, I would be careless and irresponsible
2. _______ If I worry, I will be less disturbed when unforeseen events occur
3. _______ I worry in order to know what to do
4. _______ If I worry in advance, I will be less disappointed if something serious occurs
5. _______ The fact that I worry helps me plan my actions to solve a problem
6. _______ The act of worrying itself can prevent mishaps from occurring
7. _______ If I did not worry, it would make me a negligent person
8. _______ It is by worrying that I finally undertake the work that I must do
9. _______ I worry because I think it can help me find a solution to my problem
10. _______ The fact that I worry shows that I am a person who takes care of their affairs
11. _______ Thinking too much about positive things can prevent them from occurring
12. _______ The fact that I worry confirms that I am a prudent person
13. _______ If misfortune comes, I will feel less responsible if I have been worrying about it beforehand
14. _______ By worrying, I can find a better way to do things
15. _______ Worrying stimulates me and makes me more effective
16. _______ The fact that I worry incites me to act
17. _______ The act of worrying itself reduces the risk that something serious will occur
18. _______ By worrying, I do certain things which I would not decide to do otherwise
19. _______ The fact that I worry motivates me to do the things I must do
20. _______ My worries can, by themselves, reduce the risks of danger
21. _______ If I worry less, I decrease my chances of finding the best solution
22. _______ The fact that I worry will allow me to feel less guilty if something serious occurs

APPENDIX 3.4 (continued)

23. _______ If I worry, I will be less unhappy when a negative event occurs
24. _______ By not worrying, one can attract misfortune
25. _______ The fact that I worry shows that I am a good person

WW-II Subscales:

Worry aids in problem solving: items 3, 5, 10, 14, 21
Worry helps motivate: items: 8, 15, 16, 18, 19
Worrying protects the individual from difficult emotions in the event of a negative outcome: items: 2, 4, 13, 22, 23
The act of worrying itself prevents negative outcomes: items: 6, 11, 17, 20, 24
Worry is a positive personality trait: items: 1, 7, 9, 12, 25

APPENDIX 3.5

Negative Problem Orientation Questionnaire (NPOQ)*

People react in different ways when faced with problems in their daily lives (e.g., health problems, arguments, lack of time, etc.). Please use the scale below to indicate to what extent each of the following items correspond to the way you react or think when confronted with a problem. Please enter the number that best corresponds to you for each item.

1	2	3	4	5
Not at all true of me	Slightly true of me	Moderately true of me	Very true of me	Extremely true of me

1. ______ I see problems as a threat to my well-being
2. ______ I often doubt my capacity to solve problems
3. ______ Often before even trying to find a solution, I tell myself that it is difficult to solve problems
4. ______ My problems often seem insurmountable
5. ______ When I attempt to solve a problem, I often question my abilities
6. ______ I often have the impression that my problems cannot be solved
7. ______ Even if I manage to find some solutions to my problems, I doubt that they will be easily resolved
8. ______ I have a tendency to see problems as a danger
9. ______ My first reaction when faced with a problem is to question my abilities
10. ______ I often see my problems as bigger than they really are
11. ______ Even if I have looked at a problem from all possible angles, I still wonder if the solution I decided on will be effective
12. ______ I consider problems to be obstacles that interfere with my functioning

* Reprinted from Robichaud, M., & Dugas, M. J. (2005). Negative problem orientation (part I): Psychometric properties of a new measure. Behaviour Research and Therapy, 43, 391–401. (With permission from Elsevier.)

APPENDIX 3.6

Cognitive Avoidance Questionnaire (CAQ)

People react differently to certain types of thoughts. Using the following scale, please indicate to what extent each of the following statements is typical of the way that you respond to certain thoughts. Please enter the appropriate number (1 to 5).

1	2	3	4	5
Not at all typical	A little typical	Somewhat typical	Very typical	Completely typical

1. ____ There are things that I would rather not think about
2. ____ I avoid certain situations that lead me to pay attention to things I don't want to think about
3. ____ I replace threatening mental images with things I say to myself in my mind
4. ____ I think about things that concern me as if they were occurring to someone else
5. ____ I have thoughts that I try to avoid
6. ____ I try not to think about the most upsetting aspects of some situation so as not to be too afraid
7. ____ I sometimes avoid objects that can trigger upsetting thoughts
8. ____ I distract myself to avoid thinking about certain disturbing subjects
9. ____ I avoid people who make me think about things that I do not want to think about
10. ____ I often do things to distract myself from my thoughts
11. ____ I think about trivial details so as not to think about important subjects that worry me
12. ____ Sometimes I throw myself into an activity so as not to think about certain things
13. ____ To avoid thinking about subjects that upset me, I force myself to think about something else
14. ____ There are things I try not to think about
15. ____ I keep saying things to myself in my head to avoid visualizing scenarios (a series of mental images) that frighten me
16. ____ Sometimes I avoid places that make me think about things I would prefer not to think about
17. ____ I think about past events so as not to think about future events that make me feel insecure
18. ____ I avoid actions that remind me of things I do not want to think about
19. ____ When I have mental images that are upsetting, I say things to myself in my head to replace the images

APPENDIX 3.6 (continued)

20. ____ I think about many little things so as not to think about more important matters
21. ____ Sometimes I keep myself occupied just to prevent thoughts from popping up in my mind
22. ____ I avoid situations that involve people who make me think about unpleasant things
23. ____ Rather than having images of upsetting events form in my mind, I try to describe the events using an internal monologue (things that I say to myself in my head)
24. ____ I push away the mental images related to a threatening situation by trying to describe the situation using an internal monologue
25. ____ I think about things that are worrying other people rather than thinking about my own worries

CAQ Subscales:

Suppressing worrisome thoughts: items 4, 11, 17, 20, 25
Substituting neutral or positive thoughts for worries: items 3, 15, 19, 23, 24
Using distraction as a way to interrupt worrying: items 8, 10, 12, 13, 21
Avoiding action/situation that can lead to worrisome thoughts: items 7, 9, 16, 18, 22
Transforming mental images into verbal-linguistic thought: items 1, 2, 5, 6, 14

CHAPTER 4

Treatment Overview

Over the years, a number of psychological treatments have been developed for generalized anxiety disorder (GAD). Many of these treatments are based on theoretically derived accounts of GAD (e.g., Borkovec, 2006; Roemer & Orsillo, 2002; Wells, 2006), some of which have received empirical support in randomized controlled trials (e.g., Borkovec & Costello, 1993; Borkovec, Newman, Pincus, & Lytle, 2002). Among those shown to be efficacious in controlled treatment studies, either the treatments in their entirety, or significant components thereof, can be subsumed under the heading of cognitive-behavioral therapy (CBT). Our treatment, which we shall describe at length in the following two chapters, is one such treatment. It is based on a theoretical model of GAD that has been empirically supported (see Chapter 2) and the efficacy of our protocol has been supported by four randomized controlled trials (see Chapter 6). The present chapter will provide an overview of our treatment by discussing its core modules, thereby paving the way for the next chapter, which describes the actual implementation of the treatment strategies.

TREATMENT OUTLINE

The term *CBT* is used to describe a broad range of therapeutic modalities. Although most psychological treatments that have been shown to be effective for GAD carry the CBT label, they differ greatly from one another in terms of underlying models, treatment targets, and procedures. For example, in the CBT protocol "Mastery of Your Anxiety and Worry" developed by Michelle Craske and her colleagues (Craske, Barlow, & O'Leary, 1992), treatment components include relaxation, probability estimation, and decatastrophizing, all of which are considered cognitive-behavioral interventions. However, none of these techniques is employed in our treatment package. This is largely due to our conceptualization of GAD as a syndrome that is driven by pervasive, excessive, and uncontrollable worry. As such, we consider *worry* to be the primary focus of treatment, and the somatic symptoms of GAD (that is, restlessness or feeling keyed up or on edge, being easily fatigued, difficulty concentrating or mind going blank, irritability, muscle tension, and sleep disturbance) are viewed as being largely the result of pathological worry. The noteworthy consequence of such a conceptualization is that the treatment *does not* directly target the somatic symptoms of GAD. In other words, treatment strategies such as applied relaxation and anxiety management training are not part of the treatment described in this book. Rather, all treatment modules bear directly on pathological worry, and concomitant reductions in associated somatic symptoms are expected to occur as a function of reductions in worry. Data from our clinical trials support this contention because it was found that decreases in worry lead to decreases in the somatic symptoms of GAD (see Chapter 6 for more detail).

Overall Goal of Treatment

Although the treatment described in this book aims to achieve a number of therapeutic goals, the ultimate goal of our treatment package is to help clients develop a greater tolerance for uncertainty in their everyday lives. Without a doubt, having the ability to tolerate, cope with, and even accept uncertainty is incompatible with the excessive and uncontrollable worry seen in GAD. One way to view worry is as a form of scenario building, where individuals go over every potential outcome of an uncertainty-inducing situation in order to control or be fully prepared for each outcome. If individuals have a greater acceptance and tolerance for uncertainty, the extensive "mental preparation" of worry no longer becomes necessary. However, learning to tolerate uncertainty is not as easy as it might seem. For this reason, the overarching focus of treatment is to target intolerance of uncertainty both directly (Module 2) and indirectly (Modules 3, 4, and 5). Specifically, Module 2 targets intolerance of uncertainty directly by helping clients to not only recognize uncertainty, but to become familiar with their reactions to it. In addition, they are encouraged to seek out, rather than avoid, uncertainty-inducing situations, and refrain from engaging in the many behaviors that they typically do to reduce or control uncertainty (for example, reassurance seeking). Modules 3, 4, and 5 target intolerance of uncertainty indirectly by addressing specific components that are impacted by intolerance of uncertainty and serve to maintain or exacerbate excessive worry. The focus of Module 3 is to help clients realize that they often hold positive beliefs about the function of worry and that these beliefs contribute to the perception that uncertainty can be avoided by worrying. Module 4 teaches clients to deal with their problems by devoting attention to actual problem solving rather than worry. This module targets intolerance of uncertainty indirectly due to the construct's relationship with problem solving. Given that problems are inherently uncertain, encouraging clients to approach their problems and solve them despite the uncertainty can further decrease their intolerance. Finally, Module 5 targets intolerance of uncertainty indirectly by having clients face the uncertainty involved in their worst fears through imaginal exposure. Throughout treatment, learning to tolerate uncertainty is a constant undercurrent, and issues related to intolerance of uncertainty are discussed and dealt with accordingly.

Treatment Modules

The treatment includes the following modules: (1) psychoeducation and worry awareness training; (2) uncertainty recognition and behavioral exposure; (3) reevaluation of the usefulness of worry; (4) problem-solving training; (5) imaginal exposure; and (6) relapse prevention. This chapter presents the rationale and "spirit" of each module, whereas chapter 5 will present the "nuts and bolts" of the treatment. It is important for the reader to keep in mind that the treatment strategies described in chapter 5 are in fact examples of ways of targeting the cognitive processes believed to underlie GAD. They are by no means exhaustive or even ideal for all clients. By clearly understanding the principles laid out in this chapter, the therapist* will be in a position to adapt the treatment to clients' specific needs while continuing to target the underlying processes involved in maintaining GAD.

MODULE 1: PSYCHOEDUCATION AND WORRY AWARENESS TRAINING

As with most CBT protocols, the first few sessions of treatment are devoted to psychoeducation. The therapist provides clients with information about the structure of sessions, the guiding principles of cognitive-behavioral interventions, and the primary role of worry in GAD. In addition, clients learn to monitor their worrying on a day-to-day basis.

* Whereas the term clinician was used in the discussion of the assessment of GAD, the term therapist will be used in the sections dealing with the provision of treatment.

Psychoeducation about CBT

Although the interventions used in CBT differ according to the disorder and the particular treatment protocol being used, there are certain general principles of CBT that it is important to impart to clients. Obviously, some of the principles will come as a surprise to many clients, as they may have preconceived notions about psychological treatment or may be unfamiliar with CBT. Therefore, it is necessary to take the time to explain to clients what CBT involves, so that they are fully aware of what will take place in treatment and what is expected of them. For these reasons, the following principles should be addressed at the outset of therapy:

- *CBT is based on a model that emphasizes the relationship between thoughts, behaviors, and emotions.* Given that there is a bidirectional interplay between our thoughts, behaviors, and emotions (that is, subjective affect and physiological responses), effecting change in one area can lead to changes in the others. As such, clients can willfully alter their cognitive, behavioral, and emotional reactions to situations when provided with the proper tools to do so. However, clients will primarily focus on changes to their thoughts and behaviors throughout the course of therapy, as they are often the most amenable to direct intervention (i.e., it is more difficult to manipulate or change one's emotional state in a volitional manner).

- *CBT provides a new way of understanding the problem.* Many clients begin treatment with the perception that their problem is impossible to control because it is the direct result of their genetic makeup or of deep-seated unconscious conflicts. CBT is designed to give clients a greater sense of control and mastery by helping them to understand their problem in a new way. This is done through a gradual process of guided discovery, where new concepts are presented to clients as hypotheses they can test using behavioral experiments. CBT is therefore a very empowering treatment approach, as clients are not simply "given" an explanation of their problem, but rather encouraged to test the validity of different hypotheses (with a gentle nudge in the right direction from the therapist).

- *CBT relies on active collaboration between clients and therapists.* Some clients might come into treatment with the expectation that therapists will "cure" them of their problem with little effort on their part. This is certainly not the case with CBT. Both client and therapist work together in order to effect change. If clients do not participate in their own treatment, it is very unlikely that they will see any substantive improvement in their symptoms.

- *CBT aims to provide clients with tools that allow them to deal with the problem independently.* In keeping with the collaborative nature of treatment, one of the tasks of the therapist is to assist clients in acquiring skills that will help them with their problem. Of course, it is the client's responsibility to learn and to practice the skills taught in session. Symptom reduction is largely due to the effort clients put into acquiring the necessary skills and implementing them accordingly. There is no magic cure for GAD, and clients need to be aware that it is only through their own diligence that they will improve.

- *CBT is brief and time-limited.* The number of sessions for CBT typically ranges from 12 to 20, depending upon the particular diagnosis and severity of the problem. This is done for a very good reason: the ultimate goal of CBT is to teach clients to become *their own therapist.* As such, treatment should last long enough to ensure that clients have properly acquired the necessary skills, but not so long as to foster dependency. By encouraging autonomy in clients, CBT enables them to leave treatment with a clear and concrete plan for maintaining their gains (with the possibility of making further progress).

- *CBT is structured and directive.* Given that CBT is a skill-based protocol that is also time-limited, sessions are relatively structured. As such, therapists set an agenda for sessions that typically includes reviewing the exercises carried out in the past week, revisiting material discussed in previous sessions, presenting and discussing new material, and assigning exercises for the following week. Given that this format of treatment may seem unfamiliar to certain clients, it is important to make them aware of the typical session plan.

- *CBT is based on the here and now.* A central tenet of CBT is that treatment focuses on factors that contribute to maintaining the problem (for example, what the client is doing, thinking, and feeling *now*), rather than emphasizing the factors that contributed to the development of the problem (e.g., family history, childhood conflicts). The reason for this is that identifying the origins of a problem does not, in and of itself, *solve* the problem. This is particularly true with respect to anxiety disorders, as what is maintaining the anxiety in the present might be very different from what originally led to its development. This is not to say that the therapist should never devote time to a discussion of the origins of the problem, only that it is often not necessary to do so in order to help clients with their current problem.

- *Between-session exercises are an integral part of CBT.* The hallmark of CBT is the prescription of exercises to all clients from session to session (we will use the term *between-session exercises* throughout this book in lieu of the more common *homework exercises* because the latter has a negative undertone for many clients). It is important that clients be made aware of this at the outset, and queried about their willingness to devote time and attention to home exercises throughout the duration of treatment. Clients who are unwilling to complete between-session exercises are unlikely to show substantial progress in therapy. Since CBT is skill-based, mastery of the skills discussed in treatment will only occur through repeated practice between sessions. Without the completion of home exercises, any symptom reduction that occurs might be tenuous at best because the skills are likely to be poorly acquired, rendering the client vulnerable to relapse following cessation of treatment.

Despite the fact that there are many principles to be considered, which may seem a little overwhelming, it is nevertheless necessary to review them at the outset for two major reasons. First, prior to starting any treatment, it is our opinion that clients should be fully aware of what treatment will involve and what is expected of them. They ultimately must decide whether the proposed treatment is a good match for them or not. Second, given that clients will be expected to contribute significantly to their own treatment, both in and out of session, it is important that they agree to put forth the effort. Clients who appear to have low treatment motivation should be queried extensively about this, in order to discriminate between an unwillingness to work in treatment and a fear of what will be required of them. In the case of the former, CBT might not be appropriate (at least at that time) since it is unlikely that clients will progress if they are unwilling to fully engage in treatment. In the latter case however, the therapist might choose to discuss clients' particular fears and explain that nothing will be asked of them unless they understand the rationale behind the request, feel able to do it (albeit on occasion with difficulty), and agree to it.

Psychoeducation about GAD

The second major psychoeducational component involves the provision of information about GAD. This should include two parts; specifically, a description of the diagnosis of GAD and the introduction of a model of the disorder. In terms of explaining the diagnosis, the therapist should strive to describe GAD and its associated symptoms in simple and easily comprehensible terms. Clients might have been told in the past that they have a diagnosis of GAD, but they will often be unclear about what that means. As such, it is important to take the time to explain that GAD is an anxiety disorder that is characterized by excessive and uncontrollable worry about a number of daily events, and to review the somatic symptoms of the disorder. In addition, we feel that it can be beneficial to describe anxiety problems (and certainly excessive worry) in terms of a dimensional system. The majority of clients are likely to view their problem within a medical framework, where GAD is a disease that can be "cured." From a CBT perspective, this is not only inaccurate, but it lays the groundwork for unrealistic expectations about treatment (that is, "I will be cured of my worry"). By presenting GAD and excessive worry along a continuum, clients can see their problem as an excessive manifestation of a normal phenomenon, with all individuals scattered along the worry continuum (as opposed to being clustered at each end). Moreover, it allows the therapist to discuss the realistic expectation of moving one's worry level away from the pathological dimension (that is, excessive worry) to a more manageable, or normal, level.

The second part of GAD psychoeducation involves the presentation of a model of the disorder (which is a standard element of most CBT protocols). It is essential that clients understand the role that their own thoughts, behaviors, and emotions have in keeping their problem alive, and this phenomenon is highlighted using a pictorial model. Within our treatment protocol, we utilize a preliminary model at the outset, and then continually add components as new treatment modules are introduced (see Chapter 5). Given that our protocol introduces several factors that are involved in the maintenance of GAD, it is our belief that presenting the model in its entirety right from the beginning of treatment can be overwhelming for some clients. Moreover, by presenting our model in a stepwise and gradual fashion, clients are more likely to understand it and focus on the particular component being targeted, without becoming distracted by other components of the model.

Our initial model of GAD includes the symptoms associated with a diagnosis of GAD. The therapist elaborates upon the triggers of a worry cycle, and then subsequently describes "what if" questions, worry, anxiety, demoralization, and exhaustion. The therapist also provides clients with a simple, clinically useful definition of worry. Once again, given that worry is an internal event, it is important that both the client and therapist agree on a definition of worry so that there is a common language and a common target in treatment.

Worry Awareness Training

Worry awareness training involves the identification of worry themes and the classification of worries into one of two categories: (1) worries about current problems, and (2) worries about hypothetical situations. During this phase of treatment, the between-session exercise involves the following: three times a day, clients stop what they are doing and take note of any worries they may be experiencing "in the moment," their level of anxiety, and the type of worry. Given that not all worries fall neatly into one of the two categories, worry awareness training allows clients to begin developing a greater tolerance for uncertainty. For example, clients who are experiencing pain and worrying about having a serious illness may find it difficult to place the worry into one or the other category ("The pain is real but the cancer might not be"). By going ahead and categorizing the worry as being either about a current problem or about a hypothetical situation, clients are being asked to make a decision even if they are unsure about the correct classification (in fact, there may not be a definitive correct classification in cases such as these). It should be noted, however, that in such situations, the therapist may want to encourage clients to consider the worry as a concern about a hypothetical situation because clients with GAD often worry about outcomes that do not materialize. Thus, through worry awareness training, clients learn to recognize worry episodes as they occur, distinguish between worries about current problems and worries about hypothetical situations, and tolerate uncertainty by following through with the categorization of worries despite the uncertainty-inducing nature of this task.

MODULE 2: UNCERTAINTY RECOGNITION AND BEHAVIORAL EXPOSURE

This second module of treatment lays the foundation for all subsequent modules and is therefore one of the most important. The therapist should take care not to rush through this phase of treatment in order to ensure that clients are in a position to really benefit from all treatment modules. The primary goals at this stage are the following:

- To help clients understand the relationship between intolerance of uncertainty and excessive worry.
- To recognize that uncertainty-inducing situations are largely unavoidable.
- To recognize the various manifestations of intolerance of uncertainty.
- To seek out and experience uncertainty-inducing situations.

Exploring the Relationship between Intolerance of Uncertainty and Excessive Worry

As described in Chapter 2, a great deal of research has uncovered the close relationship between intolerance of uncertainty and excessive worry. As such, it is a good idea for the therapist to spend a little time telling clients, in a confident manner, about this relationship. For example, clients should know that intolerance of uncertainty is clearly the best predictor of excessive worry (see Dugas, Schwartz, & Francis, 2004), and that when people learn to tolerate uncertainty, they tend to worry less (see Ladouceur, Gosselin, & Dugas, 2000). That is, once an individual has become tolerant of uncertainty, he or she cannot worry excessively. This is due to the fact that worry can be construed as an attempt to consider all potential eventualities of a future situation; in other words, it is an attempt to reduce uncertainty by thinking about every possible outcome for a given situation. If an individual is no longer intolerant of uncertainty, there is no need to engage in the prolonged mental activity of excessive worry. Because intolerance of uncertainty is such an important concept to the understanding and reduction of worry, clients should have a clear understanding of this information before moving on to other modules (see Chapter 5 for useful analogies for intolerance of uncertainty).

Recognizing That Certainty Is Impossible to Attain

Clients with GAD will often see the goal of treatment quite differently from the one that is truly desirable for GAD symptom reduction. Specifically, they might expect to achieve certainty in their lives as a means of worrying less. This is not, however, an achievable goal. Considering the necessarily uncertain nature of day-to-day life, seeking out absolute certainty is not only impossible, it also guarantees that one will have to continue striving for certainty on a daily basis as new situations arise. The impossibility of this goal therefore needs to be addressed early on in this stage, and it is important that clients understand and agree with the true goal of therapy (i.e., developing a greater tolerance for uncertainty), as it is more desirable for GAD symptom reduction. A good way to achieve this is to break down the construct of intolerance of uncertainty into its component parts: uncertainty and intolerance. Clients seeking to reduce their worry can either choose to address the first component (i.e., increasing certainty) or the second component (that is, increasing tolerance). In a Socratic fashion, therapists can help clients discover which of these goals is more realistic, more attainable, and more likely to lead to lasting reductions in worry and anxiety levels.

Identifying the Manifestations of Intolerance of Uncertainty

Another important goal in this treatment module involves helping clients to recognize the different ways in which their intolerance of uncertainty manifests itself in their lives. We have found that most clients are largely unaware of the profound impact intolerance of uncertainty has on their lives. Generally speaking, intolerance of uncertainty is problematic because clients will expend a great deal of energy using a myriad of behavioral and cognitive strategies in an attempt to avoid uncertainty-inducing situations. In fact, they typically have been using these strategies for such a long time that they have become automatic. For this reason, it is necessary that clients become *aware* of the various manifestations of their intolerance of uncertainty and recognize the impact of these behaviors.

The driving force behind the manifestations of intolerance of uncertainty is an overwhelming urge to eliminate or circumvent the experience of uncertainty. These manifestations fall into two general categories: approach and avoidance strategies. Approach strategies refer to the behaviors that involve approaching a given situation in order to eliminate one's feelings of uncertainty. Examples of approach strategies include repeatedly seeking reassurance from others before making a decision and obtaining excessive information about a given subject (for example, going to dozens of stores when buying a gift for someone to ensure that one has the perfect gift). Avoidance strategies, on the other hand, involve attempts to circumvent uncertainty by avoiding uncertainty-inducing situations altogether. Examples of this strategy include putting off completing a report until the last minute (so that feelings of uncertainty are present for only a short period of time) and not accepting a promotion at work (because of the uncertainty involved in taking on new responsibilities). The reader will notice that both types of strategies result from the belief that uncertainty is aversive, and that regardless of whether one approaches or avoids a given situation, the net effect is to eliminate the uncertainty-inducing elements. By having clients become aware of the extent to which they avoid uncertainty, therapeutic motivation can be further enhanced, which is of course extremely important for successful treatment.

Experiencing Uncertainty-Inducing Situations

Once clients begin to realize how much time and energy they expend on seeking to reduce uncertainty (and the futility of attempting to eliminate it), an alternate strategy is presented. Specifically, rather than avoiding uncertainty, clients are encouraged to seek out and experience it. This is essentially a form of *in-vivo* exposure, where the feared stimuli are uncertainty-inducing situations. As with more traditional forms of exposure, clients should be encouraged to experience and tolerate uncertainty in a gradual manner. With that in mind, initial uncertainty exposures might involve not checking and rereading low-priority e-mails before sending them, or refraining from seeking reassurance prior to making a minor decision. The goal is to allow clients to experience some anxiety while tolerating uncertainty, without becoming overwhelmed. Exercises in tolerating uncertainty should be conducted throughout treatment so that clients can develop "momentum" and become increasingly comfortable with uncertainty in their lives. One noteworthy advantage to seeking out uncertainty is that clients begin to add some variety and flexibility to their daily lives (which runs counter to the rigidity they are often accustomed to). In fact, many clients report that these exercises are unexpectedly positive experiences that provide a sense of mastery and freedom. The therapist should initially assist clients in devising uncertainty exposure exercises; however, clients should develop their own exercises later on in therapy.

MODULE 3: REEVALUATION OF THE USEFULNESS OF WORRY

In Module 3, the primary goal is to assist clients in identifying their beliefs about the usefulness of worry and to begin reevaluating these beliefs. This treatment target might seem counterintuitive at first glance, particularly since clients have deliberately sought help for their excessive worry and anxiety. As such, the reader might question whether clients actually hold positive beliefs about the usefulness of worry. In fact, many clients are unaware of, or hesitant to discuss, the positive beliefs they have about their worries. However, the therapist should be careful not to hastily conclude that clients do not see any usefulness in their worries, even if an initial investigation does not point to this conclusion. As discussed in chapter 2, our research suggests that individuals with GAD hold positive beliefs about worry from any of the five following categories: (1) worry helps them find solutions to their problems; (2) worrying can serve a motivating function, thereby aiding them in getting things done; (3) worry can serve as a buffer for negative emotions by preparing them for dreadful outcomes should they occur; (4) worry, in and of itself, can prevent negative outcomes from occurring (also called magical thinking or thought-action fusion); and (5) worrying about people or situations shows that they are caring and compassionate people. Although not all clients with GAD hold every one of these beliefs, our clinical experience has taught us that they typically hold at least some of them.

Before expanding upon ways to address this module of treatment, it should be noted that our position is *not* that positive beliefs about worry are always mistaken or erroneous. In fact, worry can be useful for a number of reasons. However, findings from many studies show that individuals with GAD hold these beliefs to a greater extent than people who do not have GAD (e.g., Dugas, Gagnon, Ladouceur, & Freeston, 1998; Ladouceur et al., 1999). Furthermore, it appears that the usefulness of worry decreases as worrying becomes excessive, as is the case for individuals with GAD (Pruzinsky & Borkovec, 1990). Stated differently, relative to individuals with moderate levels of worry, clients with GAD not only believe that worrying is *more* useful, but they appear to worry to such an extent that it is actually *less* useful.

Why Address Positive Beliefs about Worry?

The reader might wonder why it is that identifying and reevaluating beliefs about the usefulness of worry is a necessary treatment module. If the ultimate goal of treatment is to assist clients in reducing their worry to a more manageable level (and not to eliminate it altogether), then it might seem relatively benign to hold strong beliefs about the usefulness of worry. However, this is not the case. Although clients present for treatment to reduce their worries and anxiety, this is largely in a "general sense." There is often a paradox present when it comes to clients' relationship to their worries. For example, they may generally wish to feel less anxious and worried, while concurrently believing that it is very important to continue worrying about their children. As such, when faced with the notion of actually worrying less about specific topics (for example, one's children), clients may be ambivalent about change if their beliefs about worry have not been properly addressed. By taking the time to let clients identify their beliefs about the function of specific worries, and ultimately begin to challenge their actual usefulness, treatment motivation and compliance can be enhanced.

A second goal of this phase of treatment is to help clients think about what it really means to worry less. This can be a very emotional experience for clients. Most individuals with GAD have difficulty remembering a time when they did not worry. Although they present to treatment in order to reduce their worry and anxiety, many have not given much thought to what their lives would be like without the constant "background" of worry. Therefore, it is important for the therapist to allow clients to discuss any fears or feelings of loss they might have regarding this potentially significant change.

Identifying and Reevaluating Positive Beliefs about Worry

Returning to the issue of identifying clients' beliefs about the usefulness of worry, any strategy that will facilitate the identification and disclosure of these beliefs can be therapeutically useful. Since clients may hesitate to "admit" they are seeking treatment for something they believe has a positive dimension, it is important that the therapist take the time to explain that it is common for clients to see a positive side to their emotional problems. One of the main treatment strategies that we use to encourage disclosure is the *lawyer–prosecutor role-play*, which is described in Chapter 5. With this method, clients are encouraged to present arguments in favor of the usefulness and value of their worries. Although we have found this role-play very useful in helping clients to identify arguments for (and against) the usefulness of their worries, other strategies are useful as well (see Chapter 5 for other helpful tactics).

Once clients have identified their positive beliefs about worry, the therapist can proceed to help clients reevaluate these beliefs. In other words, clients are encouraged to begin thinking about whether their worries are as useful as originally thought. This type of reevaluation will set the stage for the next treatment modules. Specifically, if worrying is not as useful as once believed, that is, if it does not in fact help to solve problems or protect loved ones, then perhaps clients need to develop alternate strategies for achieving these goals. The problem solving and imaginal exposure modules that follow are therefore a natural progression from this treatment module. The process of reevaluation of beliefs can be viewed as the most "cognitive" of all treatment modules. The primary goal is to help clients to acknowledge that *their beliefs are thoughts and not facts*, and to ultimately develop a more flexible belief system. So rather than adopting a "search and destroy" strategy, where thoughts, assumptions, and beliefs are identified, reevaluated, and replaced by more appropriate or productive ones, this phase of treatment has a much more modest goal. Specifically, cognitive and behavioral strategies are used to help clients recognize that their beliefs about the usefulness of worry are interpretations and not facts, to see that other interpretations (or beliefs) also have some merit, and to wonder if perhaps they have overestimated the actual usefulness of their worries. At the same time, clients can begin the process of "imagining a life without worry."

MODULE 4: PROBLEM-SOLVING TRAINING

In our opinion, one of the important innovations of this treatment is the use of specific strategies for each type of worry. For worries about current problems, we have found that the application of sound problem-solving principles is an extremely helpful treatment strategy. That is, rather than worrying about a problem, it is better to actually solve it! As such, once the reevaluation of beliefs about the usefulness of worry has been completed, the treatment turns to problem-solving training for worries about current problems. Obviously, worries about hypothetical situations (for example, worries about situations that have not happened, and in most cases, never will) are not addressed with problem solving. In fact, attempting to solve a problem that may well never exist is not only unproductive, but can actually lead to increased worry. A specific treatment strategy for this type of worry is presented in the next module (see Module 5: Imaginal Exposure). However, for worries about current problems, taking an action-oriented stance such as problem solving is, in our opinion, the most appropriate treatment strategy.

There are two discrete elements involved in this treatment module, improving problem orientation and applying problem-solving skills. As mentioned previously, problem orientation refers to the way in which an individual views problems and problem solving, and is therefore considered a cognitive set. Problem-solving skills, on the other hand, refer to the steps that an individual carries out in order to actually solve a problem. These include (1) defining the problem and formulating problem-solving goals; (2) generating alternative solutions; (3) choosing a solution; and (4) implementing the chosen solution and assessing its effectiveness (see D'Zurilla & Nezu, 1999, for a detailed description of these steps). In our treatment, we devote as much time to assisting clients in enhancing their orientation toward problems as we do to the application of skills. As such, both of these problem-solving dimensions are treated as separate, albeit complementary, elements.

Given that problem-solving training was not specifically designed for individuals with GAD, it should come as no surprise that it needs to be modified to meet the specific needs of this client population. As a result, we modified "standard" problem-solving training by placing a strong emphasis on the role of uncertainty in both the problematic situation and the problem-solving process, and by consistently distinguishing between the passive process of worry and the active process of problem solving.

Improving Problem Orientation

Uncertainty in the Problem-Solving Process

Social problems (that is, problematic situations that occur in the natural social environment) have many uncertainty-inducing qualities. For example, the problem itself might be ambiguous or vague, the effects of the chosen solution are unpredictable, and the repercussions of an ineffective solution are difficult to estimate. Not unexpectedly, for a client who is intolerant of uncertainty, the problem-solving process is likely to be construed as threatening and aversive. It should therefore come as no surprise that GAD clients have a negative orientation toward problems and problem solving.

As noted earlier, learning to tolerate uncertainty in daily life is central to our treatment and is addressed either directly or indirectly in every session. The introduction of problem orientation and problem-solving skills is no exception. The presence of uncertainty in the problem-solving process is therefore discussed in session, as well as any fears that clients might have about the process. The futility of searching for certainty, particularly as it pertains to daily life problems, is also discussed. Rather than worrying about problems, clients are encouraged to "move forward" with problem solving despite the inherent uncertainty of the situation. Not only is this beneficial to clients because they learn how to deal with everyday problems, but they are also given yet another opportunity to increase their tolerance for uncertainty. Thus, in terms of initially addressing problem orientation, it is important to acknowledge the uncertainty of the problem situation, address the client's negative thoughts/emotions in relation to problem solving, and encourage action *toward* the problem.

The Impact of a Negative Problem Orientation

The impact of a negative problem orientation is best seen in the *consequences* of this cognitive set. Specifically, if clients are threatened by problems, doubt their ability to solve them, and anticipate a negative outcome irrespective of effort, then it is likely that they will react negatively on an emotional, cognitive, and behavioral level. In terms of emotions, clients are likely to be frustrated, irritated, anxious, or depressed when confronted with problems, given their predisposition to view them as threatening. In terms of cognitions, a negative evaluation of problems is likely to lead GAD clients to worry excessively about problems when they arise. In addition, if problems are left unsolved, they can generate new problems over time, which themselves can become worry topics. In this manner, holding a negative problem orientation can be seen as maintaining, and at times exacerbating, the worry cycle. Finally, in terms of behavioral consequences, clients might avoid or delay solving problems because they view the problems as threatening and have a negative outcome expectancy. This final consequence relates directly to the importance of discussing problem orientation prior to addressing problem-solving skills. Specifically, so long as problems are seen as threatening and unlikely to be effectively dealt with irrespective of effort, clients are unlikely to use their problem-solving skills (no matter how good they are). As a consequence, a series of strategies designed to encourage clients to approach problematic situations, rather than avoid them, are used in this treatment (see Chapter 5 for strategies for improving negative problem orientation).

Applying Problem-Solving Skills

In terms of problem-solving skills, the emphasis is placed on two ideas. First, the problem-solving skills component is not presented as "learning about new skills." This is because most people are intuitively aware of the general steps involved in solving problems. Rather, the emphasis is placed on learning how to use the skills *effectively*. Improperly defining a problem, setting unrealistic goals, or being unsure about how to select a potential solution are more likely to be the difficulties that people encounter with problem solving. Focusing on mastering the skills, rather than learning what they are, will be more reflective of the client's experience. Second, clients are encouraged to tolerate uncertainty throughout the problem-solving process. At each step of this process, the goal is to achieve the *best* result for that particular individual, not the *perfect* result. In other words, problem solving is expected to be a deliberate and rational process where clients do the best they can at each step. Once they have completed a problem-solving step, clients need to move forward to the next stage of problem solving, without the certainty that they made the "perfect" or the "right" choice. In essence, the implementation of one's problem-solving skills is an exercise in tolerating uncertainty.

One noteworthy point related to the use of problem solving as a way to tolerate uncertainty is that in reality, things might not turn out as expected. Even when one is highly organized, it is impossible to have complete control (or certainty) over one's social environment. Unexpected events can arise, people might not react as planned, and solutions might not work out as well as expected. However, events such as these can promote one's tolerance for uncertainty. When clients do not attain their desired goal and come to realize that they can handle unexpected adversity, they greatly benefit from their "mistake." In this way, moving forward with problem solving, despite the uncertainty of the process, represents a "win-win" situation for individuals with GAD. Once they have had some experience in dealing with current problems via problem solving, the therapist can then begin assisting clients in addressing the second type of worry; that is, worry about hypothetical situations.

MODULE 5: IMAGINAL EXPOSURE

In this treatment module, the therapist introduces clients to a strategy for dealing with worries about hypothetical situations. As noted beforehand, problem solving is not appropriate for situations that have not yet occurred (and may never happen). As such, we recommend imaginal exposure to the fears that underlie these types of worries. One of the great advantages of including both imaginal exposure and problem-solving training in the treatment of GAD is that clients acquire tools for dealing with their worries from an intrapersonal *and* interpersonal perspective. Given that internal (e.g., avoidance of threatening mental images) and external (e.g., avoidance of uncertainty-inducing situations) processes play important roles in GAD, providing clients with strategies for dealing with both types of processes is vitally important. Thus, by combining both types of treatment interventions that address the inner experience of clients (e.g., imaginal exposure), as well as their situational or interpersonal experiences (e.g., problem-solving training), therapists are in a good position to foster change in a greater proportion of their clients.

As noted previously, imaginal exposure is used to address worries about hypothetical situations. Examples of worries about hypothetical situations include worrying about a loved one being involved in a serious car accident, becoming seriously ill when one has a clean bill of health, and going bankrupt in the absence of financial difficulties. In terms of the model components, imaginal exposure is used to target cognitive avoidance. As mentioned in Chapter 2, this model component (and its corresponding treatment strategy of cognitive exposure) has been largely influenced by the research of Thomas Borkovec, who developed a compelling theory of GAD that focuses largely on *implicit* cognitive avoidance. The main element of this theory proposes that GAD worry is negatively reinforced by the automatic avoidance of threatening mental images and unpleasant emotional arousal. In other words, by worrying in "words" rather than mental images, GAD clients avoid the physiological reactions typically associated with imagery. This successful affective avoidance subsequently reinforces verbal-linguistic worry, as well as the continued avoidance of mental images. However, affective avoidance also interferes with the emotional processing of fears and ultimately contributes to the maintenance of high levels of worry and GAD.

In addition to recognizing the role of implicit cognitive avoidance in GAD, our model also acknowledges the role of *explicit* or voluntary attempts to avoid worrisome thoughts. It is our position that the use of effortful cognitive avoidance strategies (for example, thought suppression and distraction) plays an important role in GAD by interfering with emotional processing (much like the automatic avoidance of threatening mental images) and by amplifying negative beliefs about anxiety and the resulting fear of anxiety (see Chapter 2 for a more detailed account of the role of implicit and explicit cognitive avoidance in GAD).

In our model of GAD, both implicit and explicit expressions of cognitive avoidance are given equal importance. Thus, we conceptualize cognitive avoidance as a broad array of strategies that include the following:

1. Avoidance of mental imagery in favor of verbal-linguistic thoughts while worrying (implicit avoidance).
2. Attempts to suppress worrisome thoughts (explicit avoidance).
3. Attempts to replace worrisome thoughts by pleasant or neutral thoughts (explicit avoidance).
4. Attempts to use distraction to stop the worry process (explicit avoidance).
5. Avoidance of situations that might trigger worrisome thoughts (explicit avoidance).

It is our contention that clients with GAD use these cognitive avoidance strategies because, at some level, they believe that thoughts and emotional arousal can be unpleasant or dangerous. Thus, imaginal exposure, which teaches clients to fully experience threatening mental images and emotional arousal, is a treatment strategy that either directly or indirectly can impact upon all five aforementioned instances of cognitive avoidance. However, as with problem-solving training, imaginal exposure should be adapted to the specific needs of clients with GAD.

For the most part, the manner in which imaginal exposure is typically carried out is appropriate for GAD clients. Specifically, it involves being exposed to two things: (1) the mental image of a threatening situation, and (2) the subjective feelings and physiological indices of anxiety. This is ideal for GAD clients, as they tend to avoid mental images when thinking about threatening material, and they typically fear their own anxiety reactions. Furthermore, since GAD clients will often "jump" from one worry topic to another, the prolonged nature of imaginal exposure is also particularly beneficial for clients. Having said this, there is one important way in which imaginal exposure should be modified in order to meet the specific needs of clients with GAD: uncertainty-inducing information should be incorporated into the exposure scenario.

Although this might seem like a minor change to standard imaginal exposure, it is in fact a fundamental modification. Keeping in mind that current theories of exposure underscore the importance of not "holding back" when identifying the exposure material in order to fully activate the fear structure (Foa & Kozak, 1986), this information should be interpreted in terms of the fear structures that are germane to clients with GAD. Clinically, we have often observed that imaginal exposure can go "too far" with our clients, because a *clear* negative outcome may be less threatening than an *uncertain* one (that is, if the worst has already taken place, there may be little left to fear). In our treatment, it is essential that the therapist strives to attain a balance between helping clients address fearful outcomes while still being exposed to uncertainty.

In fact, the actual situation that is depicted in the exposure scenario may simply be the means by which clients emotionally process their intolerance to, or fear of, uncertainty. In order to better understand the manner in which we present imaginal exposure to clients, please refer to Chapter 5. Once clients have had considerable practice with imaginal exposure (both in and out of session), the treatment can progress to the final module, namely relapse prevention.

MODULE 6: RELAPSE PREVENTION

This final treatment module is designed to help clients maintain their gains following treatment and to potentially increase their progress over time. Although the time-limited nature of CBT is discussed at the outset of treatment, many clients experience difficulties ending treatment after only a few months. As such, it is important that when treatment ends, clients leave with a sense of confidence in their skills, and a feeling of hope and optimism in their ability to continue improving over time.

There are several ways in which therapists can foster the maintenance of gains and continued symptom improvement following treatment termination, all of which are expanded upon in Chapter 5. Essentially, the final sessions of therapy should involve a review of the knowledge and skills acquired throughout treatment. Clients should also be encouraged to continue practicing their new skills and prepare for stressors that may arise. It is worth noting that the therapist can model good habits throughout treatment, which will ultimately aid clients to continue progressing long after therapy has ended. For example, many clients will downplay their treatment gains simply because they are not fully aware of the progress they have made. It is not uncommon for clients to expect treatment success to "look" quite dramatic, with a change in their emotional state taking place from one day to the next. This, of course, does not occur very often, as progress typically takes place in a gradual fashion. As such, many clients might not fully appreciate the progress they have made. The therapist can counteract this by not only frequently praising successes, but also by keeping a written record of progress every week. Clients who see this type of behavior in their therapists are more likely to emulate it once they become their "own therapist." Both in and out of treatment, motivation is vital to continued success; as such, it is extremely important that clients learn to regularly praise and reward themselves for their progress. Clients who stay motivated and confident stand a good chance of experiencing additional symptom reduction and enhanced quality of life after treatment has ended.

SUMMARY AND CONCLUDING REMARKS

The overall goal of the treatment described in this book is to help clients develop a greater tolerance for uncertainty. This is accomplished *directly* by helping them to (1) understand the role of intolerance of uncertainty in GAD; (2) identify the many ways in which intolerance of uncertainty impacts upon their daily lives; and (3) deliberately expose themselves to uncertainty-inducing situations. Tolerance for uncertainty is also fostered *indirectly* by helping clients to (1) reevaluate their beliefs about the usefulness of worry; (2) learn to apply effective problem-solving principles to daily problematic situations; and (3) use imaginal exposure to process their worry-related fears. Throughout treatment, clients are encouraged to seek out and deal with uncertainty. Ultimately, they are encouraged to view uncertainty as not only unavoidable, but as an opportunity to grow and to develop as a human being. For GAD clients, one of the greatest benefits of dealing with unexpected events (and making mistakes now and then) is that they can begin to see how they are able to cope with adversity when it arises. As a result, clients can gain a sense of empowerment, which can greatly improve their quality of life.

As a final note, it is worth returning to the important role that therapist attitudes play in treatment success. Although our treatment protocol has received considerable empirical support (see Chapter 6), the specific treatment procedures represent only part of the "efficacy picture." Without positive therapist attitudes, such as openness and flexibility, even the best treatment protocol will not prove to be helpful for clients with GAD. Although one of our main goals in writing this book was to describe a set of theoretically driven treatment procedures, the reader should keep in mind that common therapy factors such as therapist attitudes are at least as important as the specific procedures described herein. Ultimately, increasing our ability to help individuals with GAD will not only depend on perfecting our treatment protocols, but also on focusing on *how* we deliver treatment.

CHAPTER 5

Step-by-Step Treatment

In this chapter, we will present a step-by-step illustration of our treatment protocol. Although the manual we use in our clinical trials has a session-by-session layout, the description presented in this chapter follows a more flexible format. Specifically, as with the treatment overview (see Chapter 4), this chapter is set up according to the different treatment modules. Therapists are encouraged to spend as much time as necessary on any given module before moving on to the next. Guidelines are provided as to when particular modules can be introduced with the ultimate goal of providing a flexible manual that can be tailored to the individual needs of each client. Throughout the chapter, examples of ways of presenting the material are provided. Although these formulations are based on our experience with generalized anxiety disorder (GAD) clients, they remain only examples of how to present the material; therapists will undoubtedly want to modify the wording in order to better suit their "clinical style."

MODULE 1: PSYCHOEDUCATION AND WORRY AWARENESS TRAINING

Presenting the Principles of Cognitive-Behavioral Therapy

The first objective in our treatment is to present the principles of cognitive-behavioral therapy (CBT). Clients are likely to be unsure of what will be involved, so it is important to explain the principles from the outset. This ensures that clients will have some understanding of what is required of them, and the therapist will be in a position to assist them in developing realistic expectations.

It is important that the presentation of CBT principles not be delivered in a rigid or authoritarian manner. Rather, Socratic questioning should be employed whenever possible to encourage the comprehension (and appreciation) of the principles of CBT. For example, when presenting the bidirectional relationship between thoughts, emotions, and behaviors, an illustrative example can be particularly helpful:

Therapist: One of the guiding principles of CBT is that there is a strttong relationship between the way we think (our thoughts), the way we feel (our emotions), and what we do (our behaviors). We will often represent this relationship with a triangle:

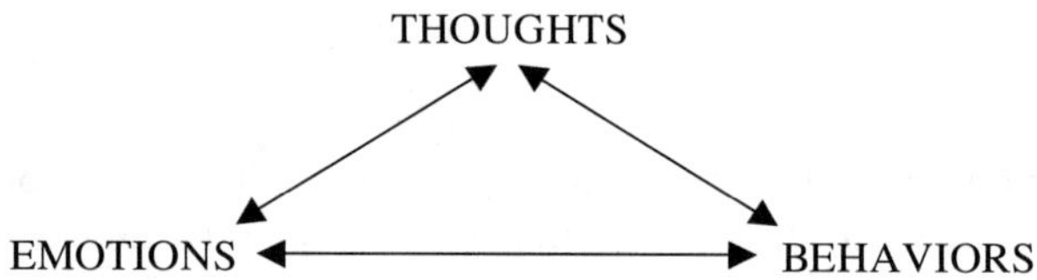

Therapist: Each one of these three factors influences the other two. For example, let's say that you are afraid of dogs. If you are walking down the street, and all of a sudden you see a dog, what are you likely to think? (Here, the emphasis is on getting clients to participate, and provide the answers themselves.)

Client: I might think: "Uh-oh, there's a dog. He might attack me!"

Therapist: That's right. And how will that influence how you feel and what you do?

Client: Well, I would probably be afraid and anxious, and I would either turn around and walk the other way or cross the street.

Therapist: Exactly. Your thought ("he might attack me") can lead you to feeling fearful and anxious, and to avoid the dog.

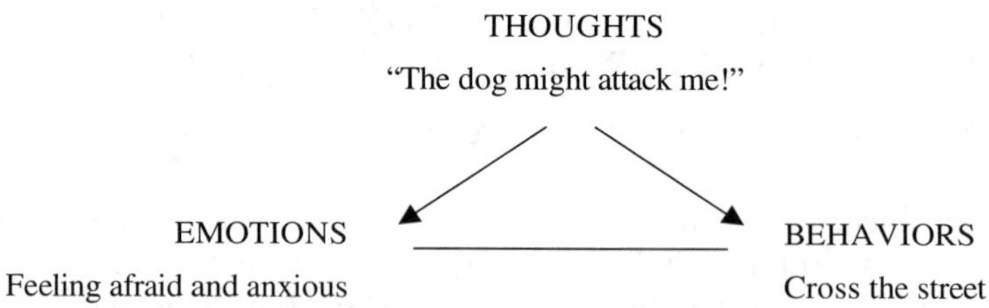

Therapist: Now, if you do cross the street and get away from the dog, what might you think and feel?

Client: I would probably feel less anxious. I might say to myself that I got away from the dog, and now he can't bite me, so I'm safe.

Therapist: Right. So, just as your thoughts can influence your behaviors and your emotions, so can that relationship go in other directions as well. Your behaviors can influence your thoughts

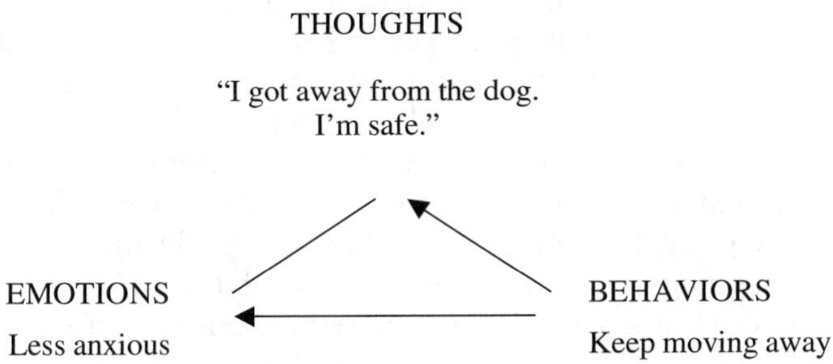

and emotions, and your emotions can have an impact on your thoughts and behaviors. CBT makes use of this relationship to help you to understand your problem in a new way, and to help you to become less anxious and worried and have a better quality of life. That is, when you have been "living" with your problem for some time, you may have developed ways of understanding and dealing with it that are actually maintaining the problem or even making it worse. CBT will help you to see your problem differently and teach you new ways of dealing with it that are more helpful and effective.

The active collaboration between client and therapist and the completion of weekly between-session exercises are also important CBT principles to address. Clients need to be aware that they will be expected to participate significantly in their own treatment. If they do not put forth the effort, both in and out of session, they are unlikely to see any notable improvement in their symptoms. Although this information is extremely important, it can sound authoritarian or intimidating to clients, particularly at the start of treatment when they are still unsure about what treatment will involve. Again, by using Socratic questioning, the information can be presented in a nonthreatening manner and can ultimately enhance client motivation. An example of how to present this is as follows:

Therapist: One of the major features of CBT is that you and I are both considered experts. You are an expert when it comes to your particular problem, so the knowledge that you have about your problem will be invaluable in treatment. On the other hand, I am an expert at understanding problems in a new way and at teaching skills that people can use to deal with their problems. That means that it is very important that we work together in session. I will need you to participate in sessions because it is the work that you put into dealing with your problem that will lead to real change. Does that make sense? I will also be giving you exercises to do between sessions every week to practice new skills or to test out new ideas. Why do you think it's important to do these exercises?

Client: I have no idea. I'm actually a little surprised about all this. I thought that you were going to be fixing my problem.

Therapist: Actually, I'm not going to "fix" the problem. You are. I am just going to help you discover ways of dealing with your problem, but it is you who will be responsible for actual change.

This point is a vital one, particularly in CBT. As noted previously, some clients might expect to adopt a passive stance, where almost all the work will be done by the therapist. If clients do not explicitly state their expectations regarding treatment, the therapist might want to take the time to ask them what they think therapy will involve. In this manner, any false preconceptions can be dispelled early on. Returning to our above example, a possible discussion of these issues might be:

Therapist: Keeping in mind your role in treatment success, why do you think that between-session exercises are necessary? Before you answer, let me give you an example. Let's say that you decide that you want to learn to play the piano, so you sign up for 12 weekly one-hour lessons. What will happen if you only play the piano during your lessons and not at home?

Client: I'd probably be a pretty mediocre piano player.

Therapist: Probably. But why is that? What's the difference between only playing during your lessons and practicing what you have learned in the time between your lessons?

Client: Well, obviously, I would play better if I practiced more.

Therapist: That's right. When you learn anything new, whether it is playing the piano, learning how to drive, or acquiring new ways to manage your anxiety, it is only through repeated practice that you improve your skills and feel confident while using them. In other words, it would be a bit of a waste of time if you didn't put your best effort into practicing the skills that you will learn in session. Without repeated practice, you wouldn't have much experience with your skills in the "real world" and you probably wouldn't feel much better.

An alternative method of presenting the rationale for between-session exercises is to present them as "behavioral prescriptions." That is, just as a physician prescribes medication when a patient is not feeling well, the therapist assigns a weekly "prescription" for between-session exercises.

As discussed in Chapter 4, the therapist should also take the appropriate steps so that clients are not fearful of what will be required of them in terms of these exercises. It is a good idea to take a few minutes to explain to clients that they will not be asked to do anything unless they understand *why* it is important, have a good idea of *how* to do it, and know *what* to expect. Moreover, clients should always be asked whether they agree with the suggested exercise. Do they clearly see its usefulness? Do they feel capable of doing it? Does it seem too overwhelming? If so, what could they do that would be less anxiety provoking, but would still be worthwhile? When between-session exercises are demystified in this manner, clients are more likely to be motivated and actually carry out their exercises.

Although the discussion of the major principles of CBT might seem to be a lengthy process, it has several notable advantages. First, it allows the therapist to ensure that clients are not holding unrealistic expectations about treatment. Second, client motivation can be enhanced by clearly outlining the reason for its importance and its contribution to treatment success. The discussion of the principles of CBT also allows clients to be fully aware of what treatment will involve and what is expected of them. Since clients must ultimately determine whether CBT is appropriate for them, this information is necessary in order for the client to make an informed decision. Finally, by taking the time to explain these principles, the therapist can also contribute to the establishment of a strong therapeutic alliance, which can make a key contribution to positive treatment outcomes.

Explaining the GAD Diagnosis

One cannot assume that a client who has been given a diagnosis of GAD has received a proper explanation of what that diagnosis entails (unless the treating clinician provided the diagnosis). As such, psychoeducation should also include a detailed description of GAD. This information is provided to ensure that clients understand their disorder and to begin to "normalize" their experience. Among the elements that can be discussed is the fact that GAD is one of the anxiety disorders and that its main feature is excessive worry about multiple daily life events. The chronicity of the disorder can also be underscored by discussing the fact that although the minimum duration is six months for a diagnosis of GAD (by definition), many individuals with GAD cannot recall a time when they did not worry excessively. The associated somatic symptoms of GAD, such as fatigue, irritability, and muscle tension, should also be reviewed. However, in keeping with our objective of targeting excessive worry, these symptoms are best described primarily as the *product* of longstanding worry.

Given that the description of GAD is meant to inform clients about their problem and to begin normalizing their experiences, some time should be taken to discuss the categorical and dimensional models of mental health as they pertain to GAD. Our position is that GAD, like many other mental health disorders, is best viewed from a dimensional perspective. Specifically, we believe that, for the most part, GAD is an excessive manifestation of a set of symptoms that everyone experiences to varying degrees from time to time. One way for the therapist to discuss this is in the following manner:

Therapist: One way to think of GAD is as an "all-or-nothing" disorder. In other words, either you have it "completely" or you don't have it at all. This is sometimes referred to as the categorical perspective of mental health.

GAD present GAD absent

Therapist: Another way to think about GAD is as a set of symptoms that can be placed on a continuum. Because everyone worries to some degree, we should all be on that continuum, albeit at different places.

No worry/anxiety Extreme worry/anxiety

Therapist: Unlike the categorical model, where everyone is placed in one of the two "boxes," the dimensional model places everyone at different points on a continuum, with some people being closer to the "no worry/anxiety" end and some closer to the "extreme worry/anxiety" end. So how do we decide when someone has GAD? Essentially, we draw a line on the continuum that represents our best estimate of clinically significant GAD symptoms; we then assign a diagnosis of GAD to people who surpass this line or threshold.

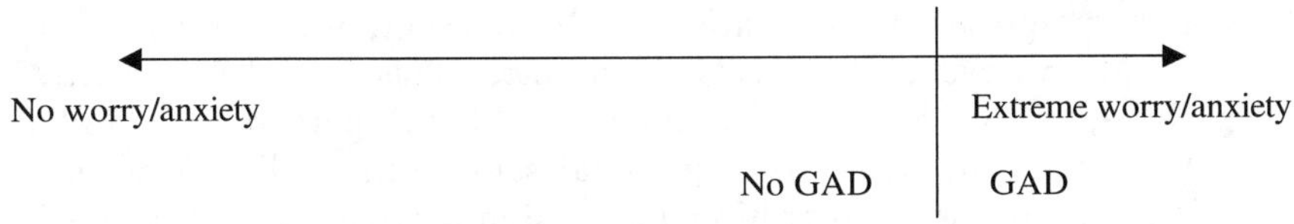

Therapist: Is there a great difference between individuals who fall just a little to the left of the line and those who fall just a little to the right? Of course, the answer is no, but in order for mental health practitioners to have a common language, we need to determine a "clinical threshold" so that we can agree on what constitutes a diagnosis of GAD. When determining a person's place on the GAD continuum, clinicians typically take into consideration the severity of the symptoms as well as the extent to which the symptoms lead to distress and impairment. In other words, in the absence of distress and impairment, a person with high levels of worry and anxiety would probably not receive a diagnosis of GAD.

As can be seen from the description of the dimensional model, emphasis is placed on the universality of anxious symptoms. As a result, assigning a GAD diagnosis becomes a matter of *degree*. For clients who are fearful about entering treatment for a "mental health problem," this type of description can be helpful in and of itself. By thinking of GAD as an extreme form of a normal phenomenon, these clients often feel less threatened by the prospect of receiving help for their worry and anxiety.

Introduction to the Model: The Symptoms of GAD

As discussed previously, our model of GAD is presented in a stepwise fashion in order to ensure that clients do not become overwhelmed from the outset. The first pictorial illustration is a basic model, where only the symptoms associated with a diagnosis of GAD are presented (see Appendix 5.1 for the first model). Before trying to modify the symptoms of GAD, clients should have a clear idea of what these symptoms are. This is especially important in GAD given that its main feature, excessive and uncontrollable worry, is a covert (or internal) event that cannot be directly observed. When presenting the initial GAD model, the therapist should walk through each step, eliciting examples from the client along the way. An example of this presentation might be the following:

Therapist: There is often a situation or trigger that starts off the chain of symptoms. This situation can be an event, or even the memory of an event, that leads to the next phase, the "What if…?" question. For example, having a difficult personal encounter, becoming aware of a physical sensation, reading a newspaper article, or watching a television newscast can all trigger a worry cycle. "What if…?" questions are thoughts that begin with "What if…" or the equivalent (for example, "Wouldn't it be terrible if…?") Can you think of an example in your own life?

Client: Well, my wife was late coming home from work yesterday, so I started thinking, what if she got into a car accident?

Therapist: Great example. In that case, your wife being late from work is the situation or trigger, and this led you to the "What if…?" thought, "What if she was in an accident?" However, the cycle does not end there. Once you said that to yourself, did you think about anything else?

Client: I started thinking all sorts of things, such as how would our children cope if she were seriously injured. At the same time, I was thinking about keeping the phone line free in case the police called to tell me she was in an accident.

Therapist: Some of those thoughts are *worries*, and they are set in motion by "What if…?" questions. They usually involve a chain of several thoughts, such as "What if my work contract doesn't get renewed; I don't know how I will pay all my debts; I won't have a penny to spare; I won't be able to keep my head above water; I might not be able to keep my car." You had a chain of similar thoughts after you said to yourself "What if my wife got into an accident?"

In order to avoid any misunderstandings, it is important that the client and therapist agree on a definition of worry. A simple and useful definition that we have used is the following: "Worry is a thought process that is concerned with future events where there is uncertainty about the outcome, the future being thought about is a negative one, and this is accompanied by feelings of anxiety" (Macleod, Williams, & Bekerian, 1991). In this definition, the emphasis is placed on the notion that worry is a *thought process* that is relatively distinct from anxiety, which is the emotional response that typically accompanies worry. The definition also highlights the idea that worry is *future-oriented* and is related to *uncertainty*. Given that this final component (that is, that worry relates to uncertainty) will be expanded upon at length throughout treatment, its introduction at the outset sets the stage for the following sessions.

Before moving on to the remaining steps in the model, more detail about worry should be provided. Specifically, therapists should discuss the types of triggers (that is, external and internal) that can set off a worry chain, as well as the two types of worries (that is, worries about current problems and worries about hypothetical situations). An example of this discussion is as follows:

Therapist: Triggers for a worry cycle can come in two general forms. Some worries are triggered by external, observable situations; for example, an argument with a friend, or in your case, your wife's lateness in returning from work. Other worries are triggered by internal events, such as a physical sensation or another worry. For example, feelings of tightness in the chest might trigger worries about heart problems, which might in turn trigger worries about finances (e.g., "What if I can't pay the medical bills?"). As for the worries themselves, they can be separated into two major types: (1) those that concern current problems (the problem already exists), and (2) those that concern hypothetical situations (the problem doesn't exist yet, and in many cases, never will). When you were worried about your wife potentially being in a car accident, you were experiencing the second type of worry; you were worrying about a situation that hadn't actually happened. However, if you were worried about the consequences of an argument with a friend, you would be experiencing the first type of worry; you would be worrying about a problem that already exists. We distinguish between these two types of worries because, in this treatment, you will use different strategies to deal with each type. Does all this make sense so far?

Client: So far so good. I had never thought about my worries as falling into different categories. That seems to make sense, though.

Therapist: Now, let's return to our model. Once you have started a worry cycle, how do you feel physically?

Client: Pretty tense. When I was thinking about my wife being in a car accident, I had knots in my stomach.

Therapist: That feeling of emotional discomfort is what we generally refer to as *anxiety*. For people who have GAD, anxiety is often a consequence of worry. In other words, chronic worry leads to anxiety, which may take the form of physical or psychological symptoms. Muscle tension and fatigue are examples of physical signs of anxiety, whereas irritability and difficulty concentrating are examples of psychological signs of anxiety. That feeling of "knots in your stomach" is an example of a physical feeling. It is important to keep in mind that worry is a type of *thought* whereas anxiety is a type of *emotion*. We know that thoughts influence emotions and emotions influence thoughts, so it follows that if you are able to better control your worrisome thoughts, you will also feel less anxious. Now, the final part of this cycle relates to something we talked about when we were discussing the criteria for a GAD diagnosis; specifically, the fact that GAD is a chronic condition. If you think about your worrying episodes, do they only happen once in a while and for brief time periods?

Client: Absolutely not! They go around and around in my head almost every day, and sometimes it can go on for hours.

Therapist: And for how long have you been experiencing this?

Client: It seems like I've been a worrier my whole life.

Therapist: Then no one knows better than you do that continually "spinning" through these worry cycles is exhausting, both physically and mentally. In the model, this state is referred to as demoralization and fatigue, and as you know, it is the consequence of months and even years of worry and anxiety.

Worry Awareness Training

Once the first model has been presented (and the importance of worry underscored), the next phase is introduced; namely, worry awareness training. As mentioned beforehand, one must first clearly "see" a symptom before attempting to reduce it. In the case of GAD, it is important that clients become experts at recognizing their own worries and classifying them as either being about a current problem or a hypothetical situation. Given that some clients feel that they already think too much about their worries, the therapist will occasionally encounter some "resistance" when asking clients to systematically monitor their worries. However, once clients begin worry awareness training, they typically realize within a short period of time how important and helpful this training can be. As such, worry awareness training is the first between-session exercise "prescribed" by the therapist.

Clients are asked to record their worries three times a day, at predetermined times, in their Worry Diary (see Appendix 5.2 for a copy of the Worry Diary). Specifically, clients record the date and time the worry occurred, the description of the worry, their level of anxiety at that time (on a scale from 0 to 8), and the worry type (about a current problem or a hypothetical situation). Once clients have completed the between-session exercise, the therapist should ask what they discovered about their worries as a result of filling out the diary. In a Socratic fashion and using client examples of worries, the following points should be covered:

- *Clients usually have recurrent worry themes.* Although most will say that they worry about "everything," most clients will have a few worry themes that consistently recur.

- *A worry chain can last a few minutes or a few hours.* Since the goal of treatment is not to eliminate worry, but rather to reduce it to more manageable levels, clients need to see just how much of their time is being consumed by worry. In addition, seeing how one worry can lead to others shows the pernicious cycle of worry chains.

- *Worries involve future events.* Even when a worry is rooted in a past event (e.g., failing an exam a week ago), it is typically about the future repercussions of the past event (e.g., "How will this affect my grade point average at the end of term?").

- *Worries can involve both a current problem and a hypothetical situation.* A client can be worried about chronic pain (which is a current problem) and also be worried that the pain is a sign that he or she may have a serious illness such as cancer in the future (which is a hypothetical situation). This is usually the result of a worry chain, where a client begins worrying about a topic, for example chronic pain, which leads to worrying about other things, such as cancer.

Although it is important to ensure that clients properly understand the distinction between both types of worry, care must be taken when expanding on this topic. Given that GAD clients are prone to reassurance seeking before making a decision, they should be encouraged to classify their worries even when they are not certain of their "proper" classification. This recommendation will become clearer as the second treatment module is introduced.

MODULE 2: UNCERTAINTY RECOGNITION AND BEHAVIORAL EXPOSURE

Intolerance of uncertainty is targeted in the second treatment module and is therefore the next component to be integrated into the model of GAD (see Appendix 5.3 for a copy of the model that includes intolerance of uncertainty). As stated in Chapter 4, developing a greater tolerance for uncertainty is the foundation on which the treatment is built; as such, it should be consistently tied in to the subsequent modules. The central goals for the therapist at this stage are (1) to ensure that clients understand the primary role of intolerance of uncertainty in the development and maintenance of excessive worry and anxiety, and (2) to encourage clients to begin recognizing and dealing with uncertainty in their day-to-day lives. There are several useful analogies that the therapist can use in integrating intolerance of uncertainty into the model of GAD, including the following:

Therapist: We are now going to begin expanding upon our initial model of GAD by adding "intolerance of uncertainty" to its background. Intolerance of uncertainty can be seen as the fuel for worry. The more someone is intolerant of uncertainty, the more that person is likely to start asking "what if" questions that lead to worry. So what is intolerance of uncertainty?

Allergy Analogy

Therapist: Obviously, most people dislike uncertainty more or less, but what do we mean when we talk about being intolerant of uncertainty? One way to think about intolerance of uncertainty is as a psychological allergy. People with an allergy, to pollen for example, will have a very strong reaction to even a minute quantity of the substance. That is, they might start sneezing, coughing, and their eyes might redden when exposed to a very small amount of pollen. In the same way, people who are intolerant of uncertainty are "allergic" to uncertainty. Even when there is only a small amount of uncertainty, they will have a strong reaction; in this case, excessive worry and anxiety. For example, someone who is intolerant of uncertainty might worry a great deal about his or her plane crashing because even though it is unlikely, there is still a small chance that it could happen.

Filtered Lenses Analogy

Therapist: Another way to think about intolerance of uncertainty is to see it as wearing special filtered glasses. Instead of wearing "rose-colored glasses," people who are intolerant of uncertainty are wearing "uncertainty glasses." These people look at the world through their filtered lenses and see uncertainty more often and faster than other people do. Even when there is only a small amount of uncertainty in a situation (like the possibility of their plane crashing), they will see it immediately and react to it. People who wear these filtered lenses put a great deal of effort into looking for uncertainty in their environment, and if the world is "colored with uncertainty," they often do not see much else. In other words, people who are intolerant of uncertainty are experts at recognizing uncertainty very quickly and thinking about all the potential bad things that could result from it.

The Manifestations of Intolerance of Uncertainty

In the next phase of this treatment module, clients become familiarized with all the strategies they use to eliminate uncertainty in their lives. Most clients are unaware of the amount of energy they expend trying to attain a sense of certainty. It is therefore important that the therapist assist them in becoming aware of all their behavioral and cognitive strategies:

Therapist: If we know that people with GAD are intolerant of uncertainty and that they do everything they can to push it away, how do you think this affects their lives? More importantly, if we agree that you have difficulty tolerating uncertainty, what do you do to deal with "uncertain" situations?

Client: I don't know. I never really thought about it. I know that I worry a lot about things that are uncertain.

Therapist: That's certainly the most obvious thing that people do when they are intolerant of uncertainty: they worry. Worrying is often used by people with GAD as a way of trying to think about every possible outcome in an uncertain situation so that the situation *feels* more predictable and less uncertain. Can you think of anything else that you do in order to feel less uncertain?

Client: I don't think that there is really anything else that I do.

Therapist: It's not surprising to hear you say that because most people are not aware of the many things they do to feel a sense of certainty. However, there are, in fact, several things that people with GAD do to either increase feelings of certainty or avoid uncertain situations altogether. For example, they might ask for reassurance from their friends and families before making even a minor decision, or they might delay completing a project until the last minute so that once it is finished they have as little time as possible to worry about it.

TABLE 5.1 Examples of Manifestations of Intolerance of Uncertainty

"Approach" Strategies

1. Wanting to do everything yourself and not delegating tasks to anyone else.

   Example: Doing all the housework yourself because otherwise you cannot be certain that it will be done right.

2. Looking for *a lot* of information before proceeding with something.

   Examples: Reading a lot of documentation on a topic; asking for the same information from a number of people; and shopping for a very long time before choosing a present for someone.

3. Questioning a decision you have already made because you are no longer certain that it was the best decision.
4. Looking for reassurance (asking others questions so that they will reassure you).
5. Rechecking and doing things over because you are no longer sure you did them correctly.

   Example: Rereading e-mails several times before sending them to make sure that there are absolutely no mistakes.

6. Overprotecting others, doing things for them (e.g., family members and children).

"Avoidance" Strategies

1. Avoiding fully committing to certain things.

   Examples: Not fully committing to a friendship or romantic relationship because the outcome is uncertain; not fully engaging in therapy because there is no "guarantee" that it will work.

2. Finding "imaginary" reasons for not doing certain things.

   Examples: Finding excuses to not move out of the family home; not doing exercise that you know is good for you by telling yourself that you might not be able to stand the discomfort of exercising.

3. Procrastinating (putting off until later what you could do right away).

   Examples: Putting off a phone call because you are not certain how the person will react; delaying making a decision because you are not certain that it is the right decision; not doing anything in the end because you are not certain about your decision (e.g., choice of film or restaurant).

The therapist can then present the client with a list of various manifestations of intolerance of uncertainty (see Table 5.1) and ask the client to think about and record which ones he or she currently engages in. The therapist may also want the client to provide personal examples of manifestations of intolerance of uncertainty. Although it is a good idea to distinguish between strategies that represent approach behaviors (for example, asking for reassurance to reduce feelings of uncertainty) and those that represent avoidance behaviors (for example, not committing to a relationship because the outcome is uncertain), the therapist should underscore that both types of strategies have the same effect. Specifically, clients are expending a great deal of time and energy trying to eliminate uncertainty at all costs. By recording this information, clients will begin to get a better idea of how intolerance of uncertainty affects their way of dealing with day-to-day activities.

Once the manifestations of intolerance of uncertainty have been reviewed, the therapist and client can begin discussing ways to address the client's intolerance of uncertainty. In this stage of treatment, clients are encouraged to acknowledge their options and to consider the implications of each by discussing the two components of the construct of intolerance and uncertainty:

Therapist: If we think about intolerance of uncertainty as the "fuel" for worry, the question then becomes: How do we change this?

Client: Yes, it certainly does seem to be easier said than done.

Therapist: Well, we can start by looking at the two parts of the term *intolerance* and *uncertainty.* If you want to decrease your worrying and anxiety, you can either increase your tolerance or increase your certainty. Does that make sense?

Therapist: Which one would you say you have been doing so far?

Client: Well, I have been trying to increase my certainty I suppose.

Therapist: And would you say that that strategy is working?

Client: I guess not, since I'm here. I still worry and have anxiety all the time.

Therapist: That's right. Why do you think that choosing to increase certainty is not an effective strategy?

Client: I don't know.

Therapist: One of the reasons is because uncertainty is absolutely unavoidable. Everyone's lives are fraught with uncertainty, and each day there is something new that comes up that has some degree of uncertainty. For example, we cannot be certain that we will be in good health in the future even if we are presently healthy. Also, we cannot know for certain if we will always have a job or if our relationships will always turn out well. No matter how much we plan our lives, there is often something unexpected that comes up. So what does that say about the strategy of increasing certainty?

Client: That it doesn't work. Actually, now that I think about it, trying to increase my certainty means that I will have to keep doing all those things every day. I guess that means my only other option is to try to increase my tolerance.

Therapist: Exactly. So that means that we need to think about *how* you can increase your tolerance for uncertainty. The challenge, of course, is that even if you can see the need to increase your tolerance for uncertainty, there is a big difference between recognizing what you want to change and actually changing it.

Client: Yes, I was about to ask you how I go about changing my attitude toward uncertainty. It seems like that might be hard to do.

Therapist: Actually, in order to change an attitude or a belief, it is best to start by changing your behavior. Let's use an analogy. If you were afraid of public speaking because you thought that the audience might scrutinize and criticize you, it would probably be more helpful to practice speaking in public rather than trying to "convince" yourself that the audience would be indulgent and noncritical. Through your actions, you could ultimately change your beliefs about public speaking. The same holds true for learning how to tolerate uncertainty. By acting "as if" you are *tolerant* of uncertainty, you can start to change your beliefs about uncertainty. A good way to do this is to ask: "If I were tolerant of uncertainty, what would I do in this situation?" From there, you can start deciding what actions to take to begin increasing your tolerance for uncertainty.

As a between-session exercise, clients are invited to complete at least one "tolerating uncertainty experiment" a week and to record their results on the Uncertainty and Behavior Monitoring form (see Appendix 5.4 for a copy of the form). These exercises are designed to help clients develop new ways of dealing with uncertainty. Like any exposure-type exercise, tolerating uncertainty experiments should follow a gradual progression.

The first experiment should be relatively simple and cause only a moderate level of anxiety to ensure success.

Examples of initial experiments include:

- Clients send a low-priority e-mail without rereading it or checking it for spelling errors.
- Clients who frequently seek reassurance from others for minor decisions (e.g., what to make for dinner), make a minor decision without asking anyone for reassurance.
- Clients go to a restaurant or a movie without reading any reviews.
- Clients call a friend unexpectedly and invite that person out for a social gathering (e.g., coffee, a movie).

Initially, clients should not conduct tolerating uncertainty experiments that are related to major worry themes. For example, if a client's primary worry is about his or her children's safety, asking that client to refrain from checking on them when they are playing outside might be too difficult at first. Rather, as clients become more comfortable with tolerating uncertainty, the exercises can gradually address more anxiety-provoking situations. As such, clients might progress from not checking low-priority e-mails to refraining from checking moderate to high-priority e-mails as their confidence grows.

Suggestions When Facing Uncertainty

The therapist can expect that clients will be quite anxious about engaging in these initial behavioral experiments because they involve behaving in a way that is in stark contrast to the way that clients have undoubtedly acted for years. As such, the following suggestions or guidelines can be presented by the therapist at the outset:

- *Record the experiment.* It is always a good idea to keep a record of the experiments you did, of how you expected them to turn out, and of how they actually went. Without a record of what you have done, you won't be able to track your progress and see all the work that you have completed.

- *Start small and be realistic.* The first time you try to tolerate uncertainty, choose something that you will find a little difficult, but not so difficult that you are unlikely to do it.

The more successful experiments you complete, the more your motivation to try new exercises will increase.

- *Expect to be anxious or uncomfortable.* The first time we attempt any new behavior, it is normal to feel anxious or nervous. This is not a sign that the behavior is inappropriate or that we should not be doing it. In fact, if you are feeling a little anxious while doing the exercise, you are on the right track. If you think about anything new that you have learned in your life, such as the first time you drove a car, you were probably quite anxious. However, with time and practice, that discomfort went away.

- *Motivation does not precede action — it follows it.* This is an extremely important principle. Many people say that they would like to change their behaviors (e.g., start an exercise regimen, quit smoking), but they are waiting for the motivation before they begin making the change. The flaw in this logic is that "waiting" for motivation is unlikely to be helpful. Once you begin to change your behavior, for example going to the gym on a daily basis, your new behavior itself will give you the motivation to continue. That is to say, the more you get, the more you want. The same holds true for these experiments. Do not "wait" for the motivation to start tolerating uncertainty, simply start facing uncertainty and the motivation will follow.

MODULE 3: REEVALUATION OF THE USEFULNESS OF WORRY

The third treatment module involves addressing positive beliefs about the usefulness of worry. As discussed in Chapters 2 and 4, individuals with GAD tend to overestimate the usefulness of their worries, which can ultimately impact upon treatment compliance. Specifically, clients are less likely to want to reduce their worries if they believe that they have a functional purpose. One way to introduce this concept to clients is in the following manner:

Therapist: We have already discussed how intolerance of uncertainty is the fuel for worry and that it is the main factor that we will address throughout treatment. However, we also want to start looking at other factors that are involved in keeping the worry cycle going. We will be introducing the first of these today. That is, we will be discussing any beliefs you might have about the usefulness of worrying. (See Appendix 5.5 for a copy of the model that includes positive beliefs about worry.)

When discussing positive beliefs about worry, it is important to take a nonjudgmental stance so that clients can feel at ease about disclosing these beliefs. It is not uncommon for clients to think that their therapist will disapprove of any admission of positive beliefs about worry because of the inherent "contradiction" in such beliefs ("I want to worry less, but I think worrying is useful"). One way to take a nonjudgmental stance is to normalize the experience for clients and to illustrate the commonality of such a belief system:

Therapist: Our beliefs about the usefulness of certain actions or behaviors obviously have a strong impact on what we do. It makes sense that we keep doing the things that we believe are useful and let go of the things that we do not find useful. In the same way, the more we feel that worrying is useful, the more likely we are to continue worrying. In fact, research has shown that people with GAD differ from people with moderate levels of worry by their tendency to believe that worrying is particularly useful. Have you ever thought that some of your worries might be useful?

Client: I don't think so. I wouldn't be here if I did.

Therapist: Well, that's true in a way. If you weren't bothered by your excessive worry and anxiety, you would not have come for treatment. However, sometimes people with GAD will say that although they dislike their worrying in general, they find that specific worries can be useful. For example, some people will say that although in general they worry too much and would like to worry less, they still believe that it is good that they worry about work because it keeps them motivated. What do you think about that?

We have often found that a good method for drawing clients out when it comes to topics they might be hesitant to disclose (such as admitting to positive beliefs about worry) is to frame the question in a "other people have said" format as illustrated above. In our experience, clients are more likely to disclose if they believe that it is a common phenomenon.

Identifying Positive Beliefs about the Usefulness of Worry

In order to assist clients in identifying their positive beliefs about worry, the therapist will first need to present the most common beliefs typically held by individuals with GAD. As stated previously, our research has shown that positive beliefs typically fall into five categories. Although at this time we encourage therapists to solely present the different belief categories, the following descriptions include an exposition of some of the "logical flaws" that clients are likely making in terms of these beliefs. During treatment, it is recommended that clients first identify their own beliefs about worry (and generate personal examples from their own worries) before introducing any challenges to those beliefs.

1. **The belief that worrying helps to find solutions to problems.** This category includes beliefs that worry helps to solve problems and find better solutions, that it increases vigilance or preparedness, that it contributes to a more well thought out or efficient reaction, and that it helps to prevent or avoid problems. An example might be: "It is good that I worry about my problems at work because it ensures that I pay attention to them and solve them efficiently." Although there is some truth to this, there are also a few problems with this belief. Although low levels of worry can, at times, be helpful in generating solutions to problems, high levels of worry actually interfere with the problem-solving process. This is because worry makes us see all the ways that our solutions might fail. So worry, in many cases, actually makes solving problems more difficult.

2. **The belief that worrying serves a motivating function that ensures things will get done.** This is a common belief among GAD clients who often believe that worrying about something that needs to get done will ensure that it does in fact get done. Examples of this include: "If I worry about my grades in school, I'll study harder and do well," and "If I worry about the way my house looks to others, I will be more likely to keep it clean." The main problem with this belief is that worrying is confused with caring. For example, "Worrying about my next exam means that it is important, so worrying will make me study harder." However, if a person worries less about an upcoming exam, this does not mean that they will suddenly become complacent. Rather, it means that they will be less anxious about the exam while preparing for it. In fact, being very worried about something often leads to inactivity because of the negative emotional reactions that are associated with

worry. This can particularly be seen with GAD clients, where a common manifestation of intolerance of uncertainty is to procrastinate or avoid. As such, worry might actually have the opposite effect from what was originally intended.

3. **The belief that worrying can protect a person from negative emotions.** This category reflects the notion that by worrying "in advance" about a potential negative event, negative feelings such as disappointment, sadness, or guilt will be prevented should the event actually occur. For example, "If I worry about my husband being injured in a car crash, I will be able to handle it without being overwhelmed by sadness if it occurs." Some individuals with GAD believe that worrying is like "putting money in the bank." They believe that if the feared event takes place, they will have already "invested" in their negative reaction in advance, thereby allowing them to be less affected by the event. Some of our GAD clients have told us that "If something happens to someone I love and I haven't worried about it in advance, I would feel very guilty." This way of thinking puts the person in a position where they must worry constantly, "just in case." One of the problems with this type of thinking is that when negative events do occur, people who have worried about them are unlikely to feel better than people who have not worried about them. Worry does not protect people from negative feelings because no one feels prepared when an unexpected negative event occurs (e.g., the sudden loss of a loved one, a car accident).

4. **The belief that worrying, in and of itself, can prevent negative outcomes.** This category reflects the belief that the act of worrying can affect the outcome of events. Specifically, that one's worries are directly responsible for the nonoccurrence of negative events or the occurrence of positive events. This type of belief is sometimes called *thought-action fusion*. For example, "I have always worried about my child being involved in a serious car accident; it has never happened, so my worrying must be working." This type of thinking is, of course, logically flawed, as the nonoccurrence of an event could be attributed to any number of things. For example, an individual might believe that his plane didn't crash because he worried about it beforehand. However, it could just as easily be due to the remoteness of the particular event (i.e., planes crash infrequently), the skill of the pilot, or the clear weather during the flight. Another problem with this type of belief is

that it usually involves *selective attention*. For example, a client might report that when he worries about presentations at work beforehand, he does well. However, has he ever not worried about a presentation and done well regardless? Conversely, has he ever worried about a presentation and not done well? Individuals with this type of belief will often search out evidence that confirms their beliefs and ignore any disconfirmatory evidence.

5. **The belief that worrying represents a positive personality trait.** This involves the belief that the act of worrying shows that an individual is caring, loving, or conscientious. An example of this might be "I'm the worrier in my family; if I worried less, my parents would be disappointed in me; they would think that I don't care about them anymore." Implicit in this belief is the assumption that individuals who worry less are less caring, loving, or conscientious. Obviously, this is untrue. In fact, most high worriers likely know someone who holds similar positive character traits in the absence of excessive worry, thereby contradicting their belief.

Once all five of the positive beliefs about worry have been presented, clients are encouraged to begin looking at their own worries and start identifying some of these beliefs. Using the Positive Beliefs about Worry form (see Appendix 5.6 for a copy of the form), which can be completed between sessions, clients are asked to write down examples for each personally relevant belief (they can use their Worry Diary to assist them in thinking about what purpose specific worries appear to serve). They can also use the form to identify any other beliefs that they might have about the usefulness of worry.

Following the identification of clients' positive beliefs about the function of their worries, the therapist should address why it is important to identify these beliefs and potentially reevaluate them:

Therapist: So, why do you think that it is a good idea to identify some of the positive beliefs you have about the usefulness of your worries?

Client: I don't know.

Therapist: As I mentioned earlier, we tend to keep doing the things that we feel are useful. So as long as you feel that some of your worries are highly useful, you are unlikely to want to reduce them. It is important that we look at what advantages you receive from worrying and whether it is in fact helpful. I am not saying that there is no usefulness to worry. Instead, I would like us to see if your beliefs are actually true by looking at the evidence and deciding whether worrying less would actually have a negative effect on your life. In addition, we want to make a distinction between worrying occasionally and worrying excessively. This is because when we talk about looking at whether worry is in fact really useful, we are actually talking about the usefulness of excessive worry and all the behaviors that go along with it (that is, reassurance-seeking, procrastination).

Strategies for Reevaluating Positive Beliefs about Worry

In this phase of treatment, the therapist walks a fine line between challenging the client's beliefs and allowing the client to express them in a nonjudgmental manner. Positive beliefs about worry are sometimes difficult to identify. One reason for this is that clients may not be fully aware of their positive beliefs. Some clients might say that although they know "intellectually" that their worries do not serve a useful purpose, they nevertheless "feel" that they do. Other clients report that although they usually believe that their worries are not helpful, at times they wonder if their worries can help them to deal with life's problems.

A second reason for the difficulty in identifying positive beliefs about worry is that clients might not be willing to acknowledge these beliefs. As mentioned above, many clients are hesitant to discuss their positive beliefs about worry because the beliefs are inconsistent with their consultation motive. Clients sometimes believe that it is unacceptable to be ambivalent and to see a positive side to a behavior they would like to decrease. In fact, some clients have mentioned that they did not think the therapist would be receptive to these ideas and wondered if disclosure of positive beliefs about worry would be interpreted as treatment resistance. Other clients fear that they will "lose face" if they admit to having these paradoxical beliefs. For all these reasons, it is important that the therapist actively encourage the client to become aware of, and acknowledge, their positive beliefs about worry. One method that we have found to be extremely useful in attaining this goal is the lawyer–prosecutor role-play.

Lawyer–Prosecutor Role-Play

In this role-play, the client is first asked to identify a specific worry, for example, "Worrying about my children shows that I am a good parent." The client is then asked to take on the role of a lawyer who must convince the members of a jury that the worry is useful. Once all arguments have been exhausted, the client then plays the role of a prosecutor who must convince the members of the jury that the worry is in fact not useful. We have found that this role-play allows clients to consider "both sides of the coin" in a nonthreatening context. Specifically, because they are taking on different roles, clients are given the opportunity to argue against their previous statements without appearing to be contradictory. Consistent with the principles of motivational interviewing (Miller & Rollnick, 2002), the therapist uses Socratic questioning to help clients reconsider the actual usefulness of worrying when playing the role of the prosecutor. In this case, examples of questions include: "Is there anything else you do that shows you are a caring parent? Do you know any 'good' parents who don't worry excessively?" The goal of this phase of treatment is to allow clients to begin questioning the actual usefulness of their worries in order to reduce ambivalence and increase motivation for change.

Specific Challenges to the Different Beliefs about Worry

When assisting clients in challenging their positive beliefs, it is important that the therapist address the beliefs regarding a *specific* worry and not the general belief itself. For example, a client might worry excessively about the health of his children because he believes it shows good parenting qualities. In this case, challenges would be to the belief, "Worrying about my children's health shows that I am a good parent," and not to the general belief "Worry represents a positive personality trait." With that in mind, a list of helpful challenging statements for each of the positive beliefs about worry is presented in Table 5.2.

Reevaluation of Positive Beliefs: A Life without Worry?

One of the by-products of discussing the actual usefulness of worry, and potentially changing clients' perceptions in such a way that they no longer see worry as particularly useful, is that they must now consider alternatives to worrying. Relatedly, many clients report feelings of grief when they realize that they have spent years engaged in the largely fruitless act of worry. As such, therapists might wish to discuss these topics following the reevaluation of positive beliefs about worry.

In terms of alternatives to worry, the upcoming modules of problem-solving training and imaginal exposure can be presented as alternative (and more action-oriented) strategies for dealing with adversity. In particular, following challenges to the beliefs that worry helps with

TABLE 5.2 Challenges to Positive Beliefs about the Usefulness of Worry

1. *Worry aids with problem solving.* Example: If I worry about problems that come up at work, I am able to find better solutions to them.

Possible Challenges:

Do you actually solve your problems by worrying, or are you just going over the problem again and again in your head?

Does worry get you to actually solve your problems, or do you become so anxious that you delay solving your problems or avoid them altogether?

Are you confusing a thought (worry) with an action (problem solving)?

2. *Worry as a motivating force.* Example: If I worry about my performance at work, then I will be motivated to succeed.

Possible Challenges:

Do you know anyone who is successful at work and who is not a worrier?

Are you confusing worrying with caring? That is, is it possible to want to succeed at work and not worry about it all the time?

Does your worry really improve your performance? Are there negative repercussions as a result of your excessive worry about work? (For example, difficulty concentrating, memory problems, intense anxiety.)

3. *Worry protects against negative emotions.* Example: If I worry about my son potentially getting a serious disease, I will be better prepared emotionally if it happens.

Possible Challenges:

Has anything bad ever happened that you had worried about before? How did you feel? Were you buffered from the pain or sadness that it caused?

Does worrying about things that might never happen actually increase your negative emotions in the here and now?

4. *Worry, in and of itself, can prevent negative outcomes.* Example: When I worry about an upcoming exam at school, I do well; when I don't worry, I don't do well.

Possible Challenges:

Have you ever done poorly on an exam even though you worried?

Is your rule about worry (that is, worry = good outcome; don't worry = bad outcome) based on real evidence or is it an assumption? For example, is it possible that you only remember the exams you did well on when you worried, and that you forget those you didn't do well on when you worried?

Were you really not worrying when things didn't go well on some exams, or are you just remembering it that way to support your assumption?

– *Continued*

TABLE 5.2 Challenges to Positive Beliefs about the Usefulness of Worry

Could you test this theory? For example, could you track your worry prior to all exams and then look at your performance on each exam?

5. *Worry as a positive personality trait.* Example: The fact that I worry about my children proves that I am a good and caring parent.

Possible Challenges:

Is there anything else you do that shows you are a good and caring parent? Is it only worrying about your children that shows caring and love?

Do you know any other parents that you would consider "good and caring" but who do not worry excessively?

Have you suffered any negative consequences from friends or family because of your excessive worry? Has anyone ever considered your excessive worry as a *negative* personality trait? For example, have your children ever said that you smother or nag them too much, or have your friends ever not taken you seriously because you worry so much?

6. *The cost of worry: Potential challenges for all worry beliefs*

Has excessive worrying about this topic impacted on your relationships with your family or friends?

Has excessive worry impacted on your work performance? Do you find that it takes you longer to complete tasks than other people who worry less?

Has your excessive worry led to high levels of stress and fatigue?

How much time and effort do you spend each way worrying about this topic? Do you get better results from your worrying (for example, a better relationship with your children, superior work or school performance) compared to people who worry less?

problem solving and motivation, the therapist can draw a sharp distinction between the passive stance of worrying about problems and the active stance of actually going out and solving one's problems. By discussing these alternatives within the module of positive beliefs about worry, the therapist can tie the upcoming modules to the current one and thus emphasize the logical flow of treatment.

A second area of discussion involves what the client's life might look like if she worried less. It is important for the therapist to keep in mind that most clients with GAD have suffered from chronic worry and anxiety for the greater part of their lives. Many cannot even conceive of a life without chronic worry. This discussion can be extremely emotional, and some clients will be quite tearful, voicing feelings of loss and frustration for time wasted. Although it is helpful to return to this discussion near the end of treatment, clients should begin giving some thought to how they would like to occupy their time if they are not spending hours worrying. As such, some alternatives to excessive worry might include taking a class or spending more time with family and friends. As with many clients with anxiety disorders, so much time is consumed by the anxious symptoms that GAD clients have probably not had the time or the energy to set treatment goals for themselves other than symptom reduction.

As a final note, this treatment module, more than any other, should be applied in a flexible manner. Specifically, although the reevaluation of positive beliefs about worry is an important part of our treatment protocol, our research findings (and clinical experience) show that these beliefs are quite variable among clients with GAD. Despite the fact that the majority of GAD clients believe that worrying is highly useful, therapists can encounter individuals who hold few, if any, of these beliefs. Thus, the therapist should not assume that all clients believe that worrying serves a functional purpose. Nonetheless, given that positive beliefs about worry can interfere with all treatment modules (for example, a client who believes that worrying less is dangerous may avoid fully engaging in treatment), it is crucial that therapists assess these beliefs early on in treatment.

MODULE 4: PROBLEM-SOLVING TRAINING

As noted in Chapter 4, the problem-solving training module is split into two phases: (1) improving problem orientation, and (2) applying problem-solving skills. In the following sections, each one of these phases is presented separately; however, the reader should keep in mind that both phases are inexorably linked. For example, until clients recognize that their problems are not entirely aversive and threatening, they are unlikely to implement their problem-solving skills no matter how good they are.

Improving Problem Orientation

When the concept of negative problem orientation is presented to clients, two main ideas should be initially introduced. First, in terms of the model, an additional factor is being incorporated into our understanding of GAD and excessive worry. Second, problem solving is introduced as a practical alternative to worry if we can agree that worrying about problems is not especially useful. This second idea, that clients can "replace" excessive worry with actual problem solving, should be underscored repeatedly throughout this module. Excessive worry about problems is not an active strategy, although clients might initially view it as such. On the other hand, the active process of problem solving can actually lead to change in a problematic situation.

Therapist: We have been spending some time talking about whether excessive worry is actually beneficial. In some instances, we have found that worrying excessively can have the opposite effect to what you previously believed. For example, worrying excessively about projects at work can make you so anxious that rather than motivating you to work on them, you procrastinate instead. So, if worry is not that useful, what do you think you could do instead?

Client: I don't know. I have been thinking a lot about that, and I assume that I should just stop worrying, but that's easier said than done. How can I just stop worrying?

Therapist: You are absolutely right. It would be great if you could just shut off worry like a light switch, but it's not that simple, is it? As I'm sure you remember, I have been having you classify your worries as either being about current problems or hypothetical situations. We are now going to start working on specific strategies for each of those worry types. The first one I will be introducing today is problem solving as a way to deal with your worries about current problems. So you are not simply going to "stop worrying," but start replacing worry with a more productive strategy.

Client: Well, I'm really not very good at solving my problems.

Therapist: Well, if that's true, then it is even more important to start working on this. But what you just said about your ability to solve problems relates exactly to what we will be discussing today: negative problem orientation. Negative problem orientation is a factor that contributes to excessive worry, and it interferes with your problem-solving ability on many levels. (See Appendix 5.7 for a copy of the model that includes negative problem orientation.)

Prior to beginning a discussion on negative problem orientation and its impact on both problem solving and the worry cycle, it is a good idea for therapists to briefly discuss with clients some of the research findings in the area. For example, it is helpful for clients to know that the research to date suggests that excessive worriers are just as skilled at problem solving as people who worry less. However, excessive worriers have a more negative problem orientation. In other words, they have more negative attitudes and beliefs about problems and problem solving. The following is a suggestion for the presentation of negative problem orientation:

Therapist: What is negative problem orientation? It refers to the way we view problems, and the way we view ourselves as problem solvers. People who have a negative problem orientation tend to (1) view problems as threatening; (2) doubt their ability to solve problems; and (3) believe that problem solving will turn out badly no matter what. In other words, people with a negative problem orientation will say to themselves: "I don't like problems, I'm not good at solving them, and when I try to solve them, it doesn't work." Have you ever thought like that?

Client: Absolutely. I hate dealing with problems and I do think that I'm not good at solving them. I usually ask other people for advice on how to deal with them.

Therapist: If you remember, when we first talked about intolerance of uncertainty, I told you that it has a number of effects on your thoughts (i.e., worry) and your behaviors (e.g., reassurance-seeking). Negative problem orientation works in the same way. When you have negative beliefs about problems and your ability to deal with them, this has a strong impact on your emotions, your thoughts, and your behaviors.

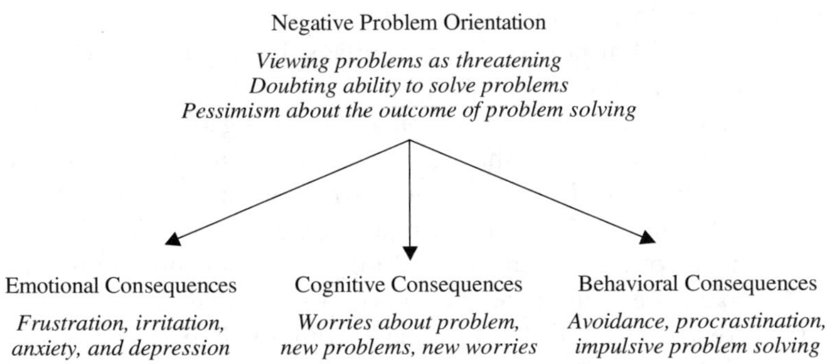

When presenting the consequences of negative problem orientation, it is best for therapists to encourage clients to generate examples through Socratic questioning. This can be achieved by logically linking the beliefs underlying negative problem orientation to the expected impact. For example:

Therapist: So, if a person saw problems as entirely threatening and believed that she was a poor problem solver, how do you think she is likely to feel when a problem comes up?

Client: Probably pretty annoyed. I hate it when there is a problem. I also get anxious.

Therapist: Exactly, so the emotional effect for you is that you have lots of negative feelings like irritation, annoyance, and anxiety whenever you encounter a problem.

When discussing the consequences of a negative orientation, there are several possibilities that can be considered. In terms of behavioral consequences, clients have a tendency to avoid or delay solving problems for as long as possible. However, if left unsolved for long enough, one problem can create new problems over time. Other behavioral consequences include asking others to solve the problem rather than dealing with it personally, or solving it impulsively in order to worry about it for the least amount of time. The cognitive consequence of a negative problem orientation, however, is what makes this construct such a central factor in the worry cycle. This can be discussed with clients in the following manner:

Therapist: So what do you think the impact of your negative orientation toward problems has on your thoughts? Do you think it makes you worry less or more?

Client: It makes me worry more.

Therapist: Why do you think that is?

Client: Well, if I'm not solving a problem, I am going to continue to worry about it.

Therapist: That's right. So long as you are not using an active strategy to deal with your problems, you are likely to continue to worry about them. In fact, if you leave problems unsolved for long enough, they can create new problems. On the other hand, have you ever tried to not think about your problems, that is, to ignore them instead of worry about them?

Client: Absolutely. I think I go back and forth between worrying about problems and ignoring them.

Therapist: That leads to another consequence of negative problem orientation, which involves not being very good at recognizing problems when they come up. If you ignore problems, you are less likely to see them early on and deal with them. Are you starting to see how your attitude toward problems is having a huge impact on your life?

At this stage in treatment, we recommend that therapists incorporate the role of intolerance of uncertainty into the discussion. This will not only highlight the consistency of intolerance of uncertainty throughout treatment, but will also allow therapists to normalize negative problem orientation with respect to GAD. It is important that clients realize that if they are intolerant of uncertainty, then having negative beliefs about problems and problem solving is a natural consequence of their intolerance.

Therapist: Why do you think that people with GAD have such a negative problem orientation? Why would you be more likely to have negative beliefs about problems and problem solving than someone who worries less?

Client: I don't know.

Therapist: A major reason for the relationship between GAD and negative problem orientation has to do with intolerance of uncertainty. As we have discussed before, intolerance of uncertainty is the fuel for worry. Even a little bit of uncertainty causes people with GAD to worry, and they tend to view the world through a filter where they are constantly searching out uncertain situations. Let's see how this relates to problems. First of all, how would you define a problem?

Client: I would say that a problem is something that does not have an obvious solution and that could turn out badly.

Therapist: So a problem is a situation that has no obvious solution and that could have a negative effect in the future. In other words, the outcome of problem solving is uncertain.

Client: I see ... problems are uncertain, so they set off my intolerance of uncertainty.

Therapist: That's right. When we look at it this way, it makes sense that you would find problems threatening. At the same time though, you have been working on changing that intolerance by repeatedly conducting tolerance of uncertainty experiments. A good way to see problem solving is as just another one of those experiments.

Client: But how am I supposed to change my negative problem orientation? Will I just have to use positive thinking?

Therapist: That's a great question. The answer to that is no. We are now going to start discussing ways to change your negative problem orientation, but that does not mean just "thinking positive." Instead, it means learning to be more realistic, flexible, and balanced in your thinking by acknowledging both the negative and the positive sides of situations.

Strategies for Improving Problem Orientation

Although there are a number of different strategies that can be used to help clients improve their problem orientation, we typically focus on three of these strategies. Specifically, we believe that it is beneficial to assist clients in (1) recognizing problems before it is too late; (2) seeing that problems are a normal part of life; and (3) seeing problems as opportunities rather than threats. For additional therapeutic strategies, the reader is referred to the work of D'Zurilla and Nezu (1999) on problem-solving therapy.

Recognizing Problems Before It Is Too Late

One of the consequences of finding problems aversive is the tendency to avoid recognizing problems as they come up in daily life. Often, problems can start out small and it is only when they are ignored that they begin to grow and become more serious and complex. For example, a client might have had a misunderstanding with a colleague at work. If left unsolved, the colleague might begin to hold a grudge and believe that the client is an uncaring or selfish person. The colleague might then begin to tell other coworkers about the problem, thereby making the problem more complex as other people are brought into the situation. From this example, it is evident that if the problem had been dealt with immediately, it probably would have been easily resolved. Instead, by ignoring or failing to see the problem, it developed into a "minor crisis" at work, with many people involved. This example clearly shows the importance of dealing with problems as soon as they arise. In order to assist clients in improving their ability to recognize problems when they arise, we recommend using two strategies: (1) using one's emotions as cues, and (2) developing a recurrent problem list.

In terms of the first strategy, a common obstacle to identifying problems is the tendency that many people have to interpret their negative emotions as the problem. For example, many clients identify their problem as frustration or stress. However, these emotions are not the problem (in terms of problem-solving theory). Rather, they are likely to be the by-product of the actual problematic situation. For example, if a person has many reports to do at work and he is very anxious and stressed about it, the problem is not that he is stressed. Instead, the problem is that he has to complete the reports; his anxiety and stress are due to the fact that he has this particular problem. With this in mind, clients can begin to use their emotions as a cue that there is a problem in their social environment:

Therapist: The first strategy is to use your emotions as cues. Your negative feelings can be used to let you know that there might be a problem. When you are feeling anxious, stressed out, or demoralized, you can ask yourself: "Is there a problem I am not seeing that is leading to these emotions?" Our emotions, when we are attentive to them, can be very useful in helping us to recognize problems. This strategy has two advantages. First, it will allow you to recognize your problems more quickly and potentially avoid having a small problem become a big problem. Second, it will help you to see your negative emotions in a more "positive" light. In this case, they serve an important function as an early detection system.

The second strategy is to encourage the client to write a list of recurrent problems. It is common to almost everyone that certain problems keep coming up again and again. Examples of recurrent problems include difficulties with a work colleague and end-of-the-month financial problems. However, every time problems recur, most of us have a tendency to react to them with surprise and disappointment, as if they were occurring for the first time. By writing out a list of recurrent problems, clients will be better able to recognize them quickly when they arise. In addition, the accompanying feelings of surprise and disappointment are less likely to develop simply because the problem is expected. This second strategy can be incorporated into a between-session exercise whereby clients are asked to keep the list accessible at all times in order to be better able to recognize problems quickly and react to them with less anger and disappointment.

Seeing Problems as a Normal Part of Life

It should come as no surprise that individuals with a negative problem orientation have a tendency to feel resentful when problems develop. One of the reasons for this is that they will often view problems as abnormal ("If I plan for everything and reduce all uncertainty in my life, no problems should ever arise. It is not normal for me to have unexpected problems come up."). However, one of the difficulties with believing that problems are abnormal is that the individual will expend a great deal of energy trying to avoid problems rather than dealing with them. As with attempting to eliminate uncertainty, this is an exercise in futility. Having to deal with problems is a normal and unavoidable part of life. As such, therapists should spend some time discussing this issue with clients. The goal is to allow them to see that everyone has problems to varying degrees in their lives:

Therapist: Having to deal with problems is a normal and inescapable part of life. Try to find someone who has no problems and you will come to the same conclusion. If a person believes that it is abnormal to have problems, that person will spend more time feeling annoyed by the problem than trying to solve it. It is much more useful to put that energy into solving the problem, getting it over with, and not worrying about it anymore. For some people, the reason why they feel that problems are abnormal is because they attribute their problem to personal incompetence or deficiencies. For example, if you believe that you have problems because you are flawed in some way ("I just don't have it when it comes to getting along with people"), you will tend to see your problems as being abnormal. However, it is important to remember that all of us have problems no matter how intelligent, sociable, attractive, or skillful we may be. It might seem that some people do not have problems, but this is probably because they deal with them quickly and efficiently. By not attributing your problems to "who you are," but instead to the fact that you are a human being (and all of us have problems from time to time), you will be better able to see your problems as a normal part of life and to start dealing with them more efficiently.

Seeing Problems as Opportunities Rather Than Threats

This final strategy for addressing a negative problem orientation is extremely important in getting clients to take action *toward* their problems. It is no secret that when a situation is viewed as entirely aversive, one is unlikely to approach it. In our daily lives, we have a tendency to avoid threats and approach opportunities. The goal of this treatment strategy is to assist clients in becoming more flexible in thinking about problems. Specifically, clients are encouraged to see some of the opportunities that exist in solving problems rather than focusing entirely on the negative aspects. It is important to note, however, that this does not mean that the threatening components of a problem are ignored. No one enjoys dealing with problems, but if there is a challenge or opportunity in a problematic situation, then clients are more likely to attempt to deal with it. As such, therapists should assist clients in starting to view problems as situations that can carry an opportunity, while at the same time remaining aware of the threat. This is accomplished by helping clients to see that problems do not need to be slotted into the following categories:

☐ Threat ☐ Opportunity

Seeing a problem as either completely negative or completely positive is an extreme way of viewing the problem. In reality, there are a multitude of points between those two extremes. Rather, clients can be encouraged to see both of these extremes as lying on a continuum:

Threat ←——————————————→ Opportunity

It is unrealistic to expect clients to see their problems as only representing an opportunity, but this continuum can allow them to view their problems as not 100% threatening either. By looking at problems and trying to extract the opportunities from the situation, clients can perhaps shift a little from the "threat" extreme and move closer to the "opportunity" extreme. This can be accomplished by getting clients to ask themselves: "What is the opportunity for me in this situation?" Opportunities that can be found in problematic situations include acquiring new skills or sharpening existing ones, and improving relationships with coworkers, friends, and family. The following are a few examples of how perceptions of threat can be shifted on the continuum toward perceptions of opportunity:

Example 1: A Job Interview. The initial reaction to this situation might be: "I hate interviews. Why do I have to go through this agony? I never do well in these types of situations. I will make a fool of myself just like the last time. I just wish it was over." A more flexible way of thinking might be:

I'm really nervous before going to an interview. What is the threat in this situation? Well, I might not do well during the interview and not get the job. Who knows, I might even make a real fool of myself. What is the opportunity for me in this situation? Maybe I need to learn to show others just what I am capable of doing. Interviews are not easy, but it would be great if I could learn to sell myself. That is a skill that I will need many times in my life. I guess I could try to look at this as an opportunity to get experience interviewing and to get better each time.

Example 2: The Illness of a Loved One. The initial reaction to this situation might be: "Someone who I am close to is suffering from a serious illness that requires expensive treatment. Why does this have to happen to our family? It's awful to have to spend so much money on this medication. One day we won't be able to afford it any longer. This is so unfair." A more flexible way of thinking might be:

I feel sad and frustrated about this whole thing. What is the threat in this situation? Well, the illness could get worse and who knows where that could lead? Even if the medication works, we could not be able to afford it for much longer. What is the opportunity for me in this situation? It is certainly difficult to see how illness can be an opportunity. I guess I could see this situation as an opportunity to show that I really care. I could help out as much as possible and try to be a model of hope and strength. Although I am certainly distressed, I see this as an opportunity to be strong for someone I love.

Therapists can use the two previous examples to help clients identify opportunities within varied problematic situations. Again, it is important that clients not be under the impression that they simply need to "think positive." Instead, the goal is to try to find a challenge or opportunity in a situation that was previously seen as altogether threatening.

A between-session exercise can be implemented here to help clients identify opportunities in problem situations. For example, clients can be asked to look through their Worry Diary and identify any current unsolved problems that are leading to worry, then try to think about (and record) the challenges or opportunities present in at least one problem with the ultimate goal of perceiving it as less threatening. Once clients have integrated some flexibility in thinking about their problems, therapists can move to the next phase of problem-solving training.

Applying Problem-Solving Skills

Although we have already discussed how problem-solving *skills* appear to be mostly unrelated to GAD, this does not mean that GAD clients have a good problem-solving *ability*. As mentioned previously, it is clear that their negative problem orientation interferes with the proper use of their problem-solving skills, which considerably decreases their ability to solve problems. Relatedly, because one's negative problem orientation can interfere in different ways with the proper application of each problem-solving skill, it is important that orientation be addressed both on its own and within the context of each skill. Furthermore, although the problem-solving skills of GAD clients do not seem to be extremely poor, they are not particularly strong either. That is, even though their skills are similar to those of people from the general population, it appears that most people are not especially skilled at effectively working through the problem-solving steps. Thus, although our model identifies negative problem orientation as the main problem-solving factor involved in GAD, our treatment includes comprehensive problem-solving training, which includes the review and practice of each problem-solving skill.

One thing that we have consistently noticed in treatment is that although GAD clients are willing to work on each step of the problem-solving process, they often have difficulty completing a stage and moving on to the next. This is likely to be due to their desire for certainty and for the "perfect" solution. As such, the goal of this phase of treatment is not only to help clients to refine their problem-solving skills, but also to encourage them to tolerate uncertainty by moving forward in the process despite the uncertainty inherent in each step (that is, problem definition and goal formulation, generation of alternative solutions, decision making, and solution implementation and verification).

Problem Definition and Goal Formulation

Before trying to solve a problem, one must first properly define it. Although this might seem obvious, our clinical experience has taught us that many people define their problems in vague or confused terms. In addition, we have observed that many of our clients do not "separate" their problems, so that their problem definition actually includes several problems at once. In many ways, this is the most important step in effective problem solving, since a poorly defined problem can have a negative impact on all the remaining steps. For example, if a person is being given more files to work on at his job than he can handle, an ill-defined problem definition might be: "My boss is a selfish man who takes advantage of me." If the problem is defined in this way, it becomes difficult to think of a goal for problem solving ("How can I make my boss more sensitive and caring?") and the remaining steps become impaired as well. In this case, a more appropriate problem definition might be: "My boss gives me more files to work on than I can handle." When the problem is defined in this way, the resultant goals and potential solutions are clearer and more achievable (for example, "My goal is to have my workload lightened.").

In order to effectively define a problem, the following guidelines can be considered. A good problem definition should:

- Be defined in clear and concrete language.
- Be comprised of facts, not assumptions.

- Answer three questions:
  - What is the situation?
  - What would I like the situation to be?
  - What is the obstacle that is interfering with the attainment of the desired situation?

- Focus on the central conflict, namely, the discrepancy between the actual and the ideal situation. When a problem is under one's direct control, emotional consequences should not be considered the main problem. In situations where one has little or no control, emotion management can be the central problem (for example, "How do I cope with the illness of my spouse?").

- Not be overly narrow in its scope. For example, a problem defined as "How can I write five reports in one hour?" is quite narrow in scope and, as such, only allows for one or two solutions. Alternatively, a problem defined as "How can I complete my reports more efficiently?" allows for a broader array of solutions.

One point to note about the problem definition stage is that it can often require readjustments throughout the problem-solving process. For example, a problem definition provided by the client may initially include more than one problem. This type of error is quite common, and will occasionally go unnoticed by the therapist upon first glance at the problem definition. However, if difficulties arise in subsequent steps of the problem-solving process as a result of a poor problem definition, the therapist and client should return to this initial step and adjust the definition as necessary.

When formulating goals, it is important to keep the following three guidelines in mind. First, goals should be *clear, concise, and defined in concrete terms*. When goals are defined in vague or unclear terms, it can be difficult to know not only how to achieve them, but also if they have been achieved. For example, if my goal is "to be happy," it is difficult to know if I have achieved it (that is, "How often do I want to be happy? How happy should I be?"). The second guideline is that goals should be *realistic and attainable*. Problem solving is most effective when the likelihood of achieving a goal (and resolving the problem) is high. If goals are unrealistic, clients will tend to become frustrated or disappointed. The final guideline is to *be aware of the timeline* for achievement of a particular goal. Depending upon the problem, clients might develop short- or long-term goals. While it is not surprising that some goals take longer to achieve than others, it is important that clients expect this so as not to experience feelings of disappointment. In addition, it can be helpful to set short-term goals even when the final goal is a long-term one. It can be quite demotivating to invest effort in a situation when no return is expected for an extended period of time. For example, if someone has decided to change her level of fitness and has set a certain weight and body fat percentage as her ultimate goal, it would be a good idea for her to set intermediary targets in order to remain motivated and driven toward the final goal.

Unlike the problem definition step, where clients are encouraged to ensure that only one problem is included in the definition, it is acceptable at this stage to have more than one goal. However, this is specifically in reference to the time in which the goal is expected to be accomplished, meaning that one can have both short- and long-term goals for a particular problem.

Generation of Alternative Solutions

This stage of problem solving is often referred to as the "brainstorming stage." The idea is to generate as many potential solutions to the problem as possible, in order to increase the chances of finding the best solution. Although this may appear to be an easy thing to do, very few people actually take the time to generate multiple solutions before making a decision. In fact, most people will think of only one solution, and then apply it without considering other possibilities. Alternatively, some people will come up with several solutions; however, they are the same solutions that they came up with in the past that were either ineffective or only worked in the short term. Why does this occur? There are two primary obstacles to the development of numerous and varied solutions. The first obstacle is *habit.* As noted previously, we tend to return to "tried and true" solutions when solving problems in our daily lives. Although this can be beneficial for many of our problems, sticking with the same strategies out of habit can, at times, prevent us from finding a better solution. The second obstacle to the generation of alternative solutions is *convention.* By doing things in a conventional manner, we might have the impression that we are doing "the right thing," even when this is not the case.

At this stage, the most effective way to generate multiple creative solutions is to use the following three principles of brainstorming:

1. **Deferment of Judgment Principle.** According to this principle, clients need to suspend any judgment or evaluation of solutions when trying to generate them. In order to come up with varied solutions, it is important not to censor oneself from the outset (e.g., "Oh, that's just a silly solution; I won't consider that one"). During the subsequent decision-making step, inappropriate solutions will be eliminated, so there is no need to screen or remove any solutions during this step. With this in mind, clients are encouraged to come up with solutions that might even be considered "crazy," since these types of solutions can facilitate the generation of other original and unconventional solutions that might be more appropriate.

2. **Quantity Principle.** From a logical standpoint, clients are more likely to come up with a good solution for a particular problem if they have many potential solutions from which to choose. As such, the second principle of brainstorming states that the more solutions that an individual can think of, the better. Therapists should encourage the generation of at least 10 or 12 solutions for a particular problem.

3. **Variety Principle.** This principle states that more good quality solutions are available when there is variety in the types of solutions generated. A mistake that many people make is to generate multiple solutions that all reflect the same general idea. For example, for a "weight" problem, solutions such as taking up jogging, swimming, or hiking are all solutions that fall within the same set: they all involve physical activity. If clients only generate potential solutions that fall within one set, there is little actual variety of choice. Varied solutions for a weight problem might include taking up jogging, changing one's diet, and spending a weekend at a health spa. Although all these solutions address the problem, they do not reflect the same set.

Although the therapist should keep in mind the "deferment of judgment" principle at all times (and not negatively evaluate a solution), once clients have completed their list of solutions, it is a good idea to initially run through the list and discuss ways to improve it. For example, the therapist and client should discuss ways of formulating as many of the solutions as possible in concrete behavioral terms. "Taking up jogging" is a good example of a concrete solution in that it is clear what would be required of the individual should this solution be chosen. However, a solution such as "develop a more positive self-esteem" is a much less concrete strategy. If a client chose this solution, he might have a new problem, namely, figuring out how to go about enhancing self-esteem!

As a final note, creative and practical solutions can sometimes be found by combining two or more solutions. We have often found that the combination of two mediocre solutions can create one excellent solution. Such modifications can also help clients to consider every solution generated, even those that initially seem crazy, unrealistic, or silly.

Decision Making

This stage involves going over the list of alternative solutions and ultimately choosing the *best* solution for the problem. This stage can be particularly difficult for GAD clients, as they will often try to find the *perfect* solution. The problem with this type of thinking is that it can prevent clients from moving forward in the problem-solving process. It is therefore important that therapists remind their clients that this stage is just another step of the problem-solving process and that it should not become another topic for excessive worry. Rather, it can be viewed as yet another way to practice tolerating uncertainty.

In order to effectively complete this stage of problem solving, clients need to look at the available solutions and pick the best one for their particular problem. This is achieved by asking clients to evaluate each solution and determine which one has the most advantages and the fewest disadvantages. Therapists can guide clients through this process by asking them to consider four questions for each alternative solution:

1. **Will this solution solve my problem?** A solution that does not address the problem or the stated goals is probably not the best one to choose.
2. **How much time and effort are involved in this solution?** From a practical point of view, a solution is probably not ideal if it involves an excessive amount of time and effort to complete.
3. **How would I feel if I use this solution?** When picking a solution, the emotional consequence of a particular solution is certainly a factor for consideration. Some options might make clients feel anxious or nervous, and others might leave clients feeling bad about themselves.
4. **What are the consequences of this solution for myself and others in both the short- and long-term?** A good solution should have more positive than negative consequences, for oneself and others, both now and in the future.

Although all four of these questions are important, the therapist should be mindful that clients are not using them to eliminate all *imperfect* solutions. That is, every solution will have some advantages and disadvantages, simply because if there existed a solution that solved the problem, required little time and effort, made the client feel good, and had no negative personal or social consequences, it would have already been found. As such, clients need to ask all four questions for each potential solution, and then decide which one *best* fits the problem.

Solution Implementation and Verification

Solution implementation involves planning how to carry out a chosen solution, and then actually implementing it. This can be a very difficult stage for GAD clients because it tends to "activate" their intolerance for uncertainty. Specifically, there are no guarantees whether a chosen solution will work as expected, and that can be quite difficult for many clients. However, because clients will have had previous experience with tolerating uncertainty, they should have developed some "momentum," such that implementing a chosen solution can be seen as just another exercise in tolerating uncertainty.

Prior to carrying out a solution, clients should plan the steps involved. This will not only ensure that they will know what to do, but will also increase the likelihood that they will actually carry out the solution. The steps involved should be concrete and specific, and depending upon the complexity of a solution, a timeline for the execution of each step can also be established. However, the therapist needs to keep in mind that the goal involves not only knowing what to do, but *actually doing it!* In other words, GAD clients should not be overly meticulous or seek excessive information when devising their plan, as this could be a way of avoiding the actual implementation of the solution. In most cases, however, by taking the time to plan the major steps involved in implementing the solution, clients are more likely to carry it out. Therapists should praise their clients for any movement toward implementing their solutions, and remind them that they are not only working toward solving their problems in an active manner, but also increasing their tolerance for uncertainty.

The second part of this final step involves the important task of verifying if the solution that was carried out is working as planned. As noted previously, one of the reasons that problems are so stressful is that it is impossible to predict exactly what will happen once a solution is implemented. As such, it is necessary to assess whether or not the solution is actually working, and this can be accomplished by setting up "markers" along the way. Clients are encouraged to think of some index that will let them know if the solution is working as planned. These indices can be observable information, such as higher grades if the problem was poor performance at school, or a check of one's mood following implementation of the solution (for example, "Am I feeling better since I put my solution into action?").

One of the major reasons why it is important to establish checks is to spot whether the solution is *not* working early on. Even with the best-laid plans, a chosen solution might not solve the problem. Clients should be able to identify this as soon as possible in order to begin taking steps toward correcting the situation. If a solution is in fact ineffective, clients can begin troubleshooting the source of the problem by returning to earlier steps. Was the solution carried out effectively? Did it best answer the decision-making questions? Was the problem correctly identified? Was the goal realistic and achievable? By walking through the various steps, clients can usually identify where problem solving went astray. If, on the other hand, a solution is working, then clients should be encouraged to reward themselves for a job well done.

One Final Note about Problem Solving

Perhaps the greatest challenge when introducing problem solving to clients is the tolerance for uncertainty required by *therapists*. There is no perfect answer for any of the problem-solving steps, and therapists themselves might initially feel unsure throughout the process. However, this can be highly beneficial in session, as there is the opportunity for therapists to model comfort with the uncertainty at various steps. Our suggestion for the ideal method of presentation in this phase of treatment is to initially use a working example to illustrate the effective use of all the problem-solving steps. This can then be followed by collaboratively working through the client's problem in session, and then having the client carry out the chosen solution. Although this will likely be difficult for clients because it involves solving their own problem, the assistance of the therapist allows this to be an intermediary stage that is less anxiety provoking (see Table 5.3 for a list of helpful questions that the therapist can ask clients when working through the problem). Finally, as a between-session exercise, clients should be encouraged to walk through the steps alone and record the results of each step on the Resolution of a Problem form (see Appendix 5.8 for a copy of the form). Once clients have developed some confidence in their problem-solving ability, treatment can move to the next module.

TABLE 5.3 Steps to Effective Problem Resolution

1. What is the problem? That is, what is the current situation, what would you like it to be, and what is the obstacle that is keeping you from achieving your ideal situation?
2. What goal would you like to achieve? Is it realistic and achievable?
3. What are all the possible solutions to this problem? Keep in mind to: (a) defer judgment ("crazy" solutions are all right); (b) come up with at least 10 solutions; and (c) generate varied solutions.
4. Which is the best (not the perfect!) solution? Specifically, which solution best answers the following questions: (a) Will this solve your problem? (b) How much time and effort is involved in this solution? (c) How would you feel if you use this solution? (d) What are the consequences of this solution to yourself and others in both the short and long term?
5. How will you carry out this solution? That is, what steps do you need to take to actually start implementing this solution?
6. How will you know if this solution is working? What checks or markers will you use that will tell you whether your solution is going as planned?

MODULE 5: IMAGINAL EXPOSURE

In this treatment module, clients learn a specific strategy for dealing with worries about hypothetical situations. These types of worries are not amenable to problem solving because the feared situation has not happened (and may never happen); therefore, any attempts at problem solving would be unproductive. Instead, clients learn how to expose themselves to a mental image of their fears in order to address their tendency to engage in cognitive avoidance (both implicit and explicit). This treatment module can be very difficult for clients because it involves focusing on thoughts and images that they have tried very hard to avoid for a long time. It is therefore extremely important that therapists take the time to properly explain the rationale behind this treatment module. The rationale for the use of imaginal exposure is somewhat complex, and as with any treatment strategy, clients must fully understand why they are being asked to do something before they actually do it.

The Futility of Cognitive Avoidance

The first aim is to illustrate to clients how attempts at avoiding thoughts can be counterproductive. As mentioned previously, research on thought suppression has shown that, in some instances, trying to suppress a thought can result in a paradoxical increase in that thought. As most clients are unaware of this phenomenon, an effective way to illustrate the effects of thought suppression is to ask them to engage in the white bear experiment.

Instructions for the White Bear Experiment

Therapist: Today we are going to talk about cognitive avoidance, which is the tendency to try to avoid certain thoughts. However, before we do, I would like you to try a little experiment with me. For 60 seconds, I am going to ask you to close your eyes and think of anything that you like. Anything at all, there are no restrictions, except for one small thing: I want you to absolutely *not* think about a white bear. I don't want you to picture a white bear or even think the words *white bear.* But other than that, you can think of anything else. I am going to time you while you do this, and I will simply ask you to raise your hand every time, if any, the thought crosses your mind. Are you ready? Go." (The therapist then records how many times the client raises his hand.) "So, how did it go? Do you remember how many times the thought of a white bear came up?"

Client: Almost the entire time; at least seven or eight times.

Therapist: That's interesting. How many times did you think of a white bear on your way over to my office today?

Client: None.

Therapist: How about yesterday? How many times did the "white bear" thought come up?

Client: None, again.

Therapist: Interesting. So all day yesterday and today you did not have a single thought about a white bear. And yet, when I specifically asked you not to think of one for one minute, you were unable to. Why do you think that is?

Client: I have no idea.

Therapist: Well, research shows that trying *not* to think about something doesn't work. In fact, it can produce two types of opposite effects. One is the *enhancement effect*, which you just experienced. That is, trying to deliberately suppress a thought can bring on that very thought while we are trying to avoid it. The second effect is the *rebound effect.* In this case, after trying to suppress a thought, it might tend to pop up in your mind. In the case of our experiment, you might find that you will think about a white bear on the way home or this evening. So what does all this say about your worries?

Client: I guess it means that if I try not to think about something unpleasant, like my children getting injured or killed in a car accident, I'll actually end up thinking about it even more.

Therapist: That's right. Trying to block or avoid upsetting worries can actually lead to more worries popping up in your mind.

An Alternative to Avoidance and Neutralization

In order to clearly illustrate the importance of exposure in reducing fears, the therapist should discuss the concepts of avoidance, neutralization, and exposure in terms of behavioral rather than cognitive avoidance. That is, it is easier to discuss these abstract concepts in reference to a specific observable fear before relating them to the cognitive construct of worry. A useful example is elaborated upon below, using a dog phobia analogy:

Therapist: Why do you think that we tend to avoid the things that we fear? Very simply, we do it because avoidance works. If I am afraid of something, once I avoid it, I feel less anxious. For example, if I am afraid of dogs, and I see someone approaching with a dog while am walking down the street, I will probably become very anxious. However, what will happen once I cross the street?

Client: You'll feel better.

Therapist: That's right. Once I avoid the dog, I'll probably feel less anxious. Let's look at this using a graph, where the horizontal line represents time and the vertical line represents anxiety.

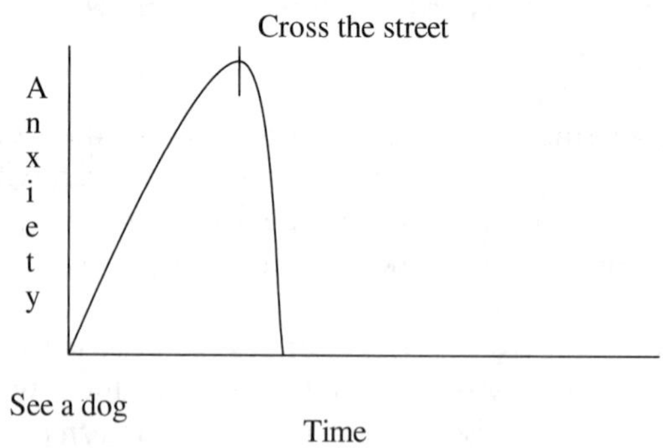

Therapist: Using this graph, we can see that once I see the dog my anxiety goes up, but the moment that I cross the street (and avoid the dog), my anxiety goes down. What is the problem with this? What do you think will happen to my fear of dogs so long as I avoid them?

Client: You'll probably continue to be afraid of them.

Therapist: That's right. In fact, I might become even more afraid of them over time, because I might say to myself: "Good thing I avoided those dogs; who knows what would have happened?" If we look at this continued avoidance on a graph, it would look like this (see below), with a dip in anxiety every time I avoid and an increase in anxiety every time I see a dog. We call this the avoidance curve, and we can see that avoidance decreases anxiety in the short term, but maintains the fear in the long term.

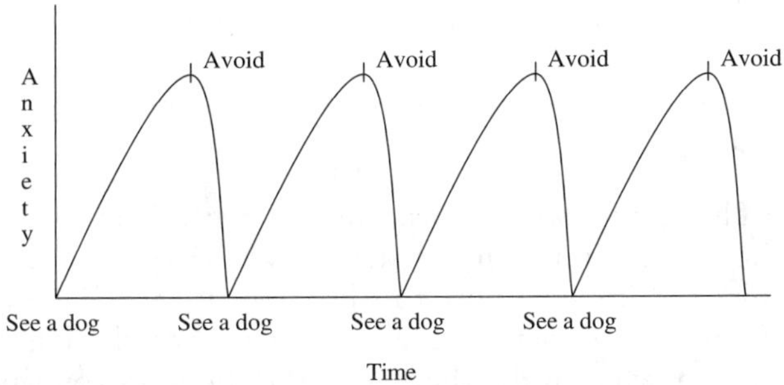

One of the reasons that we recommend discussing the maintaining effect of avoidance is to allow clients to see how exposure to a feared situation is the best way to reduce anxiety in the long term. However, it is also important that clients understand the *right* way to conduct exposure. As such, the role of neutralization is also discussed because it can pose a particular problem to the effective execution of imaginal exposure:

Therapist: Unfortunately, avoidance is not the only way that we maintain our fears. Neutralization can have a similarly negative effect. Neutralization refers to a deliberate attempt to reduce the experience of anxiety while in a fearful situation. For example, if I am afraid of dogs, I might decide that I need to confront my fear and stop avoiding them. With that in mind, I go to visit my friend at his house, since he has a dog. Once there, I get very anxious, so I decide to look out the window and think of something else. What will happen to my anxiety?

Client: It will probably go down.

Therapist: That's right. It will probably go down, but not all the way since I'm still in the same room with the dog. Also, once I look back at the dog, my anxiety goes back up. This time, I try to lower my anxiety by looking at the dog's tail instead of his teeth, which again makes me feel less uncomfortable. These behaviors are examples of neutralization, and if we were to draw this on a graph, it would look like this:

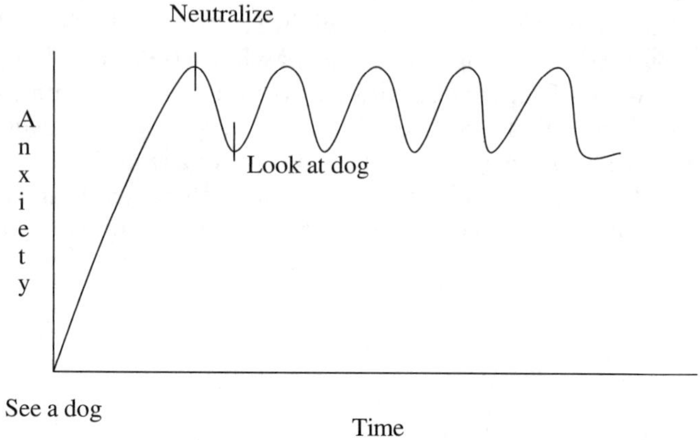

Therapist: This graph, which illustrates the neutralization curve, shows how each time I neutralize, my anxiety goes down a little bit. The problem with this behavior is that, like avoidance, it maintains anxiety in the long term, even though it decreases it somewhat in the short term. So, how do you think we can bring anxiety down in the long term?

Client: Probably by not avoiding and neutralizing.

Therapist: Exactly. Basically, we can reduce anxiety in the long term by exposing ourselves to feared situations. But when we do this, we have to do it for long enough, and often enough, for the anxiety to go down and stay down. In other words, if you stay in a feared situation long enough, without doing anything at all, your anxiety will go down naturally. (See graph below.)

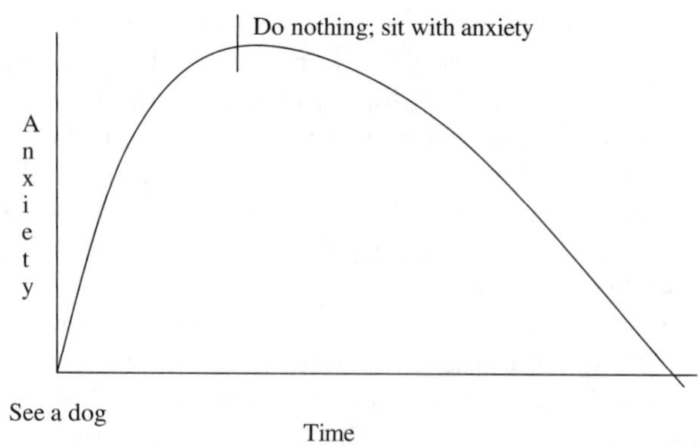

Therapist: This graph illustrates the exposure curve, and it teaches us a powerful lesson: "If I stay in a fearful situation and do nothing, my anxiety goes down. Perhaps this is not as scary as I thought." Unfortunately, we don't really believe that lesson until we conduct exposure several times. Each time we do, the feeling of anxiety does not go up quite as high, and it takes less and less time to go back down. (See graph below.)

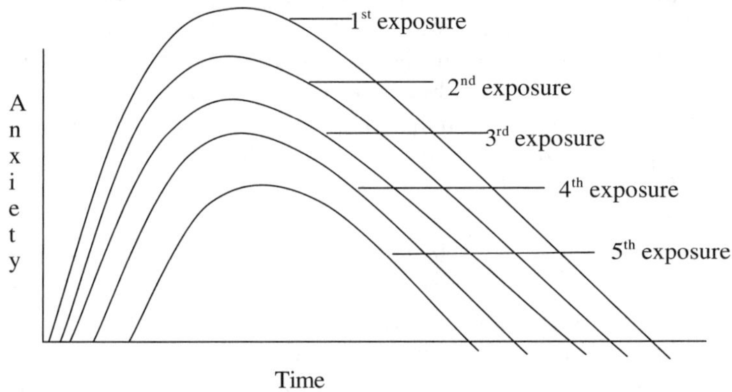

Therapist: So all of this means that if we want to reduce anxiety in the long term, it is best to face our fears through exposure, to stay in the situation until our anxiety goes down, and to do it repeatedly. Does all this make sense so far?

Once therapists have taken the time to explain the role of avoidance and neutralization in maintaining fears, as well as the therapeutic role of exposure, it is important to return the conversation back to client worries.

Therapist: So how do avoidance, neutralization, and exposure work when we think about worries? Well, the same logic applies to our thoughts. For example, if a person is very afraid that she might become seriously ill in the near future, she might try very hard not to think about that possibility. This avoidance of scary thoughts is referred to as cognitive avoidance. So by trying not to think about your fears, you are in fact maintaining them. (See Appendix 5.9 for a copy of the model that includes cognitive avoidance.) Neutralization, which in some ways is similar to cognitive avoidance, also contributes to maintaining your fears. When you are worried about a potential problem, you might tell yourself: "It won't happen" or "It won't be that bad if it does." These thoughts serve to neutralize or lessen your discomfort; however, as with neutralizing a fear of dogs, these thoughts end up maintaining your worries. When we worry about a hypothetical situation, we often think about it repeatedly and for short periods of time, all the while trying not to think about the worst that could happen. Unfortunately, this does not allow us to get over our fear of the situation. The only way to really process or *digest* the fear is to think about it intensely, for a relatively long period of time, and repeatedly. So this means that the best way to deal with worries about hypothetical situations is to conduct exposure to those fears; that is, thinking about your fear for a prolonged period of time (30 to 60 minutes) every day for a few weeks until your fear decreases.

Client: That sounds scary.

Therapist: Yes, most people do find the idea of exposure scary. But we are going to do this at *your* pace. However, it is a good idea to keep in mind that you have been trying to avoid fully thinking about these situations for a long time, and you are still worrying about them. What does that tell you about cognitive avoidance as a strategy?

Client: That it doesn't work.

Therapist: Exactly. So now it is time to try a new strategy. When it comes to dealing with anxiety, you need to face your fear in order to eliminate it in the long run. Shall we try it?

Preparing the Exposure Scenario

The preparation of the exposure scenario can be broken down into four steps: (1) identifying the exposure theme; (2) preparing a preliminary draft of the scenario; (3) finalizing the scenario; and (4) recording the scenario for repeated exposure. If difficulties are encountered in any of these steps, it might mean that the client does not fully understand the logic of exposure or does not feel prepared to undertake imaginal exposure. In either case, the therapist might find it useful to return to the rationale to increase client confidence and motivation.

Identifying the Exposure Theme: The Downward Arrow Technique

The first step in preparing the exposure scenario is to identify the exposure theme (i.e., the fear that will be targeted in imaginal exposure). One way to accomplish this is to use the downward arrow technique, which has also been referred to as the vertical descent or catastrophizing technique (see Burns, 1989; Provencher, Freeston, Dugas, & Ladouceur,

2000; Vasey & Borkovec, 1992). We recommend that therapists use the following steps in order to access core fears:

1. Therapists begin by asking clients to formulate their worry in simple terms. For example, "What if my flight runs into turbulence?"
2. Clients are then asked the following question: "If your worry came true, what might happen next?" or "If your worry actually happened, what could that lead to?"
3. Once the client has identified the next link in the worry chain (e.g., "The plane could crash"), therapists can then ask the same question a second time, with the goal of moving progressively further down the fear hierarchy.
4. Once clients respond to this second prompt, therapists repeat the question until the client is no longer able to provide an answer to the prompt, suggesting that the core fear has been identified (e.g., "I could die").

An example of a client's responses to the downward arrow technique is provided below for a work-related worry:

"I will not be able to make a deadline at work."

↓

"My boss will be upset."

↓

"I will lose my job."

↓

"I won't be able to find another job."

When using the downward arrow technique, it is important that therapists not direct clients in their answers, but simply follow their lead. Furthermore, it is important to strike a balance between accessing an important fear while not going so far that the client is unable to fully engage in the exposure process. Specifically, if a client mentions that the scenario is too "far fetched," this can indicate that an outcome identified earlier in the downward arrow would be a more appropriate exposure theme for that particular client. For example, using the work example presented above, a client might eventually come up with the fear "I could end up on the street, homeless and penniless, with all my friends becoming disgusted with me." Most likely, clients will say that this scenario is in fact ridiculous because they know that it will not happen. It is therefore not appropriate for the exposure scenario.

Preparing a Preliminary Draft of the Exposure Scenario

Once the exposure theme has been identified, the client is asked to write a first draft of an exposure scenario. This is typically done as a between-session exercise on the Scenario for Exposure form (see Appendix 5.10 for a copy of the form). Based on current conceptualizations of emotional processing (e.g., Foa & Kozak, 1986) and our own clinical experience, it is useful to provide the client with guidelines that fall into two categories: *content* and *form*. In terms of content, the scenario should include: (1) the fearful situation or context; (2) the client's reactions to the situation; and (3) the meaning ascribed to the situation and the reaction. In terms of form, the scenario should be described: (1) in the first person; (2) in the present tense; (3) with great detail, including information from the senses (i.e., sight, touch, taste, smell, hearing); and (4) without neutralization (that is, any information that might decrease the client's anxiety during exposure). If a looped audiotape will subsequently be used to record the scenario, it should last one to five minutes when read slowly and with expression (simply because looped tapes typically last one to five minutes).

Therapists should keep in mind that the client has probably been trying to avoid thinking about his fear for some time. As such, the first draft of the exposure scenario will likely need some work during the next session (although the client may have worked very hard to produce the initial scenario). For example, a client who feared that her child would be involved in a serious car accident produced the following first draft for exposure:

> I imagine that my child is involved in a car accident. I rush to the scene of the accident, and there are ambulances and bits of broken glass all over the highway. Then I see her; she is sitting in the grass beside the road, and she has blood on her. Her arm is all cut and swollen — it looks like it might be broken. The paramedics lift her onto a stretcher and put the stretcher into the back of the ambulance. I get into the back of the ambulance and sit beside the stretcher, and hold her hand in mine. She looks at me and smiles. I

> realize I'm crying uncontrollably. The paramedic puts an oxygen mask on her just to be safe; inside the ambulance little lights on machines are blinking, and there's that funny hospital smell. At the hospital they take her in to see the doctor and I have to wait outside. I feel very anxious, so I sit down and try to calm down. After a few minutes, the doctor comes out to see me. He smiles at me and says, "It looks like she'll be all right...."

Although this was a good first draft that followed most of the rules of form and content, it clearly contained many elements that served to avoid full (or functional) exposure. For example, elements such as "I hold her hand in mine. She looks at me and smiles" and "It looks like she'll be all right..." are attempts at neutralizing the scenario and reducing anxiety.

Finalizing the Scenario

Once clients bring their first exposure draft to the next session, the therapist's primary challenge is to assist them in improving the scenario. Some examples of neutralization to be on the lookout for are "I imagine..." because it reminds clients that the scenario is not real, and the inclusion of a "happy ending" that is clearly at odds with facing one's worst fear. Returning again to the example of the client's core fear that her child could be in an accident, the final scenario is reproduced below. Note that the scenario is much improved and is now appropriate for imaginal exposure:

> My child is in a terrible car accident. I rush to the scene of the accident, and there are ambulances, sirens going off, mangled cars, and bits of broken glass all over the highway. Then I see her; her little body is sprawled face down on the road, and she's covered in blood. Her face is all cut and swollen — it hardly looks like her. The paramedics lift her onto a stretcher — they have blood all over them too — and put the stretcher into the back of the ambulance. I get into the back of the ambulance and sit beside the stretcher, and hold her cold hand in mine. I realize I'm crying uncontrollably. The paramedic puts an oxygen mask on her; inside the ambulance little lights on machines are blinking, and there's that awful hospital smell. At the hospital they rush her into the emergency room and I have to wait outside. I feel like my legs are going to collapse and I'm shaking all over, so I sit down and try to control myself. After what seems like hours, the doctor comes out to see me. He clears his throat and says, "I'll get right to the point; her condition is critical...."

Recording the Scenario for Repeated Exposure

Once the scenario has been finalized, clients record it on a looped tape or compact disc, reading the text slowly, with appropriate pauses and emotional expression. Therapists might wish to hear the audio recording, as some clients will read the text quickly and in a monotone fashion in an effort to neutralize some of its emotional overtones. If this is the case, clients should record the scenario a second time, but with the appropriate pace and emotion.

Conducting Exposure

Imaginal exposure involves an important learning curve. Learning to visualize a feared scenario can take time and practice, as well as learning to sit with anxiety and tolerate it until it dissipates. Furthermore, the prospect of exposure can be daunting for someone who has used avoidance as a way to cope with his or her fears. As such, it is imperative that the first exposure session be carried out in the therapist's office.

The First Exposure Session

Therapists will want to prepare clients for exposure by presenting the first exposure session as a learning experience where clients will have an opportunity to begin learning the skill of exposure. As such, the objective of the first session is not to experience "successful" exposure, but rather to begin learning what it feels like to attempt imaginal exposure. Clients are asked to assume a comfortable sitting position, and then begin listening to the recorded exposure scenario. Prior to beginning, however, therapists should mention that it is initially quite difficult to stay focused on an exposure theme and that clients will undoubtedly find their minds wander during exposure. When this happens, they should simply return to the scenario. During the actual in-session exposure, we recommend asking clients to provide an anxiety rating from 0 to 10 (with 0 representing "no anxiety" and 10 representing "extreme anxiety") every minute of the exercise, on the therapist's cue. Following the exercise, therapists can then create a graph of the client's anxiety level throughout exposure. The imaginal exposure session should continue until the client's anxiety more or less returns to its baseline level.

Subsequent Exposure Sessions

After clients have had some in-session experience with imaginal exposure, they can begin practicing exposure at home. Clients need to perform exposure every day, with each exposure lasting approximately 30 to 60 minutes. The objective is for clients to stay focused on the scenario for as long as necessary to experience the "exposure curve," that is, a rise in anxiety, which then stays elevated for several minutes, and subsequently descends gradually to the preexposure baseline level. Therapists should encourage their clients to continue their daily exposures until they experience little to no anxiety when listening to their exposure scenario. For each exposure conducted between sessions, clients can fill out the Exposure Summary form (see Appendix 5.11 for a copy of the form) which is useful for monitoring daily progress. This form asks for their level of distress prior to the exposure, immediately after, as well as the maximum level experienced during the exposure.

Once clients have emotionally processed their fear (i.e., they no longer experience significant anxiety when listening to their scenario), they can choose to use imaginal exposure to address another core fear (i.e., a fear that underlies worries about other hypothetical situations). In our experience, because each core fear underlies worries about many hypothetical situations, the number of exposure scenarios that is required for each client is quite limited. In fact, we have found that the vast majority of clients require only one or two exposure scenarios in order to considerably decrease their worries about a vast array of hypothetical situations. When the therapist and client feel that termination of treatment is imminent, they can move to the final treatment module, relapse prevention.

MODULE 6: RELAPSE PREVENTION

The final treatment module deals with maintaining gains and preventing relapse following treatment termination. Although we refer to this stage as relapse prevention, data from our clinical trials show that many clients actually continue improving following treatment termination (see Chapter 6). As such, the goal at this stage of treatment is to help clients continue using the skills acquired in treatment with the hope that progress will be maintained long after the final session is over. We break down this module into three components: (1) daily maintenance; (2) identification of at-risk situations; and (3) preparation for at-risk situations.

Daily Maintenance

Daily maintenance is based on a very simple idea; namely, that strategies that helped clients to get better will also help them to stay better.

In other words, if clients stop using the skills acquired in therapy, it is unlikely that they will maintain their treatment gains in the long term. This means that it is in the clients' best interest to continue reevaluating their positive beliefs about worry, addressing life's problems by using effective problem-solving strategies, and processing fears through exposure. Most importantly, however, clients should continue developing an ever greater tolerance for uncertainty. The best way for clients to take charge of their own symptom maintenance is by learning to become their own therapist:

Therapist: Now that treatment is coming to an end, it is important that you learn to become your own therapist. What I mean by this is that you will start to take on the role that I have been assuming in treatment. In addition to teaching you the necessary skills you need to manage your symptoms, I monitored your progress on between-session exercises and helped you to troubleshoot any problems that came up. It is this role that you will need to fill now. Once treatment ends, you will need to assign yourself exercises, carry them out, and monitor your progress. For example, you can work on correcting your beliefs about worry, and apply strategies like problem solving or cognitive exposure to worries that come up in your daily life. Being your own therapist also implies regularly evaluating your method of reacting to worries, encouraging yourself to persevere even when it's difficult, and congratulating yourself for both your large and small successes.

Some clients enter treatment with the belief that when therapy ends, they will no longer be worried or anxious. This is obviously not the case. In our treatment, as with most other CBT protocols, clients do not typically end treatment entirely symptom-free. Rather, a successful treatment experience will see clients leaving with a significant reduction in symptoms, an array of new tools and strategies for dealing with their symptoms, and a number of successes using those skills under their belt. Considering how long most clients have suffered with GAD, it is unrealistic to expect to be symptom-free after only a few months. However, if clients continue working with the skills acquired during treatment, there is no reason to believe that further improvement will not occur. The ultimate goal of daily maintenance is that the skills learned in therapy become automatic, and that clients use these skills without being fully conscious of each decisional step. This goal, however, will only be attained if clients regularly use the strategies over extended periods of time.

Identifying At-Risk Situations

The identification of at-risk situations is important because it helps clients adopt realistic expectations about how their worry and anxiety will fluctuate following the termination of treatment. Therapists will want to help their clients become aware that everyone experiences decreases in their quality of life during periods of high stress or negative mood. For GAD clients, stressors such as moving, changing employment, or experiencing interpersonal difficulties, as well as times when they are feeling more tired or "down" than usual, can serve as triggers to increase worry and anxiety (see Appendix 5.12 for a copy of the model that includes mood state and life events). These types of fluctuations in symptoms are perfectly normal. They only become a problem when clients interpret them catastrophically (i.e., "I am so worried and anxious again! I undid all the progress I made in treatment!"). As such, it is important that clients learn to identify these periods of stress so that they will not be caught off guard when they are feeling more worried and anxious. In fact, clients can use increases in their symptoms as a "red flag" that alerts them to apply their newly acquired skills and work on them in a structured manner.

It is also equally important that clients have realistic expectations for themselves. Progress in therapy does not mean that clients will experience a smooth and regular decrease in worry and anxiety. For all clients, there are weeks where their symptoms are higher, other weeks where worry and anxiety might drop sharply, and still other weeks where there is little or no change. This intermittent fluctuation in worry and anxiety can also be expected following treatment. Experiencing a period of greater worry and anxiety should not be viewed as a failure or a relapse. Rather, it is an opportunity to continue working on the skills that will ultimately give clients a better chance at long-term protection against excessive worry and anxiety.

Preparing for At-Risk Situations

One of the best ways that therapists can assist clients in preparing for difficult situations in the future is to clearly distinguish between a lapse and a relapse. The key difference between both events is the reaction that clients have to a rise in their symptoms:

Therapist: It is important to keep in mind that there is a significant difference between a lapse and a relapse. A lapse can be understood as the result of normal fluctuations in worry and anxiety

> levels. A relapse, on the other hand, is more or less a return to the state you were in before treatment began. Therefore, to experience an increase in worry and anxiety from time to time is unavoidable and is not necessarily a relapse. However, your reaction to an increase in worry and anxiety is an important factor in determining whether a lapse will become a relapse. For example, let us suppose that two individuals worry a lot during a three-day period. In the middle of the week one of the two realizes that an accumulation of work has been causing his stress and worry. He tells himself that he will try to finish his excess workload as soon as possible, within reason, and will relax on the weekend. He can always work for two hours Sunday morning if he hasn't finished by Friday. By the end of the week, he has finished his work and is satisfied and relaxed. The other individual is also stressed and worried because of an accumulation of work. He does all that he can to finish, but he is not very optimistic about finishing by Friday. By 5 p.m. on Friday the individual has finished her work and says, "What a crazy week! I am never able to get through a surplus of work without worrying about it all week! It took all my energy! What will it be like next time? I probably won't be able to handle it...." We can see from this example that the second person is on her way to a full-blown relapse simply because she reacted to the situation catastrophically.

One way that clients can prepare themselves for both treatment termination and any at-risk situations that might occur is to develop a plan of action before the end of therapy. Since one of the goals of treatment is to teach clients how to become their own therapists, they should be encouraged to set goals for future progress without the therapist's help. For example, a client with continuing worries about her job might decide to plan additional tolerance of uncertainty experiments and to use effective problem-solving strategies for any work-related difficulties that arise. In this manner, clients can continue working regularly with their acquired skills and develop a greater sense of control over their worry and anxiety.

One Final Point

As treatment comes to an end, it may be important to return to an issue that was discussed right at the start of treatment: the distinction between normal and excessive worry. Paradoxically, if clients have made great strides during treatment, the therapist may have to encourage them to accept a certain level of worry in response to life's daily problems. We have found that some clients forget that moderate levels of worry and anxiety are unavoidable and a normal part of life. These clients may have unrealistic expectations and may be at risk for relapse. As such, they may need to be reminded that everyone has moments where they are more anxious and stressed. This is certainly not a sign that treatment was unsuccessful. In fact, clients who leave treatment feeling that their worry and anxiety are manageable and their quality of life is improved have made wonderful progress. As such, they should be heartily congratulated.

APPENDIX 5.1

Model 1: The Symptoms Associated with Generalized Anxiety Disorder

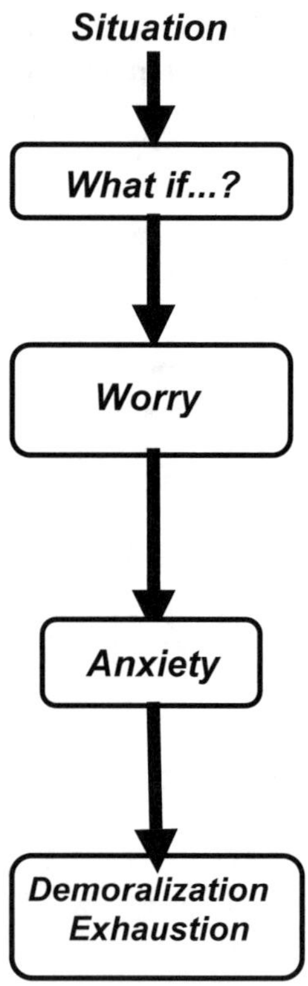

APPENDIX 5.2

Handout for Model 1: Worry Diary Form

Worry Diary

Date and time		Worry	Anxiety 0 to 8 (None to Extreme)	Worry type (current problem or hypothetical situation)
Date	Time			

APPENDIX 5.3

Model 2: The Role of Intolerance of Uncertainty

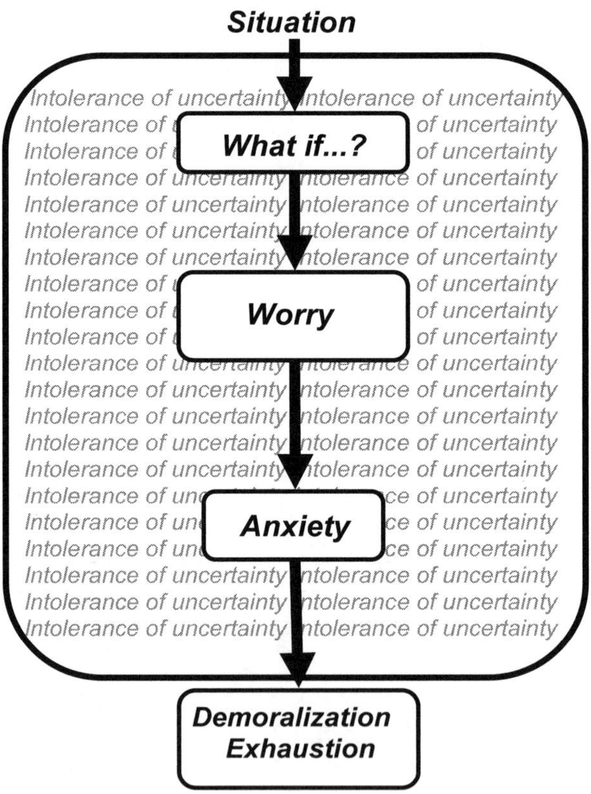

APPENDIX 5.4

Handout for Model 2: Uncertainty and Behavior Monitoring Form

What is my chosen behavior?

What, if any, discomfort did I feel while doing it?

What were my thoughts while doing it?

Now that I have done it, what do I think?

APPENDIX 5.5

Model 3: The Role of Positive Beliefs about Worry

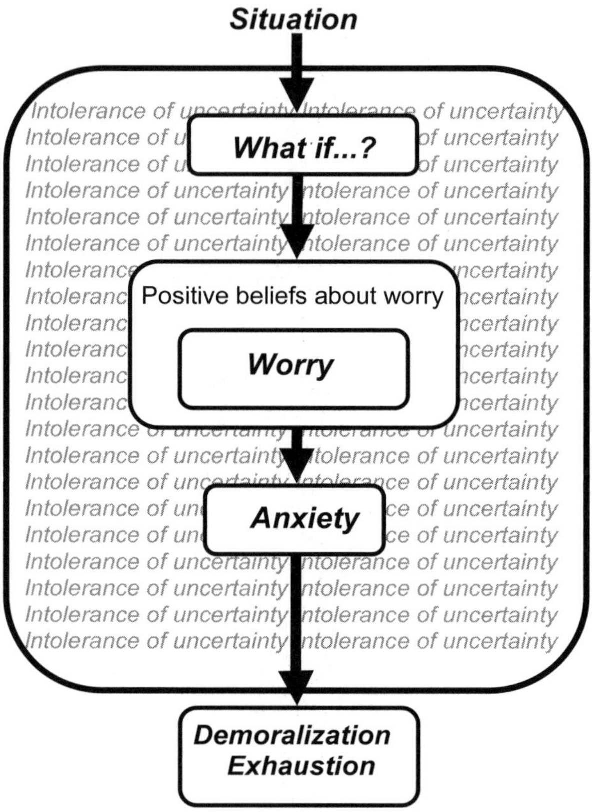

APPENDIX 5.6

Handout for Model 3: Positive Beliefs about Worry Form

Below are a number of beliefs that people can have about worry. They have been grouped into different categories. Please indicate by checking off "YES" or "NO" whether you have experienced each type of belief about worry; if "YES," write down a personal example for each.

1. Beliefs about worry as something that can help you to resolve problems. This means all beliefs that convey the idea that worrying helps to fix problems, find better solutions, become more aware of problems, be better prepared to face them, react better when problems occur, and avoid potential problems.

   YES: ______ NO: ______

   Personal example:

2. Beliefs that worry is a good way to motivate yourself. This means all beliefs that convey the idea that worrying will motivate you to do things you would otherwise avoid. These beliefs can relate to responsibilities at work, household tasks, social activities, or leisure activities.

   YES: ______ NO: ______

   Personal example:

3. Beliefs about worry as a way to protect oneself from negative emotions. This means all beliefs that convey the idea that by worrying about something beforehand, you can protect yourself from subsequent deception, disappointment, or guilt if the event actually occurs.

   YES: ______ NO: ______

   Personal example:

4. Beliefs that the act of worrying can have an effect on events. This means all beliefs that convey the idea that the act of worrying itself can have an effect on events, that worries have power over the occurrence or non-occurrence of events.

   YES: _____ NO: _____

   Personal example:

5. Beliefs about worry as a positive personality trait. This means all beliefs that convey the idea that a person who worries is considerate, prudent, and cares about the well-being of others. These beliefs also imply that worrying about someone is proof of love or caring.

   YES: _____ NO: _____

   Personal example:

Can you think of any other examples of beliefs about worry, that don't fit into the preceding categories?

YES: _____ NO: _____

If YES, please describe:

APPENDIX 5.7

Model 4: The Role of Negative Problem Orientation

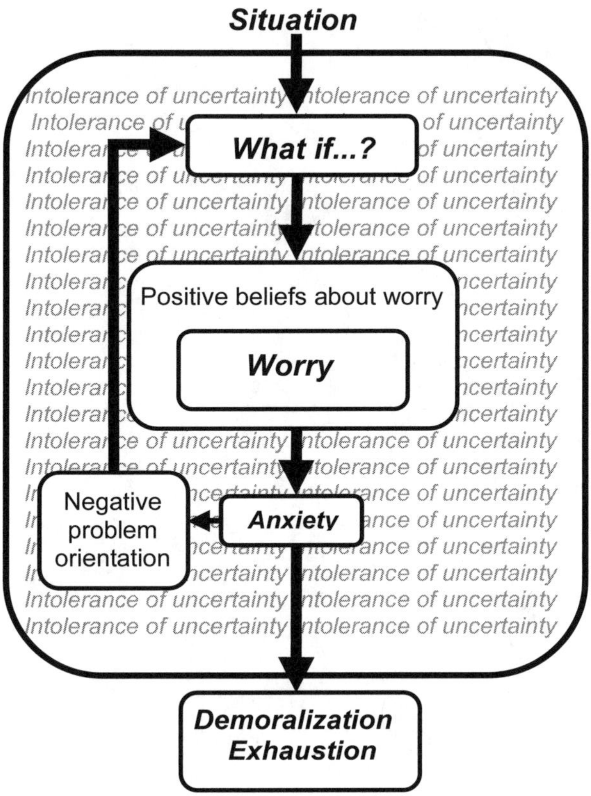

APPENDIX 5.8

Handout for Model 4: Resolution of a Problem Form

Problem definition and problem-solving goal(s):

Potential solutions:

Chosen solution:

Application of the solution and evaluation of the results:

Observations and comments:

APPENDIX 5.9

Model 5: The Role of Cognitive Avoidance

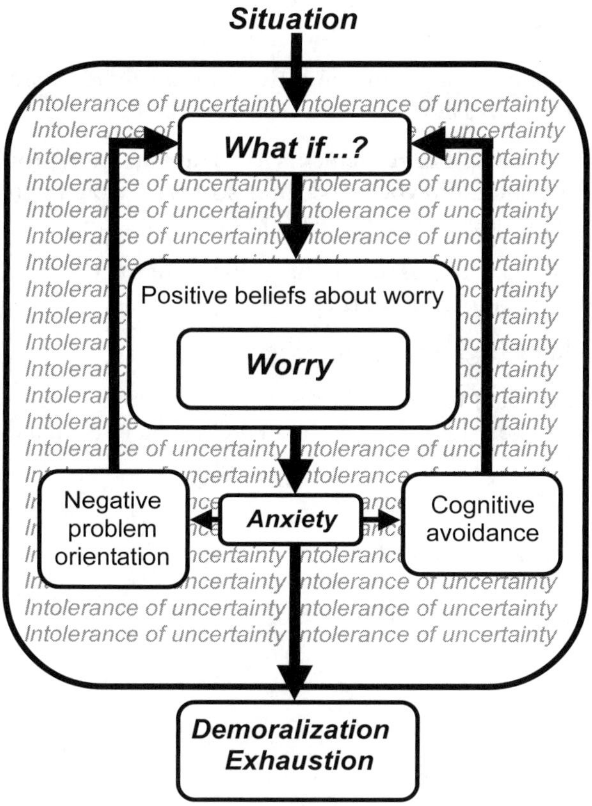

APPENDIX 5.10

Handout 1 for Model 5: Scenario for Exposure Form

The goal of this exercise is to develop a scenario for exposure that has the following characteristics:

1. It should take one to five minutes to read, when read *slowly and with expression.*
2. It should not contain elements of neutralization (for example, words like "maybe" and "not so bad," which can reduce the effectiveness of the exposure).
3. It should be composed in the present tense (as though the scenario is happening in the present).
4. It should be frightening but believable.
5. It should refer to your senses (sight, hearing, smell, etc. — including these helps you to form a clear mental image).

Please continue on another page

APPENDIX 5.11

Handout 2 for Model 5: Exposure Summary Form

Theme of scenario:

To complete before exposure:

1. Time ______:______
2. What is the level of distress associated with your thought *right now*? (Circle the number that best corresponds to your level of distress before the beginning of the exposure session.)

0	1	2	3	4	5	6	7	8
none		**a little**		**moderate**		**considerable**		**extreme**

To complete after exposure:

1. Time ______:______
2. What is the level of distress associated with your thought *right now*? (Circle the number that best corresponds to your level of distress after the end of the exposure session.)

0	1	2	3	4	5	6	7	8
none		**a little**		**moderate**		**considerable**		**extreme**

3. What was the maximum level of distress that was associated with your thought *during exposure*? (Circle the number that best corresponds to your maximum level of distress during the exposure session.)

0	1	2	3	4	5	6	7	8
none		**a little**		**moderate**		**considerable**		**extreme**

4. Did you neutralize your thought while you were listening?

Yes: ______ No: ______

If yes, in what way?

APPENDIX 5.12

Model 6: The Influence of Mood State and Life Events[1]

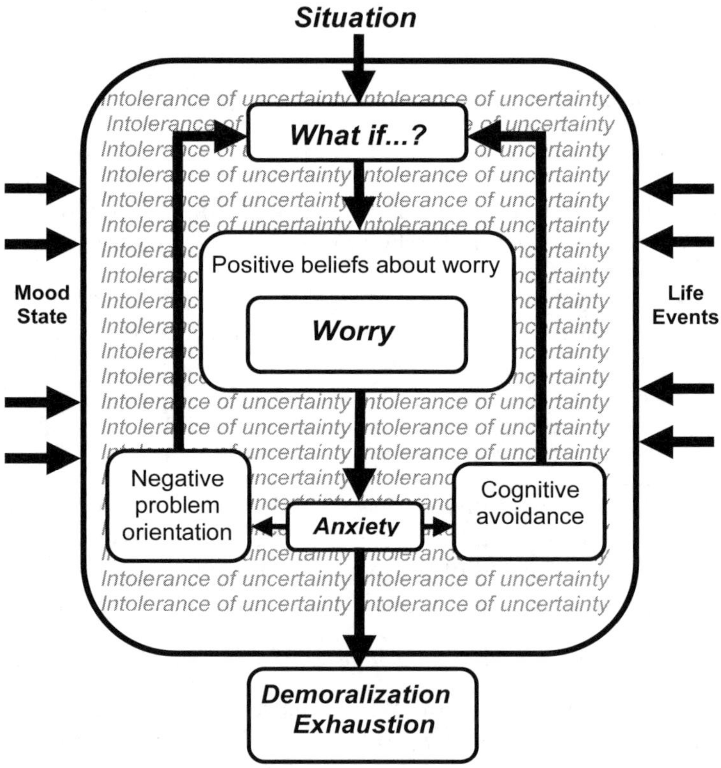

[1] Reprinted from Behaviour Research and Therapy, 36, Dugas, M.J., Gagnon, F., Ladouceur, R., Freeston, H., Generalized axiety disorder: A preliminary test of a conceptual model, 215–226, (1998), with permission from Elsevier.

CHAPTER 6

Treatment Efficacy

In Chapters 4 and 5, we presented our cognitive-behavioral treatment of generalized anxiety disorder (GAD). In the current chapter, we will review the data on the treatment's efficacy. We will begin with a discussion of the advantages and limitations of different criteria for establishing a treatment's efficacy. We will then review the main findings from four studies that have tested the treatment using a randomized controlled design, where clients are randomly assigned to one of two or more experimental conditions.

CRITERIA FOR ESTABLISHING TREATMENT EFFICACY

There are many ways of assessing treatment efficacy in clinical trials. As mentioned previously, the comprehensive assessment of GAD clients offers several advantages, the most important being that each assessment method provides different information on clients' state and progress. In the following sections, we discuss three of the most widely used criteria/methods for assessing treatment efficacy in clinical trials: diagnostic remission, statistical comparisons of mean effects, and clinically significant improvement. Whereas the criteria for diagnostic remission and clinically significant improvement are applied to each participant, statistical comparisons of mean effects are assessed for entire groups or subgroups of participants.

Diagnostic Remission

In many clinical trials for GAD, diagnostic remission (that is, not meeting GAD diagnostic criteria following treatment) is used as one of the main criteria for treatment success. The assessment of diagnostic remission is an attractive success criterion for many reasons. First, it is nonambiguous; clients are either in remission or not in remission. Second, it is based on information contained in diagnostic manuals such as the

Diagnostic and Statistical Manual of Mental Disorders, Fourth Edition (*DSM-IV*) (American Psychiatric Association, 1994). Third, the assessment of diagnostic remission facilitates communication with clients, their families, other health professionals, and third-party payers such as insurance companies. For example, insurance company representatives will not want to know if treatment led to reliable changes in standardized measures of worry and anxiety; they will want to know if clients no longer meet GAD diagnostic criteria following treatment.

Although the assessment of diagnostic remission is attractive for the aforementioned reasons, it is an incomplete (and at times, inaccurate) way of evaluating client progress. One of the main problems with using diagnostic remission as a treatment success criterion resides in its either–or nature. As mentioned in the preceding paragraph, clients either meet GAD diagnostic criteria or they do not. Like any measurement technique based on a yes/no answer, the assessment of diagnostic remission can be an unreliable method of appraising client progress. To illustrate this point, imagine a client who continues to be a very high worrier following treatment, but only has two of the six GAD somatic symptoms (e.g., restlessness and difficulty concentrating). This client would meet the conditions for diagnostic remission (three somatic symptoms are required to meet GAD criteria), but the remaining GAD symptoms would likely continue to lead to important interference and distress in the client's life. In this case, therefore, the answer to the either–or diagnostic question would not capture the interference and distress that result from the client's considerable residual symptoms.

Another notable problem with the remission criterion is that GAD has relatively low diagnostic reliability; even experienced clinicians often have difficulty agreeing on the presence or absence of GAD. This problem is further complicated by the fact that therapists tend to underestimate GAD symptoms following treatment because they "want" their clients to be in remission. This is why treatment studies typically call upon an independent evaluator (someone not involved in other aspects of the study) to assess diagnostic remission. For these reasons, the assessment of diagnostic remission is insufficient as a sole marker of treatment efficacy. Combined with the methods described in the following paragraphs, however, diagnostic remission may provide the answer to one part of the important question of treatment efficacy.

Statistical Comparisons of Mean Effects

In addition to assessing diagnostic remission, clinical trials typically submit data to statistical comparisons of mean effects. These analyses can be used to examine within-group effects (e.g., to compare post-treatment scores to pretreatment scores in one treatment condition); between-group effects (e.g., to compare posttreatment scores in two treatment conditions); and within-between group effects (e.g., to compare pre- to posttreatment changes in two treatment conditions). Generally speaking, differences are considered "real" when there is less than a 5% probability that they are the result of chance fluctuations. Thus, in most cases, the expression "statistically significant effect" means that there is a 95% probability that the observed effect is real and not due to random variations.

In recent years, statistical significance testing, which is also referred to as *probability testing*, has come under intense criticism. The main critique of probability testing is that it addresses a dichotomous question (much like diagnostic remission). Obviously, the "5% principle" should not be applied in a rigid fashion, but clear guidelines on how to carry out probability testing in a flexible and justifiable way are lacking. Given these (and other) limitations of probability testing, it is now widely recommended that researchers also report the size of the observed effects. Roughly speaking, an *effect size* can be conceptualized as a standardized measure of the magnitude of an effect. Thus, by combining the calculation of effect size (magnitude of effect) with probability testing ("realness" of the effect), statistical comparisons of mean effects can provide a considerable amount of information about treatment efficacy.

Statistical comparisons of mean effects have many advantages. First, they are firmly grounded in scientific theory and research and are widely acknowledged to be the most important means of assessing treatment efficacy. Second, as mentioned above, they allow researchers to compute the magnitude of effects as well as the probability that the observed effects are true effects and not the result of chance variations. Third, statistical comparisons of mean effects allow researchers to arrive at general conclusions about the treatment under study (for example, that on average, the treatment leads to significant change for individuals afflicted with a particular disorder).

Although statistical comparisons of mean effects have many advantages, they also have some serious limitations, not the least of which is that they do not provide information on particular individuals participating in the clinical trial. By focusing on within- and between-group differences, these tests do not offer information about treatment progress for individual clients. Further, statistical tests do not tell us if the observed changes are *clinically significant*. It may be that a group of individuals is statistically improved following treatment, but this does not necessarily imply that the individuals have made changes that translate into real improvements in their daily lives. Only tests of clinical significance directly address this question.

Clinically Significant Improvement

In addition to the assessment of diagnostic remission and statistical significance, many recent treatment studies include the evaluation of clinically significant improvement. Simply stated, clinically significant change is attained when a client returns to normal functioning following treatment. In a landmark article, Neil Jacobson and Paula Truax (1991) reviewed both a rationale and a methodology for calculating clinically significant change. Although there exist more sophisticated methods for calculating the clinical significance of change, the methods described by Jacobson and Truax have the benefit of being both relatively simple and informative. Furthermore, a study of the accuracy of different methods of calculating clinical significance suggests that those described by Jacobson and Truax are equivalent to more complex methods (Atkins, Bedics, McGlinchey, & Beauchaine, 2005). Basically, the authors argue that two questions should be addressed when assessing the clinical significance of each client's change. First, is the client's progress reliable? In other words, is the client's response to treatment most likely real or due to chance variations? Second, following therapy, does the client display greater similarity to people with GAD or to those without GAD? From a statistical perspective, this question can be formulated in the following way: do the client's posttreatment scores on measures of GAD fall closer to those of untreated GAD clients or to those of individuals from the general population? According to Jacobson and Truax, the answers to these two questions will provide key information about the clinical significance of client progress.

The assessment of the clinical significance of change is helpful in a number of ways. First, it allows one to evaluate treatment gains for each individual client. Thus, clinical significance testing provides idiosyncratic information that can ultimately help us to understand *why* some clients benefit from treatment more than others do. The measurement of clinical significance also offers information that is meaningful to clients. For example, many GAD clients want to know if they have "really" changed over the course of treatment, and if they are now "normal" in terms of their worry and anxiety. Although group analyses cannot directly answer these questions, clinical significance testing makes this type of information available to clients. Finally, the methods described by Jacobson and Truax can be easily modified for the purposes of a given study. For example, in our own treatment studies, we have typically defined treatment response (or reliable change) as a 20% reduction in pretreatment scores.

Although the assessment of clinically significant change offers many advantages, it is not without limitations. One of the problems with the assessment of clinical significance is that treatment response and end state functioning are ultimately questions requiring a yes/no answer, and as such, are prone to the limitations inherent in the evaluation of dichotomous responses. Another limitation of clinical significance testing relates to the reliability of the calculations. For example, when calculating a "cut score" that best distinguishes the GAD population from the general population on a given measure, one must rely on the available normative data for that particular measure. Obviously, the validity of the chosen cut score will be the direct result of the quality of the available normative data.

As with the other measurement methods described herein, the assessment of clinically significant change is insufficient in and of itself for the assessment of treatment efficacy. However, by combining it with the evaluation of diagnostic remission and statistical comparisons of mean effects, researchers can present a fairly comprehensive and accurate picture of the efficacy of a given treatment. In the following sections, we focus mainly on these assessment strategies in presenting the findings from our clinical trials. The reader should also know that posttreatment results presented in this chapter are based on all clients *entering* treatment. For clients not completing treatment (and thus, not attending posttreatment assessments), pretreatment scores were carried forward to posttreatment. In other words, in the absence of posttreatment data, we assume that clients made no progress. Although this is a conservative approach, it is the most appropriate way of evaluating a treatment's efficacy because one simply should not assume that a client made progress in the absence of data. Therefore, the posttreatment data presented in the following sections are based on all clients entering treatment or what is often referred to as the "intent-to-treat" sample.

STUDIES OF TREATMENT EFFICACY

Since we formulated our cognitive-behavioral treatment for GAD, we have tested its efficacy in different ways. Specifically, we have compared our treatment to a passive control condition (waiting list) and to an active control condition (applied relaxation). We have also compared our treatment to a nonspecific active control condition (active listening) in terms of its ability to facilitate medication discontinuation.

Study 1: Cognitive-Behavioral Therapy and Wait-List Control

In our initial controlled clinical trial, we assessed the efficacy of our cognitive-behavioral treatment (CBT) protocol by comparing it to a wait-list control condition (Ladouceur, Dugas, Freeston et al., 2000). The treatment, which was administered over 16 weekly sessions, consisted of the procedures outlined in chapter 5. The study sample consisted of 26 adults, 20 women and 6 men, with a mean age of 40 years. All participants had a primary diagnosis of GAD. In an effort to have a clinically representative sample, we did not exclude clients taking psychotropic medication or having other psychological conditions. We did require, however, that medication use be stable and that comorbid conditions be less severe than the GAD. Of the 26 study participants, most had comorbid anxiety disorders and one third of them were taking medication for their anxiety.

Study participants were assessed with a structured diagnostic interview, the Anxiety Disorders Interview Schedule for *DSM-IV* (ADIS-IV), which was used to diagnose and establish the overall severity of GAD and any comorbid conditions. Participants also completed a series of self-report questionnaires, which were used to assess the study's main outcome variables: pathological worry, GAD somatic symptoms, associated anxiety, and depression. In addition, participants were asked to complete a measure of intolerance of uncertainty so that we could assess the impact of treatment on underlying cognitive processes (although most measures used in our treatment studies are described in Chapter 4, the reader may want to consult the original treatment articles for a full description of all measures used in each study). Although participants completed other questionnaires (such as measures of common therapy factors), we will restrict our discussion to the variables mentioned above because they represent the study's main outcomes and processes.

In the first phase of the study, participants were randomly selected to receive treatment (n = 14) or be placed on a 16-week waiting list (n = 12). As expected, we found that relative to participants in the wait-list condition, treated participants had higher rates of GAD diagnostic remission and showed greater statistical and clinical change on all outcomes (overall GAD severity, pathological worry, GAD somatic symptoms, associated anxiety, and depression). Although these results were encouraging, they were not surprising given that the treatment condition was being compared to a wait-list control condition. Although waiting lists typically lead to some improvement in symptoms (mostly because clients have positive expectations about the treatment they will soon be receiving), they nonetheless represent the least stringent of control conditions. Therefore, in this type of study, one must take a close look at the magnitude of change (or effect size) that results from receiving the treatment (see below).

In the second phase of the study, the 12 participants in the wait-list condition were offered the same 16-week treatment. Once wait-listed participants had received treatment, we examined treatment effects for the entire sample of 26 participants and found that 20 of 26 participants (77%) no longer met GAD diagnostic criteria at posttreatment. We also noted statistically significant decreases on all outcomes from pre- to posttreatment. More importantly, effect sizes were large (by convention, $d' = 0.8$ or greater is considered a large effect size) for all outcome variables: $d' = 3.2$ for overall GAD severity, $d' = 2.4$ for pathological worry, $d' = 1.6$ for GAD somatic symptoms, $d' = 0.9$ for associated anxiety, and $d' = 1.1$ for depression. When we examined the clinical significance of change, we found that 65% of participants were high responders (20% change on at least two thirds of outcome measures) and that 62% met criteria for high end state functioning (within nonclinical range on at least two thirds of outcome measures).

In the final phase of the study, we examined the maintenance of treatment gains during the year following treatment termination. Remarkably, all participants were available for follow-up assessments as none had dropped out during the treatment or follow-up phases of the study. Overall, we found that participants maintained their treatment gains over the follow-up period. In terms of diagnostic status, 77% of participants continued to be in diagnostic remission at six-month and one-year follow-ups. Moreover, statistical comparisons of posttreatment and follow-up means showed that treatment gains were maintained on all measures of outcome. Finally, at one-year follow-up, there was a slight and nonsignificant decrease in the percentage of participants who were high responders (62% as opposed to 65% at posttreatment) and who met criteria for high end state functioning (58% compared to 62% immediately following treatment).

Of interest, we found that changes in intolerance of uncertainty closely paralleled changes in symptoms during treatment and follow-up, supporting the idea that intolerance of uncertainty is an important treatment target. In particular, the treatment led to statistically significant decreases in intolerance of uncertainty, and these changes were maintained at six-month and one-year follow-ups. Furthermore, for most clients, changes in intolerance of uncertainty preceded changes in time spent worrying over the course of therapy, further supporting the notion that intolerance of uncertainty is an important treatment target (Dugas, Langlois, Rhéaume, & Ladouceur, 1998). In fact, the latter finding suggests that the treatment may exert its effects on pathological worry by first leading to changes in intolerance of uncertainty.

Overall, the results from our first randomized clinical trial indicated that approximately three out of four participants were GAD-free following treatment and at one-year follow-up. Moreover, about 60% of participants met conditions for high end state functioning immediately following treatment and at one-year follow-up. Although the treatment did not lead to ideal outcomes, the results indicated that the majority of clients benefited greatly in both the short and long term.

Study 2: Group CBT and Wait-List Control

In our second clinical trial, we set out to test the efficacy of our treatment when offered in a group format (Dugas, Ladouceur, Léger, Freeston et al., 2003). We hypothesized that therapeutic factors unique to group therapy such as altruism, vicarious learning, interpersonal learning, role flexibility, and group cohesiveness might be advantageous for many clients with GAD. We also wondered if the group therapy format might help reduce client demoralization, which is a common complication of GAD. Finally, we noted that the group format has produced impressive treatment gains in individuals with other anxiety disorders.

As we had done in our first clinical trial, we assessed the efficacy of the treatment by using a wait-list control condition. The total sample consisted of 52 adults (37 women and 15 men) with a mean age of 41 years. All study participants had a primary diagnosis of GAD. Again, we did not exclude clients with comorbid conditions (if the comorbid conditions were less severe than the primary diagnosis of GAD) or taking psychotropic medication for their anxiety (if the medication use was stable). Most participants (35) had at least one additional disorder and 9 of them were taking medication for their anxiety. The study's main outcome variables were similar to those of the previous treatment study. Namely, we assessed overall GAD severity, pathological worry, GAD somatic symptoms, associated anxiety, and depression. Participants also completed a measure of social adjustment (adaptive functioning within various social contexts) as well as the Intolerance of Uncertainty Scale.

In the first phase of the study, the participants either received treatment immediately (n = 25) or were placed on a waiting list (n = 27). Those in the immediate treatment condition were divided into five groups, with four to six participants per group. The treatment, which consisted of the procedures described in Chapter 5, was administered over 14 weekly two-hour sessions by two clinical psychologists. As anticipated, results from the first study phase showed that compared to those on the waiting list, treated participants had higher rates of remission and showed greater statistical and clinical change on all measures of outcome: overall GAD severity, pathological worry, GAD somatic symptoms, associated anxiety, depression, and social adjustment. Again, these results are not surprising given that the treatment was compared to a waiting list, which is a nonstringent control condition.

During the second phase of the study, which began after the 14-week waiting period, wait-listed participants were divided into five treatment groups, with four to six participants per group. Once all participants had received treatment, we examined posttreatment outcomes for the entire sample. The percentage of participants no longer meeting GAD diagnostic criteria was 60%. Not surprisingly, we found statistically significant decreases on all study measures. Pre- to posttreatment effect sizes were medium to large for all outcomes: $d' = 1.8$ for overall GAD severity, $d' = 1.6$ for pathological worry, $d' = 1.2$ for GAD somatic symptoms, $d' = 0.9$ for associated anxiety, $d' = 1.0$ for depression, and $d' = 0.7$ for social adjustment. Although the effects sizes obtained with group treatment were considerable, they were nonetheless not as large as those obtained in the previous study of individual treatment.

The clinical significance of pre- to posttreatment change was again assessed according to treatment response and end state functioning. Consistent with our previous study, treatment response was defined as a 20% change in pretreatment scores, and end state functioning was defined as a score that was within one standard deviation of the mean of normative nonclinical samples. Following group treatment, 60% of participants were high responders (20% change on at least two-thirds of outcome measures) and 65% of participants met criteria for high end state functioning (within nonclinical range on at least two-thirds of outcome measures).

In the study's final phase, we assessed all available participants over a two-year follow-up period (at six months, one year, and two years following treatment). The percentage of participants no longer meeting diagnostic criteria was 88% at six-month follow-up, 83% at one-year follow-up, and 95% at two-year follow-up. When we looked at the question of change in various outcomes from posttreatment to follow-up assessments, we found no evidence of deterioration on any of the outcome measures over the two-year period. In fact, we found that worry scores actually *decreased* during the two-year follow-up. Thus, in terms of pathological worry, participants were doing better two years after treatment than immediately after the end of treatment. Finally, we examined clinically significant improvement over the two-year follow-up period and found an increase in the percentage of high responders (72% at two-year follow-up as opposed to 60% at posttreatment) as well as in the percentage of participants meeting criteria for high end state functioning (72% at two-year follow-up compared to 65% at posttreatment).

Although the follow-up data are impressive, they may represent an overestimation of continued progress as the number of participants available for each assessment steadily decreased over time, with only 39 participants being available for the two-year follow-up evaluation. It may be that participants not doing as well over the follow-up phase of the study were less motivated to attend all assessments, thus leading to an overestimation of remission rates during follow-up. Nonetheless, at the very least, it appears that clients typically maintained their treatment gains in the two years following treatment termination.

With the goal of investigating treatment mechanisms, we subsequently examined the relationship between intolerance of uncertainty and the various treatment outcomes (Dugas, Ladouceur, Léger, Langlois et al., 2003). When examining pre- to posttreatment changes, we found that changes in intolerance of uncertainty predicted changes in pathological worry and GAD somatic symptoms, above and beyond common therapy factors such as therapist characteristics, treatment credibility, and client motivation. In terms of pretreatment to follow-up changes, the results indicated that only client motivation and pre- to posttreatment changes in intolerance of uncertainty predicted changes in pathological worry and GAD somatic symptoms at two-year follow-up. Thus, it appears that the extent to which clients become more tolerant of uncertainty over the course of treatment predicts their GAD symptoms immediately after treatment, as well as up to two years following treatment termination. These findings further add to the evidence indicating that intolerance of uncertainty is an important target when treating individuals with GAD.

Overall, the findings from the individual and group treatment studies suggest that both treatment formats are efficacious. Individual treatment, however, appears to be more effective than group treatment in terms of short-term progress, as evidenced by higher GAD remission rates and larger effect sizes on most outcome measures. Interestingly, the follow-up data suggest that individual and group treatment provide clients with similar long-term gains. As a case in point, when remission rates were calculated in the most conservative way possible for the group treatment study (by assuming that clients unavailable for follow-up assessments had relapsed), the percentage of participants in remission was 71 at one-year follow-up and 77 at two-year follow-up. A final notable comparison of the individual and group treatment studies concerns dropout rates. None of the participants in the individual treatment study dropped out of treatment, whereas 10% of those in the group treatment study did not complete the full treatment. Thus, it may be that individual treatment is an acceptable format to a greater proportion of clients with GAD. This, in turn, may be the result of the greater flexibility of individual treatment, which provides the therapist with more "room" to adapt treatment to the specific needs of each client. In summary, although the findings of the group treatment study are very encouraging, the data suggest that individual treatment is the optimal treatment format for those who suffer from GAD.

Study 3: CBT, Applied Relaxation, and Wait-List Control

In this ongoing study, we are in the process of comparing our CBT protocol to applied relaxation and wait-list control (Dugas, Savard et al., 2004). Given that our previous treatment studies had shown that our CBT protocol leads to statistically and clinically significant change, our main objective in carrying out this study was to test our treatment against a well-established intervention, namely applied relaxation. We chose applied relaxation as an active control condition for a number of reasons. First, applied relaxation has received empirical support for the treatment of GAD (Chambless et al., 1998). Thus, we reasoned that it would allow for a relatively stringent test of our treatment's comparative efficacy. Second, applied relaxation is widely used in clinical settings. We felt that this was important to increase the study's clinical usefulness. And finally, the therapeutic procedures involved in applied relaxation are very different from those involved in our treatment. We wanted the comparison condition to be distinct from our treatment so that we could draw firm conclusions about treatment differences in terms of both outcomes and treatment mechanisms. We also included a wait-list condition in order to replicate the finding that both treatments were superior to being placed on a waiting list.

One of the main challenges we faced in designing this study was dealing with potential allegiance effects. In simple terms, allegiance effects may occur when researchers wittingly or unwittingly favor a condition to which they feel a certain loyalty. This can occur when researchers compare a treatment they have developed with other treatments. To counter potential allegiance effects, we took a series of steps. First, we hired independent assessors (senior doctoral students not involved with other aspects of the study) to administer diagnostic interviews and other assessment procedures at all measurement times. Most importantly, the assessors were not involved in treatment delivery and were unaware of participants' experimental condition. Second, we hired a psychologist who was not trained in CBT (she had received training in eclectic therapy) to be the main therapist for both treatment conditions. In this way, we hoped to limit biases concerning one type of therapy over the other. We also reasoned that by using a therapist who had not trained in CBT, the study's results would generalize to more therapists, not only those who had extensive training in cognitive-behavioral theory and treatment. Finally, weekly clinical supervision was offered by one "expert" in each treatment condition. In the applied relaxation condition, clinical supervision was provided by an experienced psychologist who was not previously involved in the development and validation of our cognitive-behavioral treatment.

For this study, we recruited 65 adults with a primary diagnosis of GAD. The sample consisted of 43 women and 22 men, with a mean age of 39 years. Once again, comorbid diagnoses and medication use were allowed, but within the limits described in the previous treatment studies (57% had comorbid conditions and 55% were taking medication for their anxiety). The treatment outcome variables were similar to those of our previous treatment studies; participants completed measures of overall GAD severity, pathological worry, GAD somatic symptoms, associated anxiety, and depression. Given that we were also interested in comparing treatment mechanisms across conditions, we assessed all components of our cognitive model. That is, participants completed measures of intolerance of uncertainty, positive beliefs about worry, negative problem orientation, and cognitive avoidance.

The participants were first randomly allocated to the experimental conditions: 23 were assigned to CBT, 22 to applied relaxation, and 20 to the waiting list. Participants in the treatment conditions received 12 weekly individual sessions of CBT or applied relaxation, with all sessions lasting 50 to 60 minutes. We decided to offer our CBT protocol in a slightly "condensed" format (12 sessions as opposed to 16 sessions in our previous individual treatment study) because we felt that 12 sessions might prove sufficient to cover all treatment modules. In hindsight, it appears we were somewhat overly optimistic, as is discussed below. The applied relaxation condition, which was also offered over 12 weekly sessions, included training in: (1) tension awareness; (2) tension-release for 16, 7, and 4 muscle groups; (3) relaxation by recall; (4) relaxation by counting; (5) conditioned relaxation; and (6) relapse prevention. The treatment conditions were matched on a number of important features such as duration of treatment, use of a clearly articulated theoretical model, and number of between-session exercises. At the time of writing this chapter, only the pre- to posttest data have been published and will therefore be presented here.

At posttest, the results indicated that participants in the CBT condition had made the most gains, followed by those in the applied relaxation condition, and finally by those in the wait-list condition. This pattern held up for every measure we administered. For example, we found GAD diagnostic remission rates of 70% for CBT, 55% for applied relaxation, and 15% for the waiting list. In addition, effect sizes for change in overall severity of GAD were 2.4 in the CBT condition, 1.4 in the applied relaxation condition, and 0.7 in the wait-list condition (in this study, wait-listed participants made surprisingly large gains). Perhaps the most meaningful finding at posttreatment was that effect sizes followed the same pattern for GAD somatic symptoms, which were not targeted in the CBT condition yet were directly addressed in the applied relaxation condition. Effect sizes for change in GAD somatic symptoms were 1.1 for CBT, 0.7 for applied relaxation, and 0.5 for the waiting list. This finding lends support to the hypothesis that treatments for GAD do not necessarily need to directly target the somatic symptoms of clients in order to help them attain important change in these symptoms. Thus, it seems that decreases in pathological worry lead to reductions in GAD somatic symptoms, suggesting that anxiety reduction strategies such as applied relaxation may not be essential in helping clients with their somatic symptoms.

Although the findings reviewed in the previous paragraph support the differential efficacy of CBT, it should be noted that effect sizes for the CBT condition were generally smaller than in our previous individual treatment study. For example, the pre- to posttreatment effect size was $d' = 1.1$ (as opposed to $d' = 2.4$) for the measure of pathological worry. Thus, although worry scores decreased by an average of a little over one standard deviation after 12 sessions of CBT (this study), they decreased by over two standard deviations following 16 sessions of CBT (the previous individual treatment study). Moreover, our clinical experience in offering the 12-session treatment was that most clients would have benefited from a few additional sessions to more fully integrate the implications of the treatment's underlying principles. We have thus come to the conclusion that in this particular case *more is better* and that 14 to 16 regular 50-minute sessions are generally required to fully cover the treatment modules and their various applications.

In terms of treatment mechanisms, preliminary analyses show that all model components significantly improved from pre- to posttreatment in the CBT condition. In other words, clients receiving CBT became more tolerant of uncertainty, had less positive beliefs about worry, had a less negative problem orientation, and were less likely to engage in cognitive avoidance. By contrast, clients receiving applied relaxation only attained change on one of the four underlying processes, namely intolerance of uncertainty. Stated differently, applied relaxation did not help clients to reevaluate their positive beliefs about worry, to change their problem orientation, or to "face their fears." It is our view that the greater efficacy of CBT can be explained by the fact that all model components are directly targeted and consequently modified. At this time, however, this conclusion remains speculative and further research on the mechanisms of treatment is needed.

The finding that applied relaxation led to greater tolerance for uncertainty is certainly intriguing. Here, we offer two hypotheses that might account for this finding. First, applied relaxation provides clients with a skill to manage their anxiety. As mentioned previously, clinical cognitive theory has taught us that fundamental beliefs (in this case, about uncertainty) may be activated by negative mood states such as anxiety. Thus, it seems probable that negative beliefs about uncertainty are less apparent (and thus, less disturbing) when clients have concrete anxiety management skills such as applied relaxation. A second explanation for the finding resides in the fundamental nature of relaxation. When in a relaxed state, clients learn to "let go" of their physiological arousal and subjective anxiety. It may be that some clients generalize the idea of letting go and begin to let go of their desire to predict and control the uncertainty of everyday life. Thus, applied relaxation can (indirectly) lead to the reevaluation of fundamental beliefs about uncertainty. Our clinical experience suggests that this is indeed the case with a significant minority of clients receiving training in applied relaxation. It is worth repeating, however, that only CBT led to positive changes in the other three model components; as such, applied relaxation does not adequately address the underlying processes identified by our cognitive model.

Study 4: CBT and Medication Discontinuation

It is well established that many individuals with GAD struggle with long-term medication use (Ashton, 2001). In particular, the use of benzodiazepines over extended periods of time can lead to a number of problems. First, their long-term use is associated with both physical dependency and tolerance effects. Second, their extended use sometimes leads to important side effects such as nausea and difficulty concentrating. And finally, many long-term benzodiazepine users report high levels of psychological dependency and are unable to cease their medication use. Given these considerations, we were interested in knowing if our treatment could help GAD sufferers who are long-term benzodiazepine users to discontinue their medication.

In this study (Gosselin, Ladouceur, Morin, Dugas, & Baillargeon, in press), we recruited 61 individuals with a primary diagnosis of GAD. The sample consisted of 36 women and 25 men, with a mean age of 50 years. All participants had been taking benzodiazepines for at least one year, with a mean duration of use of over seven years. All participants reported a desire to discontinue their medication use, and 59% reported having already unsuccessfully tried to cease taking benzodiazepines. In line with our previous treatment studies, comorbid diagnoses were allowed. Eighty percent of participants had at least one secondary disorder, with social anxiety disorder being the most frequently diagnosed condition. Participants were randomly assigned to CBT plus medication taper ($n = 31$) or active listening plus medication taper ($n = 30$). The CBT condition was again based on the procedures described in this book. In the active listening condition, clients explored their life experiences with the goal of facilitating both self-awareness and understanding of their anxiety. The therapist's role was to provide an empathetic and nonjudgmental environment within which clients could talk about themselves. By using a nonspecific psychotherapy condition such as active listening, we hoped to determine if the specific modules of our treatment were responsible for group differences, as opposed to common therapy factors such as the therapist–client working alliance and the change expectations that come with working with a competent health care provider. As for the medication taper procedure, it aimed for a decrease of the daily dose of benzodiazepines by 25% every two to three weeks over the course of treatment.

Each participant received 12 combined sessions of medication taper and psychotherapy (either CBT or active listening), with each combined session lasting 90 minutes. In the first part of the session, the participant met with a physician for about 20 minutes to review progress, assess withdrawal symptoms, and determine the following week's dose. In the second part of the session, the participant met with a clinical psychologist to receive either CBT or the nonspecific active listening intervention. Participants were assessed at pretreatment, posttreatment, and at three follow-ups (three months, six months, and one year after treatment termination). The assessment instruments and procedures were similar to those used in the previously described studies, with the addition of a medication self-monitoring agenda (and the use of urine tests to confirm the validity of the self-reports of medication intake).

Overall, the results show that CBT was more efficacious than active listening in combining with medication taper to produce benzodiazepine discontinuation. At posttreatment, 74% of participants in the CBT condition had attained complete benzodiazepine cessation whereas only 37% of those in the active listening condition had attained a similar result. Furthermore, these findings remained fairly stable during the year following treatment termination, with significantly more participants in the CBT condition having attained complete cessation of their benzodiazepines at all follow-up times. It should be noted, however, that we found no between-group differences on the quantity of benzodiazepines taken. Although this latter finding stands in sharp contrast to the rates of complete discontinuation, it is nonetheless consistent with the findings of other studies involving medication taper procedures. Specifically, many studies suggest that the final stage of medication tapering (complete cessation) is the most difficult for long-term users. Consequently, it may be that one of the main benefits of CBT is to provide clients with "tools" that allow them to successfully navigate the challenges involved in the final stage of medication tapering, namely complete cessation.

We were also interested in comparing CBT and active listening in terms of their respective impacts on the presence and severity of GAD. We first looked at diagnostic remission at posttreatment and found that 65% of participants in the CBT condition no longer met GAD criteria whereas only 20% of participants in the active listening condition achieved similar results. Over the follow-up phase of the study, the rates of diagnostic remission increased in both conditions, but percentages remained significantly higher in the CBT condition than in the active listening condition. For example, at one-year follow-up, remission rates were 71% in the CBT condition and 40% in the active listening condition. We also examined the statistical significance of change on several measures of GAD severity. Overall, we found that both conditions led to decreases in the symptoms of GAD and associated depression. Analyses comparing both groups showed that relative to participants in the active listening condition, those in the CBT condition reported significantly lower levels of worry and intolerance of uncertainty at posttreatment. Furthermore, these between-group differences were maintained over most follow-up assessments.

In summary, the findings from this study suggest that the combination of CBT and a supervised medication taper is helpful for individuals with GAD who are long-term benzodiazepine users. First, it appears that CBT plus taper is more effective than active listening and taper in helping clients to *discontinue* their use of benzodiazepines. Second, relative to active listening, CBT leads to greater treatment gains in terms of diagnostic remission and symptomatic improvement. It is noteworthy that most clients receiving CBT plus taper were able to both discontinue their use of medication and attain diagnostic remission of GAD. It may be that the 65% post-CBT remission rate is actually a conservative estimate because some participants may have been struggling with increases in anxiety due to medication cessation. Thus, it seems that receiving a combination of CBT and supervised medication taper can be doubly beneficial for many long-term benzodiazepine users with GAD: they can rid themselves of both their medication and their GAD.

GENERAL CONCLUSIONS

The general conclusions that can be drawn from the above review of the four randomized clinical trials of the treatment described in this book are presented in Table 6.1.

Short-Term Effects

Taken together, the general conclusions about the short-term effects of our CBT protocol presented in Table 6.1 suggest that 12 to 16 weekly sessions of treatment lead to very positive outcomes for approximately two thirds of clients with GAD. In fact, across studies, the data are quite consistent, with remission rates ranging from 60 to 77% and high end state functioning rates ranging from 62 to 65%. Furthermore, when one considers that all analyses were carried out using the full intent-to-treat sample (with pretreatment scores carried forward to posttreatment for noncompleters), the results are very encouraging indeed. In fact, the results appear to be superior to those reported in treatment studies using general anxiety reduction interventions. It is noteworthy that the diagnostic remission rate of 55% obtained in the applied relaxation condition of Study 3 is similar to those of other studies of general anxiety reduction interventions (e.g., Öst & Breitholtz, 2000, found that 53% of GAD clients were below the GAD diagnostic threshold following applied relaxation). Based on the findings from the individual treatment studies, it could be argued that relative to a general anxiety reduction intervention such as applied relaxation, the GAD-specific treatment helps about 20% more clients attain diagnostic remission. Given that the GAD literature is replete with studies showing that different treatments are roughly equivalent, this difference in remission rates is certainly notable.

It is also worth noting that treatment efficacy did not seem to be adversely affected by the gradual withdrawal of medication, in this case benzodiazepines. In Study 4, not only did the treatment lead to an increment in the efficacy of a supervised medication taper procedure, it also led to diagnostic remission in 65% of GAD clients (as opposed to 20% in the active listening condition). Given that many individuals enter therapy with the hope of decreasing or ceasing their use of medication, these findings suggest that this may be an attainable goal for many clients with GAD. Considering the great number of individuals who suffer from GAD *and* who are long-term benzodiazepine users, the importance of offering concrete "tools" to assist them in their efforts to stop using their medication cannot be overstated.

In terms of treatment acceptability and adherence, the data show that very few clients drop out of treatment before all modules have been covered. In the four treatment studies, dropout rates never exceeded 10% (with the highest rate being observed in the group treatment study). Thus, the data show that at least 90% of clients who enter therapy actually go on to complete all phases of the treatment. This suggests that the vast majority of clients perceive the treatment as being credible, acceptable, and relevant to their situation. In fact, this is exactly what clients reported on a measure of treatment credibility that we administered in every study (because the measure was not used to assess treatment efficacy, it was not systematically presented in this chapter). On a more general note, these data suggest that the treatment "makes sense" to those who suffer from GAD. In fact, the vast majority of participants mentioned that the focus on worry rather than the physiological symptoms of anxiety was helpful. As mentioned previously, given that the treatment led to important gains in terms of both pathological worry and GAD somatic symptoms, it certainly does not seem necessary to directly target the somatic symptoms for most clients.

Long-Term Effects

As evidenced from the long-term effects listed in Table 6.1, treatment gains are for the most part maintained over extended periods of time. For example, diagnostic remission rates tend to stay the same or increase over periods of one to two years. Furthermore, group treatment appears to lead to further reductions in pathological worry over a two-year follow-up period. Finally, although the percentage of individuals no longer using benzodiazepines decreased from posttreatment to one-year follow-up in Study 4, there was an increase in the percentage of remitted clients over the same period of time. It is a truism that helping anxiety-disordered individuals to "get better" is much easier than helping them to "stay better." Thus, it is our position that the follow-up data are just as important as the posttreatment data when considering the treatment's impact. In terms of personal and social costs, the long-term maintenance of treatment gains and the prevention of recurrent bouts of GAD have the potential to make the greatest difference not only to those afflicted with GAD, but also to their families and the health care system in general. Considering that GAD typically has a chronic and unrelenting course, the finding that over three quarters of treated individuals are in remission one and two years after treatment is encouraging indeed.

Although it is vital that we obtain data on the long-term effects of treatment, it should be noted that follow-up assessments present

TABLE 6.1 General Conclusions Based on the Studies of Treatment Efficacy

Short-Term Effects

1. Most clients attain GAD remission (60 to 77%) and high end state functioning (62 to 65%) following treatment.
2. The treatment leads to statistically significant decreases (with effect sizes ranging from 3.2 to 0.9) in GAD symptoms, associated anxiety, and depression.
3. The treatment appears to be more efficacious than applied relaxation.
4. Combined with medication taper, the treatment helps most GAD clients who are long-term benzodiazepine users to cease their medication (74%) or attain GAD remission (65%).
5. Adherence is high as very few clients (0 to 10%) drop out before all treatment modules have been covered.

Long-Term Effects

1. Treatment gains in terms of diagnostic remission, GAD symptoms, associated anxiety, and depression are maintained for at least one year after treatment termination (two years for group treatment).
2. In terms of pathological worry, further gains are made over the two years that follow treatment termination (for group treatment).
3. Combined with medication taper, the treatment leads to the maintenance of treatment gains over a one-year period (slight decrease in the percentage of clients no longer using benzodiazepines but slight increase in the percentage of clients in remission of GAD).

certain problems. Most notably, as researchers, we are unable to properly control for the impact of participants' various life experiences during the extended follow-up phases of treatment studies. In all our studies, we systematically take note of instances where clients change their medication or receive additional therapy following treatment. However, there are many other life experiences that can impact upon the maintenance of treatment gains, many of which we are unable to properly take into account. For example, a work promotion can lead to an increase or a decrease in worry and anxiety. Thus, although the assessment of the maintenance of treatment gains is extremely important, one should keep in mind that researchers have no control over day-to-day events that may contribute to further improvement or relapse in treated individuals.

Finally, it should be noted that preliminary data are consistent with the notion that the treatment exerts its effects on worry and anxiety by way of changes in the model components. For instance, the data show that the treatment leads to reductions in intolerance of uncertainty, positive beliefs about worry, negative problem orientation, and cognitive avoidance. Furthermore, pre- to posttreatment changes in intolerance of uncertainty typically precede changes in worry and predict the severity of GAD symptoms as much as two years after treatment. Although much work remains to be done to grasp the complexity of the mechanisms underlying the successful treatment of GAD, these initial data suggest that identifying variations in the model components can be helpful in understanding how the treatment exerts its effects on the symptoms of GAD.

CHAPTER 7

Addressing Complicating Factors

In this, the final chapter, we will review the factors that can complicate treatment and discuss ways that therapists can deal with them. It is easy to consider complicating factors exclusively from the perspective of the client. For example, the problems that are typically discussed in the psychotherapy literature include the presence of comorbidity and low treatment motivation. Although these are important factors (and will be discussed below), there are a number of characteristics that relate both to the therapist and to the context in which the treatment is offered that should not be overlooked. Thus, what follows is a discussion of complicating factors organized into three categories: client factors, therapist factors, and contextual factors.

CLIENT COMPLICATING FACTORS

Client complicating factors can be divided into what the client brings to the therapy session (intratherapeutic factors) and what the client experiences outside of therapy (extratherapeutic events). Although extratherapeutic events (for example, an important deadline at work or an argument with a close relative) can play an important role in treatment, they will not be discussed here because we know very little about how the myriad of life events experienced by generalized anxiety disorder (GAD) clients combine and interact to influence the outcome of treatment. On the other hand, based on the empirical data and our clinical experience, we are in a position to discuss the impact of intratherapeutic factors on the delivery, receipt, and success of treatment. Specifically, we will review the following client complicating factors: comorbidity (Axis I, Axis II, and medical comorbidity), medication use, and low treatment motivation.

Comorbidity with Axis I Disorders

As mentioned at the outset of this book, comorbidity in individuals with GAD is the norm rather than the exception. In fact, epidemiological surveys have found that over 65% of individuals with GAD have at least one additional *Diagnostic and Statistical Manual of Mental Disorders, Fourth Edition (DSM-IV)* diagnosis. Given this high rate of comorbidity, the possibility that additional diagnoses can interfere with the treatment of GAD needs to be addressed. However, a perusal of the GAD treatment literature suggests that Axis I comorbidity is not as much of a problem as was once thought. For example, there is evidence that the presence of comorbid conditions does not necessarily have a negative impact on treatment adherence and efficacy. Moreover, the successful treatment of GAD often leads to decreases in the severity of comorbid conditions, even when the conditions were not addressed in therapy (Borkovec, Abel, & Newman, 1995). There is also evidence, however, that suggests that the presence of some comorbid conditions, in particular panic disorder, can have a detrimental impact on the treatment of GAD (Brown & Barlow, 1992). Thus, it seems that the question of Axis I comorbidity is a complex one, and that some comorbid conditions have a greater impact on treatment efficacy than others.

In analyzing the data from our own treatment studies, we have consistently found that Axis I comorbidity does not negatively impact treatment outcome. In other words, successfully treated participants had just as many comorbid Axis I conditions as those who did not fully benefit from treatment. However, it is possible (and even probable) that each of our treatment studies did not have a sufficient sample size to allow us to properly test the hypothesis of lower efficacy in comorbid participants. In order to correctly address this question, we recently pooled the data from three completed treatment studies and reexamined the impact of Axis I comorbidity on treatment outcome (Provencher, Ladouceur, & Dugas, 2006). We found that 73% of participants had at least one comorbid Axis I condition, with the most common additional diagnoses being specific phobia, social anxiety disorder, panic disorder, and major depressive disorder. The pooled data also showed that following the treatment of GAD, there was a decrease in the number of comorbid conditions despite the fact that they were not addressed in treatment. Finally, we found that although comorbidity did not affect outcome immediately following the end of treatment, a different pattern emerged at six-month follow-up. Specifically, follow-up outcomes were less favorable for participants with panic disorder or with multiple comorbid conditions. Thus, it appears that clients with comorbid panic disorder or with several additional conditions might receive significantly fewer benefits in the long term from the treatment described in this book.

Although it is difficult to speculate on the many ways in which the presence of multiple comorbid conditions can have a negative impact following therapy (and we will not do so here), our experience with clients who have a comorbid diagnosis of panic disorder suggests that their *anxiety sensitivity* (that is, the tendency to interpret anxious responding in a catastrophic way) may interfere with the maintenance of treatment gains. Specifically, we have found that these clients sometimes fall back into the habit of trying to avoid or neutralize their distressing thoughts in an effort to avoid experiencing anxiety. Obviously, avoidance and neutralization run counter to the principles of exposure and can lead to a return of excessive worry and anxiety following treatment. Thus, for clients with a comorbid diagnosis of panic disorder, the therapist might want to spend additional time on the exposure module of the treatment in order to help them to continue facing their occasional distressing thoughts and anxiety once therapy has ended. The therapist might also want to schedule a few booster sessions following treatment so that emerging difficulties can be dealt with before they lead to a significant deterioration in the client's state.

Although the data from the study described above did not show that a diagnosis of major depressive disorder can negatively impact treatment, our clinical experience suggests that extra care should be taken when treating depressed clients with the procedures described in this book. Specifically, we have observed that high levels of depression can complicate the proper use of imaginal exposure. For clients with elevated levels of depression, it is particularly important that the therapist pay close attention to the exposure scenario to ensure that it does not contain too many depressogenic elements. For example, we recently treated a client with primary GAD, secondary (but relatively severe) depression, and a medical diagnosis of irritable bowel syndrome. Not surprisingly, one of his major worry themes concerned the potential consequences of his medical condition. In his first attempt at imaginal exposure, he developed a scenario wherein he was socially isolated because of complications due to his irritable bowel syndrome (for example, having to wear a colostomy bag). Rather than provoking an anxious response, exposure to this scenario led to feelings of sadness and loss. The client was asked to modify his exposure scenario with the goal of accessing more fear and less sadness. The final scenario described a dating situation in which the client felt quite anxious because he did not know if he would be able to hold off his symptoms of irritable bowel syndrome until he got home. In contrast to the first exposure scenario, the final scenario led to elevated levels of anxiety and the processing of his fear.

In summary, the presence of Axis I comorbidity does not generally complicate the treatment described in this book. However, long-term outcomes can be compromised in clients with multiple comorbid conditions or in those with comorbid panic disorder. As for clients who also suffer from depression, the client and therapist should work together closely to ensure that the content of the exposure scenario leads to an anxious response rather than feelings of sadness. Having said this, the presence of comorbid depression does not seem to interfere with the short- or long-term efficacy of the treatment.

Comorbidity with Axis II Disorders

A second complicating factor that clients can bring to therapy relates to personality style or the presence of comorbid personality disorders. Although many therapists believe that clients who have rigid and inflexible ways of relating to others benefit less from anxiety disorder treatments, the data do not clearly support this position in the case of GAD. In fact, most findings suggest that the presence of personality disorders has a negligible impact on the efficacy of cognitive-behavioral therapy (CBT) for GAD (e.g., Dreessen, Arntz, Luttels, & Sallaerts, 1994). Thus, there seems to be a discrepancy between the perceptions and beliefs of therapists, and the findings of empirical studies in terms of the impact of comorbid personality disorders. One reason for this might be that different personality disorders have dissimilar effects on treatment processes and outcomes (which is highly likely). If this is indeed the case, the proper assessment of the impact of each comorbid personality disorder would require an extremely large sample of GAD clients. To our knowledge, a GAD treatment study of this size, with the proper assessment of personality disorders, has never been carried out. Thus, we are left with clinical anecdotal reports and insufficiently powered studies to estimate the impact of comorbid personality disorders on the processes and outcomes of CBT for GAD.

In terms of the treatment described in this book, we have yet to examine the relationship between comorbid personality disorders and treatment outcome. This is quite simply because we did not systematically assess clients for the presence of personality disorders in our previous clinical trials (although we are doing so in a current trial). However, our clinical experience has been similar to that of many other therapists. That is, we have observed that certain types of personality styles appear to be associated with lower treatment adherence and enactment, as well as poorer treatment outcomes. For example, we have noticed that GAD clients with elevated levels of avoidant-related beliefs often have difficulty with the problem-solving and imaginal exposure modules of treatment. Given that both these treatment modules require clients to endure discomfort in the short term in order to make progress in the longer term, beliefs such as "I should avoid unpleasant situations at all costs" and "I cannot tolerate unpleasant feelings" can seriously interfere with treatment adherence and enactment. When working with these clients, we have found it useful to proceed at a slower pace and address the avoidant-related beliefs and low distress tolerance as they come up during therapy. Similarly, we have also found that clients with high levels of histrionic-related beliefs such as "people will pay attention only if I act in extreme ways" and "I don't have to bother to think; I can go with my gut feeling" often have difficulty applying sound problem-solving principles. In cases such as these, we typically extend the problem-solving module of treatment to allow clients to "experiment" and compare impulsive and rational problem-solving approaches.

Although the actual impact of specific personality disorders on the efficacy of our GAD treatment has not been formally assessed, the aforementioned examples of how some personality disorders can interfere with treatment certainly make intuitive sense. Now that we have systematically incorporated the measurement of Axis II disorders in our pretreatment assessment protocol, we hope to be able to eventually address this issue with more than anecdotal clinical evidence. In the meantime, we will continue to pay close attention to the interactions between the various personality styles of our GAD clients and their treatment outcomes.

Comorbidity with Medical Conditions

Comorbidity with medical conditions can also affect the treatment of GAD. Although, to our knowledge, there is no published data on the relationship between the presence of medical conditions and the efficacy of psychological treatments for individuals with GAD, it is clear that some medical conditions require special attention. For example, a client with a heart condition requires medical clearance to proceed with imaginal exposure given the potential impact of exposure on heart rate and exertion. Having said this, we have found that in the vast majority of cases, clients with heart conditions are given the "green light" by their cardiologist to engage in imaginal exposure. Thus, our experience has been that only a small minority of cardiac patients should not employ exposure methods. Typically, these individuals have serious heart conditions that require them to avoid most forms of physical exertion. Obviously, very few individuals have such serious heart conditions.

A second medical issue that may impact the course of treatment is when a client has had a serious disease that is in remission. For GAD clients who have had a serious medical condition such as cancer, it is no surprise that cancer relapse is often a central worry theme. In such situations, the therapist may wonder if imaginal exposure to a scenario involving cancer relapse is appropriate, both from a clinical and ethical point of view. Although we have not encountered many of these situations, we have found it useful to address them on a case-by-case basis. If the client is excessively worried about relapse, is not at high risk for relapse, and is willing to undergo exposure to mental images depicting relapse, then the use of imaginal exposure is probably appropriate. However, if these conditions are not met, then worry about relapse may be dealt with using other strategies such as problem solving with either an instrumental or emotional focus.

A final issue that we have encountered from time to time is a related one, but not a medical condition per se. We have found that some pregnant women are reluctant to experience the "negative thoughts" that make up their worst case scenarios during exposure. For these women, the idea of focusing on threatening mental images during pregnancy runs counter to the notion of a harmonious pregnancy filled with positive and calming thoughts. The desire to avoid exposure to threatening mental images may be particularly strong when the exposure scenario concerns childbirth or the health of the child. Furthermore, many pregnant women follow preparatory classes (such as Lamaze classes) that emphasize the importance of relaxation and positive thoughts. In situations such as these, we have found it useful to again treat each client on a case-by-case basis. Although we are steadfast proponents of imaginal exposure for worries about hypothetical situations, it is our opinion that the therapist should show the utmost sensitivity to the pregnant client's wishes. Given that pregnancy is such a significant life event and that it is time-limited, we believe that it might be most appropriate to forego imaginal exposure for women who have pregnancy-related worries, but are opposed to engaging in exposure. For these women, it might be more helpful to simply encourage them to experience these worries without using neutralization or avoidance strategies. In this way, at the very least, the clients will not contribute to their worry cycle by validating the dangerousness of the worrisome thoughts.

Use of Medication

As mentioned previously, many individuals with GAD use some form of medication for their worry, anxiety, and associated symptoms. It is interesting to note that although the impact of medication on CBT for GAD is the subject of considerable debate, no study has yet to systematically address this question. For some, the use of medication can enhance the efficacy of CBT because clients are better able to fully engage in treatment and develop new skills if their worry and anxiety are to some extent under control. For others, the use of medication can reduce the short- and long-term efficacy of CBT because (1) it interferes with specific treatment interventions (for example, anxious responding may be insufficient during exposure); (2) clients may ascribe their treatment gains to their medication rather than to the psychotherapeutic interventions; or (3) medication discontinuation might bring about a relapse of GAD. In our opinion, the use of medication is most problematic when clients attribute their progress to their medication rather than to the day-to-day changes that result from CBT. In particular, these clients may be at risk for relapse when medication is eventually decreased or discontinued. Thus, for clients taking medication, the therapist should systematically assess attributions about progress, and address beliefs that reflect an *external locus of control* ("My progress is the result of my medication and not a consequence of my hard work"). The more that medicated clients can ascribe their progress to their own efforts, the more they will be in a position to fully benefit from CBT both in the short and long term.

In an excellent review article on the compatibility of medication and cognitive-behavioral approaches to anxiety disorders, Henny Westra and Sherry Stewart (1998) conclude that medication can in fact interfere with CBT and that the use of high potency benzodiazepines is most problematic for the success of CBT for the anxiety disorders. In particular, it appears that high potency benzodiazepines can have a detrimental impact on CBT for anxiety because both modes of treatment are based on somewhat contradictory premises (for example, benzodiazepines aim to decrease anxiety whereas CBT aims to modify catastrophic beliefs about anxiety). Although the authors make some compelling arguments against combining benzodiazepines with CBT for the treatment of anxiety, the general issue of combination treatments for GAD awaits study in a sufficiently powered, well-controlled study.

In our clinical trials, the percentage of participants taking medication for their GAD was 35% in the initial individual treatment study (Ladouceur, Dugas, Freeston et al., 2000), 21% in the group treatment study (Dugas, Ladouceur, Léger, Freeston et al., 2003), and 57% in the CBT/applied relaxation treatment study (Dugas, Savard et al., 2004). Although none of our studies were designed to assess the impact of medication on treatment efficacy, we were able to compare outcomes for participants with and without medication in all three studies. Simply stated, medication status was unrelated to treatment outcome in each study; clients taking medication did no better and no worse than clients who were not taking medication. For example, in a preliminary and unpublished analysis of the data from the CBT/applied relaxation study, we found that medication status was unrelated to treatment outcome in terms of overall GAD severity, pathological worry, GAD somatic symptoms, associated anxiety, and depression. It should be noted, however, that because of the limited sample size, we were unable to properly test for the impact of specific types of medication on treatment outcome. Further, because we required that participants taking medication have a stable dose (i.e., at intake, no change in dose for the past four weeks for benzodiazepines and the past 12 weeks for antidepressants), we were unable to assess the impact of medication for clients who start both medication and CBT *at the same time*. Given that this is often the case, future studies should contrast CBT alone and CBT with medication when both are initiated concurrently.

To summarize, although the impact of medication use on the efficacy of CBT for GAD is the subject of heated debate, no study has yet to properly address this issue. It seems safe to say, however, that medication does not have a prominent effect on the treatment described in this book as preliminary analyses of the data from all treatment studies show that medication use is unrelated to short- and long-term outcomes. For now, therefore, it appears that the use of medication does not typically pose a serious threat to the treatment procedures described in this book.

Low Treatment Motivation

A final client factor that will be discussed here is treatment motivation. Like all "action-oriented" therapies, CBT requires a considerable amount of motivation on the part of the client. Given that clients are expected to actively collaborate with the therapist and carry out between-session exercises that involve considerable time and energy, one can easily see how low treatment motivation can interfere with CBT. In fact, one could argue that treatment motivation is particularly important for anxious clients receiving CBT because they are typically expected to face their fears and experience relatively high levels of anxiety. It is surprising, therefore, that few treatment studies have examined the impact of varying levels of treatment motivation on the efficacy of CBT for GAD.

In our own clinical trials, we typically assess treatment motivation and other common therapy factors (that is, client expectations vis-à-vis therapy and client perceptions of the therapist's characteristics) using standardized self-report questionnaires. In line with other treatment studies, we assess common therapy factors following the third treatment session. In our opinion, this is the most appropriate timing because it strikes a balance between clients being able to form an opinion about the treatment and the therapist, without being so far along in therapy that their opinion is unduly influenced by their progress. Overall, the findings from our treatment studies suggest that level of client motivation significantly predicts both short- and long-term outcomes. In fact, it appears that motivation is a stronger predictor of outcome than either client expectations or therapist characteristics. For example, by combining the data from our first two clinical trials, we found that although ratings of motivation, expectations, and therapist characteristics were related to each other, only treatment motivation predicted the extent of pre- to posttreatment change in pathological worry (Léger, Dugas, Langlois, & Ladouceur, 1998). Moreover, subsequent analyses of the follow-up data from the group treatment study showed that treatment motivation (again, assessed following the third therapy session) predicted overall GAD severity at six-month and two-year follow-ups (Dugas, Ladouceur, Léger, Langlois et al., 2003). Once more, although client expectations and therapist characteristics were related to treatment motivation, they did not predict long-term outcomes. Therefore, it appears that low treatment motivation is a considerable complicating factor for the treatment protocol described in this book.

Having acknowledged the potential negative impact of low treatment motivation, we now turn our attention to the two following questions:

(1) What are the sources of low motivation?

(2) What can be done to increase client motivation?

In terms of the first question, we believe it is important to underscore that low treatment motivation may be attributable to either the client or therapist. In fact, the therapist should be careful not to "lay the blame" on the client when treatment is unsuccessful and the client appears unmotivated. Low client motivation may result from any number of therapist factors such as an unconvincing presentation of the general principles of CBT and the specific treatment rationale, a rigid and insensitive approach to treatment delivery, and an unreceptive attitude toward the client (see the following section for a more detailed discussion of therapist complicating factors). In cases where the client's low treatment motivation does not appear to be the result of therapist factors (although this is always a difficult call), it may be that the client is simply ambivalent about change. For example, the client may have many positive beliefs about worry that are resistant to change, either because they are difficult to disprove or because they are closely tied to the client's value system (e.g., "Good people worry about others"). Similarly, the client may perceive important secondary gains to having GAD such as not being asked to take on certain responsibilities at home or at work. Finally, the client may not be "ready for action;" in terms of stages of change theory, most of these clients are in the stages of contemplation (that is, aware of the problem but not committed to action) or preparation (that is, ready to take only small steps) of readiness for change (Prochaska & Norcross, 2001). Thus, there are many sources leading to low client motivation, some of which are the "responsibility" of the client, and some of which are not. Below, we address potential solutions to some of these sources of low motivation.

For unmotivated clients who do not seem to be ambivalent about change, the therapist should consider the possibility that the treatment's rationale has not been properly presented or discussed. If this appears to be the case, the therapist should of course revisit the treatment's underlying principles and address all client questions and concerns about the logic behind the treatment procedures. The therapist may also want to reflect on relationship factors that may be contributing to the client's low motivation. For example, it may be that the therapist's "natural style" is not ideally suited to the needs of a particular client and that a slight adjustment in how the therapist relates to the client is warranted. For a client with marked dependent personality traits, for example, the therapist may want to adopt a more "nurturing" attitude in the initial stages of treatment and progressively move to a true collaboration with the client in the later stages of therapy. Thus, when unmotivated clients do not appear to be ambivalent about change, therapists should reflect on how they might be contributing to low motivation. As always, an open and nondefensive discussion about potential sources of low motivation can be very useful in helping therapists better respond to the client's needs in order to foster greater treatment motivation.

In some cases, low treatment motivation is the result of the client's ambivalence about change (for any of the reasons listed above). One way the therapist can help clients to become less ambivalent is to ensure that positive beliefs about worry have been properly addressed. If the client's ambivalence appears to be the result of broader issues, then the therapist may want to add motivational interviewing to the treatment protocol (see Miller & Rollnick, 2002, for a detailed discussion of motivational interviewing). That is, the therapist may want to temporarily move away from an action orientation to explore the sources of client ambivalence using specific interventions. For example, clients can be asked to "explore both sides of the change coin" by elaborating on the reasons why the status quo is both desirable (for example, "Having GAD means taking on less responsibility at work") and undesirable (for example, "Having GAD also means not taking advantage of what life has to offer"). Motivational interviewing exercises can also be used to increase client motivation. For example, clients can be asked to write two letters describing themselves one year from that moment, with the first letter describing the status quo (continuing to suffer from GAD) and the second letter describing change (no longer having GAD). In this way, clients can be helped to more fully appreciate the potential benefits of fully engaging in treatment. In summary, obvious client ambivalence can at times be dealt with by temporarily moving away from an action orientation and using strategies such as motivational interviewing. In our recent work, we have found that using motivational interventions for a subset of unmotivated clients with GAD has been quite useful.

THERAPIST COMPLICATING FACTORS

When treatments lead to positive outcomes, this is often understood in terms of appropriate treatment strategies and skillful therapist interventions. When treatments do not lead to positive outcomes, on the other hand, client characteristics are often invoked. It is important to keep in mind that the client and therapist both contribute to the success or nonsuccess of the therapy endeavor. For this reason, therapist characteristics should also be addressed in any discussion of the factors that can complicate treatment. Unlike client complicating factors, however, therapist complicating factors have received almost no research attention in terms of CBT for the various anxiety disorders. Thus, the following discussion is a reflection of our clinical impressions of some of the most significant therapist complicating factors: insensitivity to specific client needs, low treatment confidence, and the rigid use of treatment manuals.

Insensitivity to Specific Client Needs

All clients have specific needs. For example, some clients need to spend some time discussing the childhood origins of their adult worry and anxiety, whereas others need to get right down to "the business" of change. Some clients need the therapist to be directive during the first few treatment sessions, whereas others need to be involved in all treatment decisions right from the outset of therapy. Finally, some clients react well to (appropriate) therapist self-disclosure, whereas others feel uncomfortable when the therapist self discloses. These are just a few examples of the many specific needs that clients bring to therapy.

Obviously, if the therapist adopts a "one size fits all" attitude, many clients will not fully benefit from treatment.

One way to think about how the therapist can adapt to each client's needs and still offer a treatment of choice for GAD (whether it be the treatment described in this book or another empirically supported treatment), is to distinguish treatment procedures from how they are presented to clients. That is, meeting a client's specific needs does not mean that the therapist does away with empirically supported procedures such as imaginal exposure (much to the dismay of some clients…), but it might mean that exposure is presented and carried out in a way that is "palatable" to the client. Returning to the example of a client with significant dependent personality traits, the therapist might take on a more directive and supportive role in the beginning of therapy to facilitate client engagement. It can also be a good idea to proceed at a slightly slower pace with dependent clients so that they do not feel overwhelmed during the initial phases of treatment. Thus, the modules of the treatment described in this book can be "wrapped" differently for each client. As a result, the examples of therapist dialogue provided in chapter 5 should be adapted to fit not only with the therapist's clinical style, but also with the needs of each individual client.

Low Treatment Confidence

A second therapist factor that can seriously complicate the therapy enterprise is low treatment confidence. Given that clients are asked to engage in a treatment that is quite demanding in terms of time and effort, it is very important that the therapist model a high level of confidence in the treatment's rationale and procedures. For example, if during the problem-solving phase of treatment, a client applies a solution that does not lead to the desired outcome, the therapist should model a calm and confident attitude to help the client see that it is quite normal that initial problem-solving attempts are sometimes unsuccessful. In line with having a confident attitude, the therapist could point out that the ultimate goal of problem solving is not that clients solve all their problems, but rather that they acquire a "tool" that is known to be helpful for dealing with most problems. This illustrates an important point for therapists to keep in mind. That is, being confident in treatment does not mean that one is confident that every strategy will be helpful at all times; it simply means that one is confident that the underlying principles are sound and that the strategies will be helpful in most cases.

Low treatment confidence on the part of the therapist can be particularly obstructive when a client encounters bad luck in carrying out a between-session exercise. For example, it has happened more than once that the event described in an exposure scenario actually occurred during or after the exposure phase of treatment. In one particular instance, the client was a woman who was in remission for cancer and who was excessively worried about a potential relapse of the cancer. After having discussed the pros and cons of targeting the fear of relapse in an exposure scenario with the therapist, the client decided to proceed with imaginal exposure to cancer relapse. Unfortunately, the client actually experienced a relapse of her cancer during treatment, which led to her doubting the appropriateness of imaginal exposure. Although the therapist was very sensitive to the client's situation, he was able to not confuse the unfortunate event (cancer relapse) with the appropriateness of treatment (decreasing worry via imaginal exposure). Therefore, the therapist's high level of confidence in the treatment allowed him to be very empathetic toward the client without calling into question the treatment's rationale and procedures. The reader may be interested to know that this story has a happy ending: the client was successfully treated for her cancer relapse and she continues to enjoy an active and pleasurable life today.

Rigid Use of Treatment Manuals

Since the rise of the use of treatment manuals, there has been much debate about their clinical usefulness. Proponents of manualized treatments argue that they are useful for guiding therapists and clients through the different phases of specific treatment protocols, most of which have received at least some empirical support. Opponents of treatment manuals disagree with this position, and argue that the use of manuals leads to a rigid and one-size-fits-all approach to therapy that often devalues the role of common therapy factors such as therapist empathy and the therapeutic relationship. As the reader may guess, our position is closer to the former: we believe that manualized treatments per se are not the problem; rather, it is their improper use that can interfere with the therapist's ability to help clients benefit from treatment. Although manualized treatments can be improperly used in any number of ways, we will restrict our discussion to a common error that therapists make when using treatment manuals; namely, applying the manual in a rigid, inflexible manner.

One of the challenges faced by authors of treatment manuals (ourselves included) is to present the procedures in a way that invites their flexible use. We believe that this can best be accomplished by thoroughly discussing the theory behind the interventions, and presenting the specific procedures as *examples* of interventions that can target the underlying model components (such as intolerance of uncertainty). In this way, therapists are better able to adapt the treatment to the client's needs because they have a "theoretical blueprint" that guides them through the different phases of treatment. That is, what is most important is not the "what" (the specific treatment procedure) but the "why" (the goal of a procedure). For example, to help a client increase her tolerance for uncertainty, the therapist may use cognitive reevaluation procedures to directly challenge the client's beliefs about uncertainty. Although the cognitive reevaluation of beliefs about uncertainty is not explicitly included in the treatment described in this book, it may be helpful for some clients who are unable to deliberately face uncertainty because they have strongly held beliefs about the dangerousness of uncertainty. Thus, therapists who have a good grasp of the principles that underlie the procedures described in a treatment manual are often able to apply the treatment in a flexible and individualized manner. Consequently, one of the most effective ways that therapists can counter the tendency to use manualized treatments in a rigid fashion is to ensure that they have a firm grasp of the theoretical underpinnings of the suggested procedures.

Another way that therapists can resist the temptation to use a manualized treatment in a nonflexible fashion is to consistently remind themselves that common therapy factors make a vital contribution to successful treatment outcomes (e.g., Asay & Lambert, 1999). For example, a number of therapist characteristics appear to be decisive in the establishment of a positive therapeutic alliance and, ultimately, positive treatment outcomes. These include having a caring and involved attitude, modeling self-confidence, unconditionally accepting the client, challenging the client when appropriate, presenting material and issues in a clear and explicit way, and being willing to self-disclose when suitable (K. E. Williams & Chambless, 1990). Returning to a point made earlier, many empirical and review articles on the treatment of GAD start out by saying that up to half of individuals with GAD do not fully benefit from treatment. These articles often go on to say that this implies that our theoretical models of GAD require further refinement, without any mention of the possibility that common therapy factors such as therapist characteristics may be contributing to the fact that many clients do not fully benefit from treatment. This is surprising given that common therapy factors, such as those mentioned above, play such a vital role in the success or nonsuccess of treatment. Thus, the fact that 25 to 50% of GAD clients do not fully benefit from different forms of CBT might be the result of specific therapy factors (i.e., a lack of refinement of GAD-specific theories and treatments), common therapy factors (i.e., client, therapist, and contextual factors), or both specific and common therapy factors. It seems reasonable to assume that a combination of both types of therapy factors ultimately plays a role in the less than optimal success rates of all GAD treatments, including the treatment described in this book. By keeping this is mind, therapists may be better able to display the positive attitudes and behaviors listed above and consequently apply the principles and procedures of manualized treatments in a flexible and personalized way.

CONTEXTUAL COMPLICATING FACTORS

Many contextual factors can complicate treatment delivery and interfere with successful outcomes. Here, we discuss two such factors. First, we will address one of the most common contextual factors that can complicate the proper delivery of any psychological treatment: namely, the restricted number of psychotherapy sessions typically covered by insurance companies and managed care organizations. Afterwards, we will address a contextual factor that is specific to treatments that include audiotape- or compact disc-assisted imaginal exposure; that is, the lack of proper equipment to record the client's exposure scenario.

Restricted Insurance or Managed Care Coverage

The treatment presented in this book is typically administered over 12 to 16 sessions. Given the multiple treatment modules (psychoeducation and worry awareness training, uncertainty recognition and behavioral exposure, reevaluation of the usefulness of worry, problem-solving training, imaginal exposure, and relapse prevention), 12 sessions is probably the minimum number of sessions required to cover all of the elements of treatment (with 14 to 16 sessions being preferable in most cases). In the current health care context, however, where less than 10 treatment sessions are typically covered by insurance companies and managed health care organizations, the full treatment described in this book cannot always be offered. In situations such as these, the therapist might be at a loss as to what to do. Should each treatment module be covered briefly, or should some modules be eliminated from the treatment in order to maintain the full duration of the remaining modules? Although a case could be made either way, the findings from one of our recent studies suggest that providing training in a subset of the treatment modules might be helpful for some clients with GAD.

In our study (Provencher, Dugas, & Ladouceur, 2004), we used a case formulation approach to identify the main worry type (that is, worry about current problems or worry about hypothetical situations) for 18 clients with a primary diagnosis of GAD. First, we found that it was possible to reliably determine the main worry type for each client, with 8 clients mainly reporting worries about current problems and 10 clients mainly reporting worries about hypothetical situations. We then proceeded to offer different scaled-down versions of the treatment to each group of participants: those who worried mainly about current problems received the treatment protocol *minus imaginal exposure*, and those who worried mainly about hypothetical situations received the treatment protocol *minus problem-solving training*. Overall, we found that both versions of the treatment were effective, with no significant differences between the two treatments. Although this truncated approach to the treatment of GAD does not appear to be as effective as the full treatment protocol, the data suggest that it represents a relatively effective way of treating GAD. Thus, it appears to represent a promising alternative when insurance or managed care coverage limits the number of therapy sessions.

Although the findings of the case formulation study are encouraging, it is our position that therapists should make every effort to offer 14 to 16 sessions in order to properly cover all treatment modules. Although we have yet to systematically dismantle the treatment protocol to compare the efficacy of each module to the overall treatment, there are strong theoretical reasons why all modules should be offered to clients with GAD. In our opinion, one of the strengths of the treatment protocol is that clients learn to better deal with outside sources of worry (real-life problems) as well as internal processes that contribute to worry (cognitive and affective avoidance). It stands to reason that when clients can better deal with both external and internal sources of worry, they stand a better chance of achieving significant gains in therapy and maintaining these gains after treatment has ended. Moreover, problem-solving training and imaginal exposure are strategies that can be used for a broad range of anxiety-related problems. When clients become "believers" in these strategies, they arguably possess two of the most important sets of skills for the prevention of further anxiety-related problems. Thus, if possible, the therapist should strive to provide the full treatment protocol to all clients suffering from GAD.

Lack of Proper Equipment for Imaginal Exposure

In all of our previous clinical trials, imaginal exposure was carried out using a looped audiotape (that is, a cassette for a telephone answering machine) or a compact disc. Specifically, clients prepared a written exposure scenario, recorded the scenario on the audiotape or disc, and then repeatedly listened to the scenario until it no longer provoked an anxious response. This procedure has many advantages. For example, it provides the therapist with an opportunity to review and correct the scenario before it is recorded, it allows the therapist to know exactly what the client is exposed to, and it (arguably) facilitates exposure because clients only have to focus on the recorded message rather than actually formulating the scenario themselves during exposure. On the flip side, however, audiotape- or compact disc-assisted exposure requires that the therapist has the proper equipment available to record the scenario (which is typically done in the therapist's office). Furthermore, technical problems can sometimes be encountered when recording the scenario or using the recording to carry out exposure. For example, the quality of the recording may be poor (e.g., too much background noise) or the cassette/compact disc may become defective at some time during the exposure phase of treatment. For any one of these reasons, the therapist may wish to offer a "technology-free" form of exposure to clients. Given that exposure can be carried out in a number of ways, we have recently begun to experiment with another form of exposure which does not require that the scenario be recorded on an audiotape or a compact disc.

In the field of health psychology, a method known as *written emotional disclosure* has been shown to lead to positive health outcomes. Specifically, when individuals systematically and repeatedly write about emotionally charged past events, they typically report positive health outcomes in the weeks and months that follow the writing episodes (e.g., Pennebaker, Colder, & Sharp, 1990). Although the benefits of written emotional disclosure were originally conceived of in terms of psychodynamic theory, recent studies suggest that it is basically a form of exposure, and that its benefits can be understood in terms of exposure theories of cognitive and emotional processing (Sloan & Marx, 2004). Surprisingly, written forms of exposure have rarely been used in the treatment of anxiety disorders in general and GAD in particular. Given that written exposure can serve as a structuring context that facilitates the activation and processing of core fears, we have recently come to the conclusion that it may represent an appropriate substitute for audiotape- or compact disc-assisted imaginal exposure.

Although we have just begun to collect data on the efficacy of written exposure for worry and GAD, our initial findings are encouraging. For example, in a nonclinical sample of 30 high worriers, we found that written exposure led to decreases in worry, whereas a control condition where participants were asked to write about a nonthreatening future event did not (Goldman, Sexton, Gervais, & Dugas, 2006). In clinical participants, we have begun using written exposure for some

GAD clients and have obtained positive results. Specifically, clients first use the downward arrow procedure to identify one or more core fears. They then write about the core fear for 30 minutes every day and are encouraged to go "deeper" into their fear with each writing session. Thus far, we have found that two to three weeks of written exposure is sufficient for clients to process their fears (about the same number of sessions as for imaginal exposure). In summary, although we are just beginning to assess the efficacy of written exposure for the treatment of GAD, we have reason to believe that it represents a suitable procedure when audiotape- or compact disc-assisted imaginal exposure is not feasible.

In the preceding sections, we have reviewed the main factors that can complicate the delivery, receipt, and enactment of the treatment described in this book. Although there are many other potential complicating factors, we have tried to focus on those that are most frequently encountered by therapists using our treatment protocol. In Table 7.1, we present a summary of the complicating factors and potential solutions discussed in this chapter.

CONCLUDING REMARKS

When we set out to write this book, we had a number of goals in mind. First, we wanted to provide therapists with up-to-date general information on GAD. This seemed particularly important given the widely held assumptions that individuals with GAD are "worried well" and that the symptoms of GAD lead to only minor distress and impairment. As anyone with GAD will attest, experiencing chronic and excessive worry and anxiety on a daily basis is highly distressing and seriously interferes with one's quality of life. A second goal of ours was to present therapists with a theoretical model that could guide their clinical practice with GAD clients. In doing so, we hoped that therapists would be in a better position to conceptualize their clients' behaviors, thoughts, and emotional reactions in terms of a "theoretical blueprint" that could aid in making sense of the apparently contradictory manifestations of GAD. For example, approach behaviors such as information seeking and avoidance behaviors such as procrastination can both be seen as manifestations of an underlying intolerance of uncertainty, and as such may ultimately serve a similar function.

Our third (and perhaps primary) goal in writing this book was to strike a balance between presenting a clearly articulated treatment protocol that clinicians would find helpful in their everyday practice, and respecting the complex, dynamic, and idiosyncratic nature of the

TABLE 7.1 Complicating Factors and Potential Solutions

Complicating Factors	Potential Solutions
Client Factors	
Axis I Comorbidity	
Panic disorder	Spend additional time on exposure Schedule booster sessions
Major depressive disorder	Keep depressogenic elements in exposure scenario to a minimum
Axis II Comorbidity	Present treatment procedures differently according to comorbid personality disorders
Medical Comorbidity	
Heart condition	Obtain medical clearance Model confidence with regards to exposure
Cancer remission	Determine appropriateness of exposure on a case-by-case basis Proscribe avoidance and neutralization
Pregnancy[1]	Determine appropriateness of exposure on a case-by-case basis Proscribe avoidance and neutralization
Use of Medication	Address attributions about the sources of progress as necessary
Low Treatment Motivation	Return to treatment rationale Adjust therapeutic style Integrate motivational interviewing
Therapist Factors	
Insensitivity to Client Needs	Distinguish between treatment procedures and how they are presented and prescribed
Low Treatment Confidence	Conceptualize confidence in terms of process rather than outcome Remember that "bad luck" does not invalidate treatment rationale
Rigid Use of Manual	Thoroughly understand the theory behind the treatment See treatment procedures as examples of strategies to target underlying model components Seek out knowledge of common therapy factors

– Continued

TABLE 7.1 Complicating Factors and Potential Solutions

Complicating Factors	Potential Solutions
Contextual Factors	
Limited Number of Covered Sessions	Focus on problem-solving training *or* cognitive exposure according to the client's needs
Exposure Recording is Not Practical	Use written exposure

[1] *Although pregnancy is not a medical syndrome, we have placed it within the category of "Medical Comorbidity" because it is a physical condition that can complicate treatment.*

treatment of individuals with GAD. As discussed in this chapter, many factors can complicate treatment delivery, receipt, and enactment. In most cases, the therapist can deal with the complicating factors by having a thorough understanding of the theoretical underpinnings of the treatment, the specific treatment procedures, and the common factors that underlie all forms of psychological treatments. Having said this, however, the therapy enterprise remains an extremely complex (and rewarding) endeavor that requires a great deal of knowledge, clinical judgment, and "positive attitudes" on the part of the therapist. Given this state of affairs, our goal was to make available our treatment protocol to clinicians working with GAD clients, but to present it in a way that did not encourage a "cookbook" approach to treatment (the reader may have noticed that the word *technique* rarely appears in this book as we believe that it may give the impression that a given treatment procedure is not grounded in theory).

It was also our hope that this book would present the findings from our clinical trials in a way that would be "palatable" to clinicians. To accomplish this, we focused on the main findings of each study and emphasized the interpretation of the data over the presentation of the findings. Relatedly, we made every effort to present the data in a way that would help clinicians to truly feel confident about the treatment procedures. In our experience, when the therapist models self-confidence, clients stand a much better chance of fully benefiting from the treatment protocol.

On a final note, we would like to emphasize that the model and treatment described in this book are both works in progress. We are currently pursuing a number of lines of research that we hope will allow us to modify our theory and treatment in ways that are increasingly reflective of the clinical reality of GAD. By "following the data," we hope to be able to help more and more individuals suffering from GAD to finally break out of their worry and anxiety cycles and enjoy a greater quality of life.

References

Akiskal, H. S. (1998). Toward a definition of generalized anxiety disorder as an anxious temperament type. *Acta Psychiatrica Scandinavica, 98*, 66–73.

American Psychiatric Association. (1980). *Diagnostic and statistical manual of mental disorders* (3rd ed.). Washington, D.C.

American Psychiatric Association. (1987). *Diagnostic and statistical manual of mental disorders* (3rd ed. revised). Washington, D.C.

American Psychiatric Association. (1994). *Diagnostic and statistical manual of mental disorders* (4th ed.). Washington, D.C.

American Psychiatric Association. (2000). *Diagnostic and statistical manual of mental disorders: Text revision* (4th ed. rev.). Washington, D.C.

Asay, T. P., & Lambert, M. J. (1999). The empirical case for the common factors in therapy: Quantitative findings. In M. A. Hubble, B. L. Duncan, & S. D. Miller (Eds.), *The heart and soul of change: What works in therapy* (pp. 23–55). Washington, D.C.: American Psychological Association.

Ashton, C. H. (2001). *Benzodiazepines: How they work and how to withdraw.* Newcastle upon Tyne, U.K.: Newcastle University.

Atkins, D. C., Bedics, J. D., McGlinchey, J. B., & Beauchaine, T. P. (2005). Assessing clinical significance: Does it matter which method we use? *Journal of Consulting and Clinical Psychology, 73*, 982–989.

Bakerman, D., Buhr, K., Koerner, N., & Dugas, M. J. (2004, November). *Exploring the link between positive beliefs about worry and worry.* Poster presented at the Annual Convention of the Association for Advancement of Behavior Therapy, New Orleans, LA.

Barlow, D. H., Rapee, R. M., & Brown, T. A. (1992). Behavioral treatment of generalized anxiety disorder. *Behavior Therapy, 23*, 551–570.

Barlow, D. H., & Wincze, J. (1998). DSM-IV and beyond: What is generalized anxiety disorder? *Acta Psychiatrica Scandinavica, 98,* 23–29.

Barrett, J., Oxman, T. E., & Gerber, P. D. (1988). The prevalence of psychiatric disorders in primary care practice. *Archives of General Psychiatry, 45,* 1100–1106.

Beck, A. T., & Clark, D. A. (1997). An information processing model of anxiety: Automatic and strategic processes. *Behaviour Research and Therapy, 35,* 49–58.

Beck, A. T., & Emery, G. (1985). *Anxiety disorders and phobias: A cognitive perspective.* New York: Basic Books.

Beck, A. T., Epstein, N., Brown, G., & Steer, R. A. (1988). An inventory for measuring clinical anxiety: Psychometric properties. *Journal of Consulting and Clinical Psychology, 56,* 893–897.

Beck, A. T., Steer, R. A., & Brown, G. K. (1996). *Beck depression inventory manual* (2nd ed.). San Antonio, TX: Psychological Corporation.

Becker, E. S., Rinck, M., Roth, W. T., & Margraf, J. (1998). Don't worry and beware of white bears: Thought suppression in anxiety clients. *Journal of Anxiety Disorders, 12,* 39–55.

Beekman, A. T. F., Bremmer, M. A., Deeg, D. J. H., Van Balkom, A. J. L. M., Smit, J. H., De Beurs, E. et al. (1998). Anxiety disorders in later life: A report from the Longitudinal Aging Study Amsterdam. *International Journal of Geriatric Psychiatry, 13,* 717–726.

Behar, E., Vescio, T. K., & Borkovec, T. D. (2005). The effects of suppressing thoughts and images about worrisome stimuli. *Behavior Therapy, 36,* 289–298.

Blazer, D., Hughes, D., & George, L. K. (1987). Stressful life events and the onset of a generalized anxiety syndrome. *American Journal of Psychiatry, 144,* 1178–1183.

Blazer, D. G., Hughes, D., George, L. K., Schwartz, M., & Boyer, R. (1991). Generalized anxiety disorder. In L. N. Robins & D. A. Regier (Eds.), *Psychiatric disorders in America. The Epidemiologic Catchment Area Study* (pp. 180–203). New York: Free Press.

Borkovec, T. D. (2006). Applied relaxation and cognitive therapy for pathological worry and generalized anxiety disorder. In G. C. L. Davey &, A. Wells (Eds.), *Worry and psychological disorders: Theory, assessment and treatment* (pp. 273–287). Chichester, U.K.: Wiley.

Borkovec, T. D., Abel, J. L., & Newman, H. (1995). Effects of psychotherapy on comorbid conditions in generalized anxiety disorder. *Journal of Consulting and Clinical Psychology, 63,* 479–483.

Borkovec, T. D., & Costello, E. (1993). Efficacy of applied relaxation and cognitive-behavioral therapy in the treatment of generalized anxiety disorder. *Journal of Consulting and Clinical Psychology, 61*, 611–619.

Borkovec, T. D., & Hu, S. (1990). The effect of worry on cardiovascular response to phobic imagery. *Behaviour Research and Therapy, 28*, 69–73.

Borkovec, T. D., & Inz, J. (1990). The nature of worry in generalized anxiety disorder: A predominance of thought activity. *Behaviour Research and Therapy, 28*, 153–158.

Borkovec, T. D., Newman, M. G., Pincus, A. L., & Lytle, R. (2002). A component analysis of cognitive-behavioral therapy for generalized anxiety disorder and the role of interpersonal problems. *Journal of Consulting and Clinical Psychology, 70*, 288–298.

Brown, T. A., & Barlow, D. H. (1992). Comorbidity among anxiety disorders: Implications for treatment and *DSM-IV*. *Journal of Consulting and Clinical Psychology, 60*, 835–844.

Brown, T. A., Barlow, D. H., & Liebowitz, M. R. (1994). The empirical basis of generalized anxiety disorder. *American Journal of Psychiatry, 151*, 1272–1280.

Brown, T. A., Chorpita, B. F., & Barlow, D. H. (1998). Structural relationships among dimensions of the *DSM–IV* anxiety and mood disorders and dimensions of negative affect, positive affect, and autonomic arousal. *Journal of Abnormal Psychology, 107*, 179–192.

Brown, T. A., Di Nardo, P. A., Lehman, C. L., & Campbell, L. A. (2001). Reliability of *DSM-IV* anxiety and mood disorders: Implications for classification of emotional disorders. *Journal of Abnormal Psychology, 110*, 49–58.

Brown, T. A., Moras, K., Zinbarg, R. E., & Barlow, D. H. (1993). Diagnostic and symptom distinguishability of generalized anxiety disorder and obsessive–compulsive disorder. *Behavior Therapy, 24*, 227–240.

Brown, T. A., O'Leary, T. A., & Barlow, D. H. (1993). Generalized anxiety disorder. In D. H. Barlow (Ed.), *Clinical handbook of psychological disorders* (pp. 137–189). New York: Guilford.

Buhr, K., & Dugas, M. J. (2002). The Intolerance of Uncertainty Scale: Psychometric properties of the English version. *Behaviour Research and Therapy, 40*, 931–945.

Buhr, K., & Dugas, M. J. (2006). Investigating the construct validity of intolerance of uncertainty and its unique relationship with worry. *Journal of Anxiety Disorders, 20*, 222–236.

Burns, D. D. (1989). *The feeling good handbook: Using the new mood therapy in everyday life*. New York: William Morrow.

Carter, R. M., Wittchen, H.-U., Pfister, H., & Kessler, R. C. (2001). One-year prevalence of subthreshold and threshold *DSM-IV* generalized anxiety disorder in a nationally representative sample. *Depression and Anxiety, 13,* 78–88.

Chambless, D. L., Baker, M. J., Baucom, D. H., Beutler, L. E., Calhoun, K. S., Crits-Christoph, P. et al. (1998). Update on empirically validated therapies, II. *The Clinical Psychologist, 51,* 3–15.

Cole, D. A., Peeke, L. G., Martin, J. M., Truglio, R., & Seroczynski, A. D. (1998). A longitudinal look at the relation between depression and anxiety in children and adolescents. *Journal of Consulting and Clinical Psychology, 66,* 451–460.

Craske, M. G., Barlow, D. H., & O'Leary, T. A. (1992). *Mastery of your anxiety and worry*. San Antonio, TX: The Psychological Corporation.

Davey, G. C. L. (1994). Worrying, social problem-solving abilities, and social problem-solving confidence. *Behaviour Research and Therapy, 32,* 327–330.

Davey, G. C. L., Tallis, F., & Capuzzo, N. (1996). Beliefs about the consequences of worrying. *Cognitive Therapy and Research, 20,* 499–520.

Di Nardo, P. A., Brown, T. A., & Barlow, D. H. (1994). *Anxiety disorders interview schedule for DSM-IV: Lifetime version (ADIS-IV-L)*. San Antonio, TX: Psychological Corporation/Graywind.

Doucet, C., Ladouceur, R., Freeston, M. H., & Dugas, M. J. (1998). Thèmes d'inquiétudes et tendance à s'inquiéter chez les aînés. [Worry themes and the tendency to worry among older adults.] *Revue Canadienne du Vieillissement, 17,* 361–371.

Dreessen, L., Arntz, A., Luttels, C., & Sallaerts, S. (1994). Personality disorders do not influence the results of cognitive behavior therapies for anxiety disorders. *Comprehensive Psychiatry, 35,* 265–274.

Dugas, M. J., Freeston, M. H., & Ladouceur, R. (1997). Intolerance of uncertainty and problem orientation in worry. *Cognitive Therapy and Research, 21,* 593–606.

Dugas, M. J., Freeston, M. H., Ladouceur, R., Rhéaume, J., Provencher, M., & Boisvert, J.-M. (1998). Worry themes in primary GAD, secondary GAD, and other anxiety disorders. *Journal of Anxiety Disorders, 12,* 253–261.

Dugas, M. J., Freeston, M. H., Provencher, M. D., Lachance, S., Ladouceur, R., & Gosselin, P. (2001). Le Questionnaire sur l'inquiétude et l'anxiété: Validation dans des échantillons non cliniques et cliniques. [The Worry and Anxiety Questionnaire: Validation in clinical and nonclinical samples.] *Journal de Thérapie Comportementale et Cognitive, 11,* 31–36.

Dugas, M. J., Gagnon, F., Ladouceur, R., & Freeston, H. (1998). Generalized anxiety disorder: A preliminary test of a conceptual model. *Behaviour Research and Therapy, 36,* 215–226.

Dugas, M. J., Gosselin, P., & Ladouceur, R. (2001). Intolerance of uncertainty and worry: Investigating specificity in a nonclinical sample. *Cognitive Therapy and Research, 25,* 551–558.

Dugas, M. J., Hedayati, M., Karavidas, A., Buhr, K., Francis, K., & Phillips, N. A. (2005). Intolerance of uncertainty and information processing: Evidence of biased recall and interpretations. *Cognitive Therapy and Research, 29,* 57–70.

Dugas, M. J., Ladouceur, R., Léger, E., Freeston, M. H., Langlois, F., Provencher, M. D. et al. (2003). Group cognitive-behavioral therapy for generalized anxiety disorder: Treatment outcome and long-term follow-up. *Journal of Consulting and Clinical Psychology, 71,* 821–825.

Dugas, M. J., Ladouceur, R., Léger, E., Langlois, F., Provencher, M. D., Boisvert, J.-M. et al. (2003, November). *Group CBT for generalized anxiety disorder: Does change in tolerance for uncertainty predict symptom change beyond non-specific therapy factors?* Poster session presented at the Annual Convention of the Association for Advancement of Behavior Therapy, Boston, MA.

Dugas, M. J., Langlois, F., Rhéaume, J., & Ladouceur, R. (1998, November). Intolerance of uncertainty and worry: Investigating causality. In J. Stöber (Chair), *Worry: New findings in applied and clinical research.* Symposium conducted at the Annual Convention of the Association for Advancement of Behavior Therapy, Washington, D.C.

Dugas, M. J., Letarte, H., Rhéaume, J., Freeston, M. H., & Ladouceur, R. (1995). Worry and problem-solving: Evidence of a specific relationship. *Cognitive Therapy and Research, 19,* 109–120.

Dugas, M. J., Marchand, A., & Ladouceur, R. (2005). Further validation of a cognitive-behavioral model of generalized anxiety disorder: Diagnostic and symptom specificity. *Journal of Anxiety Disorders, 19,* 329–343.

Dugas, M. J., Savard, P., Gaudet, A., Turcotte, J., Brillon, P., Leblanc, R. et al. (2004, November). Cognitive-behavioral therapy *versus* applied relaxation for generalized anxiety disorder: Differential outcomes and processes. In H. Hazlett-Stevens (Chair), *New advances in the treatment of chronic worry and generalized anxiety disorder.* Symposium conducted at the Annual Convention of the Association for Advancement of Behavior Therapy, New Orleans, LA.

Dugas, M. J., Savard, P., Gaudet, A., Turcotte, J., Laugesen, N., Robichaud, M. et al. (in press). Can the components of a cognitive model predict the severity of generalized anxiety disorder? *Behavior Therapy.*

Dugas, M. J., Schwartz, A., & Francis, K. (2004). Intolerance of uncertainty, worry, and depression. *Cognitive Therapy and Research, 28,* 835–842.

Dupont, R. L., Rice, D. P., Miller, L. S., Shiraki, S. S., Rowland, C. R., & Harwood, H. J. (1996). Economic costs of anxiety disorders. *Anxiety, 2,* 167–172.

D'Zurilla, T. J., & Nezu, A. M. (1999). *Problem-solving therapy : A social competence approach to clinical intervention.* New York: Springer.

D'Zurilla, T. J., Nezu, A. M., & Maydeu-Olivares, A. (1998). *Manual for the social problem-solving inventory* (Revised). North Tonawanda, NY: Multi-Health Systems.

Eysenck, M. W., Mogg, K., May, J., Richards, A., & Mathews, A. (1991). Bias in interpretation of ambiguous sentences related to threat in anxiety. *Journal of Abnormal Psychology, 100,* 144–150.

First, M. B., Spitzer, R. L., Gibbon, M., & Williams, J. B. W. (1996). *Structured clinical interview for DSM-IV axis I disorders, clinician version (SCID-CV).* Washington, D.C.: American Psychiatric Press.

First, M. B., Spitzer, R. L., Gibbon, M., & Williams, J. B. W. (2002). *Structured clinical interview for DSM-IV-TR axis I disorders, research version, patient edition. (SCID-I/P).* New York: Biometrics Research, New York State Psychiatric Institute.

Foa, E. B., & Kozak, M. J. (1986). Emotional processing of fear: Exposure to corrective information. *Psychological Bulletin, 99,* 20–35.

Freeston, M. H., Rhéaume, J., Letarte, H., Dugas, M. J., & Ladouceur, R. (1994). Why do people worry? *Personality and Individual Differences, 17,* 791–802.

Frisch, M. B. (1994). *Quality of life inventory: Manual and treatment guide.* Minneapolis, MN: National Computer Systems.

Goldman, N., Sexton, K. A., Gervais, N. J., & Dugas, M. J. (2006, May). *The efficacy of written exposure for worry.* Poster session presented at the Annual Convention of the American Psychiatric Association, Toronto, ON, Canada.

Gosselin, P., Ladouceur, R., Langlois, F., Freeston, M. H., Dugas, M. J., & Bertrand, J. (2003). Développement et validation d'un nouvel instrument évaluant les croyances erronées à l'égard des inquiétudes [Development and validation of a new instrument evaluating erroneous beliefs about worry.] *European Review of Applied Psychology, 53,* 199–211.

Gosselin, P., Ladouceur, R., Morin, C. M., Dugas, M. J., & Baillargeon, L. (in press). Benzodiazepine discontinuation among clients with generalized anxiety disorder: A randomized trial of cognitive-behavioral therapy. *Journal of Consulting and Clinical Psychology.*

Gosselin, P., Ladouceur, R., & Pelletier, O. (2005). Évaluation de l'attitude d'un individu face aux différents problèmes de vie: le Questionnaire d'Attitude face aux Problèmes (QAP) [Evaluation of an individual's attitude toward daily life problems: The Negative Problem Orientation Questionnaire.] *Journal de Thérapie Comportementale et Cognitive, 15,* 141–153.

Gosselin, P., Langlois, F., Freeston, M. H., Ladouceur, R., Dugas, M. J., & Pelletier, O. (2002). Le Questionnaire d'évitement cognitif (QEC): Développement et validation auprès d'adultes et d'adolescents. [The Cognitive Avoidance Questionnaire (CAQ): Development and validation among adult and adolescent samples.] *Journal de Thérapie Comportementale et Cognitive, 12,* 24–37.

Greenberg, P. E., Sisitsky, T., Kessler, R. C., Finkelstein, S. N., Berndt, E. R., Davidson, J. R. T. et al. (1999). The economic burden of anxiety disorders in the 1990s. *Journal of Clinical Psychiatry, 60,* 427–435.

Hoehn-Saric, R., Hazlett, R. L., & McLeod, D. R. (1993). Generalized anxiety disorder with early and late onset of anxiety symptoms. *Comprehensive Psychiatry, 34,* 291–298.

Holaway, R. M., Heimberg, R. G., & Coles, M. E. (2006). A comparison of intolerance of uncertainty in analogue obsessive–compulsive disorder and generalized anxiety disorder. *Journal of Anxiety Disorders, 20,* 158–174.

Holowka, D. W., Dugas, M. J., Francis, K., & Laugesen, N. (2000, November). *Measuring beliefs about worry: A psychometric evaluation of the Why Worry-II questionnaire.* Poster presented at the Annual Convention of the Association for Advancement of Behavior Therapy, New Orleans, LA.

Hoyer, J., Becker, E. S., & Roth, W. T. (2001). Characteristics of worry in GAD patients, social phobics, and controls. *Depression and Anxiety, 13,* 89–96.

Hunt, C., Issakidis, C., & Andrews, G. (2002). *DSM-IV* generalized anxiety disorder in the Australian National Survey of Mental Health and Well-Being. *Psychological Medicine, 32,* 649–659.

Jacobson, N. S., & Truax, P. (1991). Clinical significance: A statistical approach to defining meaningful change in psychotherapy research. *Journal of Consulting and Clinical Psychology, 59,* 12–19.

Kennedy, B. L., & Schwab, J. J. (1997). Utilization of medical specialists by anxiety disorder patients. *Psychosomatics, 38,* 109–112.

Kessler, R. C., Keller, M. B., & Wittchen, H.-U. (2001). The epidemiology of generalized anxiety disorder. *Psychiatric Clinics of North America, 24,* 19–39.

Kessler, R. C., McGonagle, K. A., Zhao, S., Nelson, C. B., Hugues, M., Eshleman, S. et al. (1994). Lifetime and 12-month prevalence of *DSM-III-R* psychiatric disorders in the United States. *Archives of General Psychiatry, 51,* 8–19.

Kessler, R. C., Walters, E. E., & Wittchen, H.-U. (2004). Epidemiology. In R. G. Heimberg, C. L. Turk, & D. S. Mennin (Eds.), *Generalized anxiety disorder: Advances in research and practice* (pp. 29–50). New York: Guilford.

Koerner, N., Dugas, M. J., Savard, P., Gaudet, A., Turcotte, J., & Marchand, A. (2004). The economic burden of anxiety disorders in Canada. *Canadian Psychology, 45,* 191–201.

Kraemer, H. C., Kazdin, A. E., Offord, D. R., Kessler, R. C., Jensen, P. S., & Kupfer, D. J. (1997). Coming to terms with the terms of risk. *Archives of General Psychiatry, 54,* 337–343.

Laberge, M., Dugas, M. J., & Ladouceur, R. (2000). Modification des croyances relatives aux inquiétudes après traitement du trouble d'anxiété généralisée [Modification of beliefs about worry following treatment for generalized anxiety disorder.] *Revue Canadienne des Sciences du Comportement, 32,* 91–96.

Ladouceur, R., Blais, F., Freeston, M. H., & Dugas, M. J. (1998). Problem solving and problem orientation in generalized anxiety disorder. *Journal of Anxiety Disorders, 12,* 139–152.

Ladouceur, R., Dugas, M. J., Freeston, M. H., Léger, E., Gagnon, F., & Thibodeau, N. (2000). Efficacy of a cognitive-behavioral treatment for generalized anxiety disorder: Evaluation in a controlled clinical trial. *Journal of Consulting and Clinical Psychology, 68,* 957–964.

Ladouceur, R., Dugas, M. J., Freeston, M. H., Rhéaume, J., Blais, F., Boisvert, J.-M. et al. (1999). Specificity of generalized anxiety disorder symptoms and processes. *Behavior Therapy, 30*, 191–207.

Ladouceur, R., Gosselin, P., & Dugas, M. J. (2000). Experimental manipulation of intolerance of uncertainty: A study of a theoretical model of worry. *Behaviour Research and Therapy, 38*, 933–941.

Ladouceur, R., Talbot, F., & Dugas, M. J. (1997). Behavioral expressions of intolerance of uncertainty in worry. *Behavior Modification, 21,* 355–371.

Laugesen, N., Dugas, M. J., & Bukowski, W. M. (2003). Understanding adolescent worry: The application of a cognitive model. *Journal of Abnormal Child Psychology, 31,* 55–64.

Lecrubier, Y., Sheehan, D., Weiller, E., Amorim, P., Bonora, I., Sheehan, K. et al. (1997). The Mini International Neuropsychiatric Interview (M.I.N.I.), a short diagnostic structured interview: Reliability and validity according to the CIDI. *European Psychiatry, 12,* 224–231.

Léger, E., Dugas, M. J., Langlois, F., & Ladouceur, R. (1998, November). *Motivation, expectations and therapeutic relationship as predictors of outcome in the treatment of GAD.* Poster session presented at the Annual Convention of the Association for Advancement of Behavior Therapy, Washington, D.C.

Logue, M. B., Thomas, A. M., Barbee, J. G., Hoehn–Saric, R., Maddock, R. J., Schwab, J. et al. (1993). Generalized anxiety disorder patients seek evaluation for cardiological symptoms at the same frequency as patients with panic disorder. *Journal of Psychiatric Research, 27,* 55–59.

MacLeod, A. K., Williams, J. M. G., & Bekerian, D. A. (1991). Worry is reasonable: The role of explanations in pessimism about future personal events. *Journal of Abnormal Psychology, 100,* 478–486.

Maier, W., Gansicke, M., Freyberger, H. J., Linz, M., Heun, R., & Lecrubier, Y. (2000). Generalized anxiety disorder (ICD–10) in primary care from a cross–cultural perspective: A valid diagnostic entity? *Acta Psychiatrica Scandinavica, 101,* 29–36.

Maser, J. D. (1998). Generalized anxiety disorder and its comorbidities: Disputes at the boundaries. *Acta Psychiatrica Scandinavica, 98,* 12–22.

Mathews, A., & Milroy, R. (1994). Effects of priming and suppression of worry. *Behaviour Research and Therapy, 32,* 843–850.

Mennin, D. S., Heimberg, R. G., Turk, C. L., & Fresco, D. M. (2002). Applying an emotion regulation framework to integrative approaches to generalized anxiety disorder. *Clinical Psychology: Science and Practice, 9,* 85–90.

Metzger, R. L., Miller, M. L., Cohen, M., & Sofka, M., Borkovec, T. D. (1990). Worry changes decision making: The effect of negative thoughts on cognitive processing. *Journal of Clinical Psychology, 46,* 78–88.

Meyer, T. J., Miller, M. L., Metzger, R. L., & Borkovec, T. D. (1990). Development and validation of the Penn State Worry Questionnaire. *Behaviour Research and Therapy, 28,* 487–495.

Miller, W. R., & Rollnick, S. (2002). *Motivational interviewing: Preparing people for change* (2nd ed.). New York: Guilford.

Mogg, K., Bradley, B. P., Miller, T., & Potts, H. (1994). Interpretation of homophones related to threat: Anxiety or response bias effects? *Cognitive Therapy and Research, 18,* 461–477.

Molina, S., & Borkovec, T. D. (1994). The Penn State Worry Questionnaire: Psychometric properties and associated characteristics. In G. C. L. Davey, & F. Tallis (Eds.), *Perspectives on theory, assessment, and treatment* (pp. 265–283). Chichester, U.K.: Wiley.

Nolen–Hoeksema, S. (1998). The other end of the continuum: The costs of rumination. *Psychological Inquiry, 9,* 216–219.

Öst, L. G., & Breitholtz, E. (2000). Applied relaxation vs. cognitive therapy in the treatment of generalized anxiety disorder. *Behaviour Research and Therapy, 38,* 770–790.

Pennebaker, J. W., Colder, M., & Sharp, L. K. (1990). Accelerating the coping process. *Journal of Personality and Social Psychology, 58,* 528–537.

Prochaska, J. O., & Norcross, J. C. (2001). Stages of changes. *Psychotherapy, 38,* 443–448.

Provencher, M. D., Dugas, M. J., & Ladouceur, R. (2004). Efficacy of problem-solving training and cognitive exposure in the treatment of Generalized Anxiety Disorder: A case replication series. *Cognitive and Behavioral Practice, 11,* 404–414.

Provencher, M. D., Freeston, M. H., Dugas, M. J., & Ladouceur, R. (2000). Catastrophizing assessment of worry and threat schemata among worriers. *Behavioural and Cognitive Psychotherapy, 28,* 211–224.

Provencher, M. D., Ladouceur, R., & Dugas, M. J. (2006). La comorbidité dans le trouble d'anxiété généralisée: Prévalence et évolution suite à une thérapie cognitivo-comportementale [Comorbidity in generalized anxiety disorder: Prevalence and course after cognitive-behavioural therapy.] *Canadian Journal of Psychiatry, 51,* 91–99.

Pruzinsky, T., & Borkovec, T. D. (1990). Cognitive and personality characteristics of worriers. *Behaviour Research and Therapy, 28,* 507–512.

Rapee, R. M. (1991). Generalized anxiety disorder: A review of clinical features and theoretical concepts. *Clinical Psychology Review, 11,* 419–440.

Robichaud, M., & Dugas, M. J. (2005a). Negative problem orientation (part I): Psychometric properties of a new measure. *Behaviour Research and Therapy, 43,* 391–401.

Robichaud, M., & Dugas, M. J. (2005b). Negative problem orientation (part II): Construct validity and specificity to worry. *Behaviour Research and Therapy, 43,* 403–412.

Robichaud, M., Dugas, M. J., & Conway, M. (2003). Gender differences in worry and associated cognitive-behavioral variables. *Journal of Anxiety Disorders, 17,* 501–516.

Robichaud, M., Dugas, M. J., & Radomsky, A. S. (2006). *The role of intolerance of uncertainty in problem-solving ability.* Manuscript submitted for publication.

Roemer, L., & Orsillo, S. M. (2002). Expanding our conceptualization of and treatment for generalized anxiety disorder: Integrating mindfulness/acceptance-based approaches with existing cognitive-behavioral models. *Clinical Psychology: Science and Practice, 9,* 54–68.

Roy-Byrne, P. P., & Katon, W. (1997). Generalized anxiety disorder in primary care: The precursor/modifier pathway to increased health-care utilization. *Journal of Clinical Psychiatry, 58,* 34–38.

Sexton, K. A., & Dugas, M. J. (2004, November). *An investigation of the factors leading to cognitive avoidance in worry.* Poster presented at the Annual Convention of the Association for Advancement of Behavior Therapy, New Orleans, LA.

Sexton, K. A., Dugas, M. J., & Hedayati, M. (2004, November). *The cognitive avoidance questionnaire: Validation of the English translation.* Poster presented at the Annual Convention of the Association for Advancement of Behavior Therapy, New Orleans, LA.

Sheehan, D. V., Lecrubier, Y., Harnett–Sheehan, K., Janavs, J., Weiller, E., Bonara, L. I. et al. (1997). Reliability and validity of the MINI International Neuropsychiatric Interview (M.I.N.I.): According to the SCID-P. *European Psychiatry, 12,* 232–241.

Sheehan, D. V., Lecrubier, Y., Sheehan, H., Amorim, P., Janavs, J., Weiller, E. et al. (1998). The Mini International Neuropsychiatric Interview (M. I. N. I.): The development and validation of a structured diagnostic psychiatric interview for *DSM-IV* and ICD-10. *Journal of Clinical Psychiatry,* 59 (Suppl. 20), 22–33.

Sloan, D. M., & Marx, B. P. (2004). A closer examination of the structured written disclosure procedure. *Journal of Consulting and Clinical Psychology, 72,* 165–175.

Sprujit–Metz, D., & Sprujit–Metz, R. (1997). Worries and health in adolescence: A latent variable approach. *Journal of Youth and Adolescence, 26,* 485–501.

Stanley, M. A., & Novy, D. M. (2000). Cognitive-behavior therapy for generalized anxiety in late life: An evaluative overview. *Journal of Anxiety Disorders, 14,* 191–207.

Stein, M. B. (2004). Public health perspectives on generalized anxiety disorder. *Journal of Clinical Psychiatry, 65,* 3–7.

Stein, M. B., & Heimberg, R. G. (2004). Well-being and life satisfaction in generalized anxiety disorder: Comparison to major depressive disorder in a community sample. *Journal of Affective Disorders, 79,* 161–166.

Talbot, F., Dugas, M. J., & Ladouceur, R. (1999). Intolérance à l'incertitude et inquiétude: Effet de l'induction d'anxiété [Intolerance of uncertainty and worry: Effect of anxiety induction]. *Revue Francophone de Clinique Comportementale et Cognitive, 4,* 5–10.

Tallis, F., Eysenck, M., & Mathews, A. (1991). Elevated evidence requirements and worry. *Personality and Individual Differences, 12,* 21–27.

Üstün, T. B., & Sartorius, N. (Eds.). (1995). *Mental illness in general health care: An international study.* Chichester, U.K.: Wiley.

Vasey, M. W., & Borkovec, T. D. (1992). A catastrophizing assessment of worrisome thoughts. *Cognitive Therapy and Research, 16,* 505–520.

Vrana, S. R., Cuthbert, B. N., & Lang, P. J. (1986). Fear imagery and text processing. *Psychophysiology, 23,* 247–253.

Wegner, D. M., & Zanakos, S. (1994). Chronic thought suppression. *Journal of Personality, 62,* 615–640.

Wells, A. (2006). Metacognitive therapy for worry and generalized anxiety disorder. In G. C. L. Davey, & A. Wells (Eds.), *Worry and psychological disorders: Theory, assessment and treatment* (pp. 259–272). Chichester, U.K.: Wiley.

Wells, A., & Carter, K. (1999). Preliminary tests of a cognitive model of generalized anxiety disorder. *Behaviour Research and Therapy, 37,* 585–594.

Westra, H. A., & Stewart, S. H. (1998). Cognitive behavioural therapy and pharmacotherapy: Complementary or contradictory approaches to the treatment of anxiety? *Clinical Psychology Review, 18,* 307–340.

Williams, K. E., & Chambless, D. L. (1990). The relationship between therapist characteristics and outcome of *in vivo* exposure treatment for agoraphobia. *Behavior Therapy, 21,* 111–116.

Williams, J. B. W., Gibbon, M., First, M. B., Spitzer, R. L., Davies, M., Borus, J. et al. (1992). The structured clinical interview for DSM-III-R (SCID): II. Multisite test-retest reliability. *Archives of General Psychiatry, 49*, 630–636.

Wittchen, H.-U. (2002). Generalized anxiety disorder: Prevalence, burden, and cost to society. *Depression and Anxiety, 16*, 162–171.

Wittchen, H.-U., Carter, R. M., Pfister, H., Montgomery, S. A., & Kessler, R. C. (2000). Disabilities and quality of life in pure and comorbid generalized anxiety disorder and major depression in a national survey. *International Clinical Psychopharmacology, 15*, 319–328.

Wittchen, H.-U., Kessler, R. C., Beesdo, K., Krause, P., Höfler, M., & Hoyer, J. (2002). Generalized anxiety and depression in primary care: Prevalence, recognition, and management. *Journal of Clinical Psychiatry, 63*, 24–34.

Wittchen, H. –U., Zhao, Z., Kessler, R. C., & Eaton, W. W. (1994). DSM-III-R generalized anxiety disorder in the National Comorbidity Survey. *Archives of General Psychiatry, 51*, 355–364.

Yonkers, K. A., Warshaw, M. G., Massion, A. O., & Keller, M. B. (1996). Phenomenology and course of generalised anxiety disorder. *British Journal of Psychiatry, 168*, 308–313.

Zanarini, M. C., Skodol, A. E., Bender, D., Dolan, R., Sanislow, C., Schaefer, E. et al. (2000). The collaborative longitudinal personality disorders study: Reliability of Axis I and II diagnoses. *Journal of Personality Disorders, 14*, 291–299.

Index

D

E

H

I

U

V

W